How to Write a Novel in 20 Pies

Sweet and Savory Secrets for Surviving the Writing Life

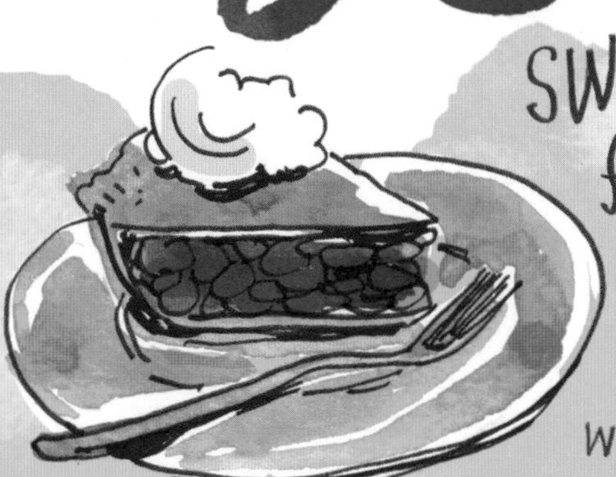

by Amy Wallen

with drawings by Emil Wilson

How to Write a Novel in 20 Pies

SWEET and SAVORY SECRETS for SURVIVING the WRITING LIFE

by AMY WALLEN
with drawings by EMIL WILSON

Andrews McMeel
PUBLISHING®

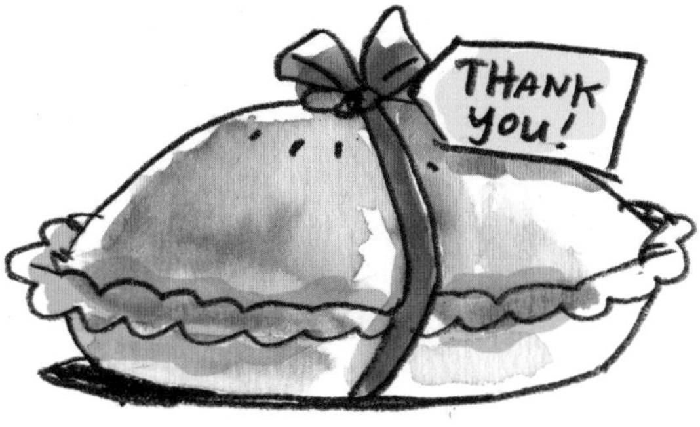
THANK YOU!

FOR JENN,
YOU CAN ALWAYS COME BACK FOR SECONDS.
-Amy

FOR MY MOTHER,
WHO'S NEVER MET A PIE SHE HASN'T LIKED.
-Emil

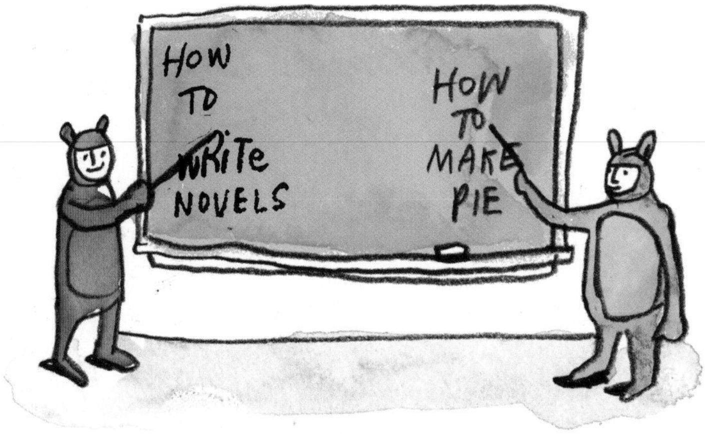
HOW
TO
WRITE
NOVELS
HOW
TO
MAKE
PIE

INTRODUCTION

How to Read THIS Book

This book is titled *How to Write a Novel in 20 Pies*, but it's not just about novels. Inside you'll find instructions based on my years of teaching classes like Novel Writing, Personal Narrative, and other creative writing workshops. You'll also find anecdotes of my firsthand experiences. Sometimes, they are based on my first novel, which was my first book, and the trials and tribulations of how I wrote it, found an agent, and made it through to publication. Sometimes, I use examples from my writing and publishing experience with my memoir, which was my second book to be published, but not my second book written. Sometimes, I share my ups and downs on the novel I'm working on concurrently while writing this book. Sometimes, I write about my miscarriages of books written but lost. They are all books, not all novels.

The instructional part is both *do as I do*, and *don't do as I do*. You can read the book from start to finish, or you can go straight to the end and read about being published and the kind of celebrations to start planning for. You can flip through to find answers to questions you are wondering about like, "When will this damn book be done?" There's a chapter on that. Or "Why do I even need an agent?" There's a chapter on that too. Maybe you want to just flip through and read the pie recipes because each one has a little story to go with it. Pie is what got me through. Maybe you want to use the book to procrastinate on your

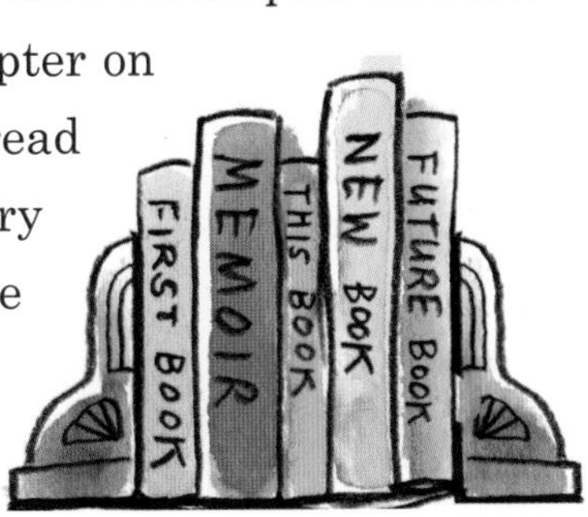
FIRST BOOK
MEMOIR
THIS BOOK
NEW BOOK
FUTURE BOOK

writing. You're welcome to do that too, as breaks are important, but get back to the writing before too much time has passed.

The most important part—the part I hope you'll take most to heart—is that books come in all shapes and sizes, but all take one thing to get to THE END—perseverance. I also hope that this book inspires you to have fun along the way, no matter how much the publishing world might try to trick you into thinking it's all business. This book provides tips on how to outfox the business side of your brain and encourages you to keep the whole process—from pen to paper to publication—creative and exhilarating.

So, the best way to read this book is to put your butt in a chair, pick up your fork, and dig in.

The EAT PIE Icon

Writing and publishing a book is a challenge; there are specific moments that especially test our spirits, and at these points I have included a special "EAT PIE HERE" icon indicating that any pie-tary indulgence in this moment will not only be forgiven but encouraged. How many books ask you to stop reading and go get a piece of pie? I wish more did.

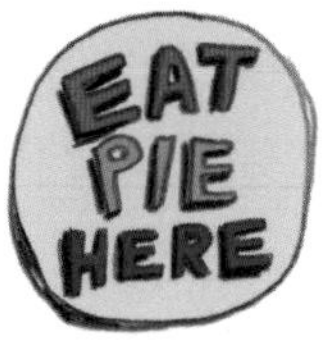
EAT
PIE
HERE

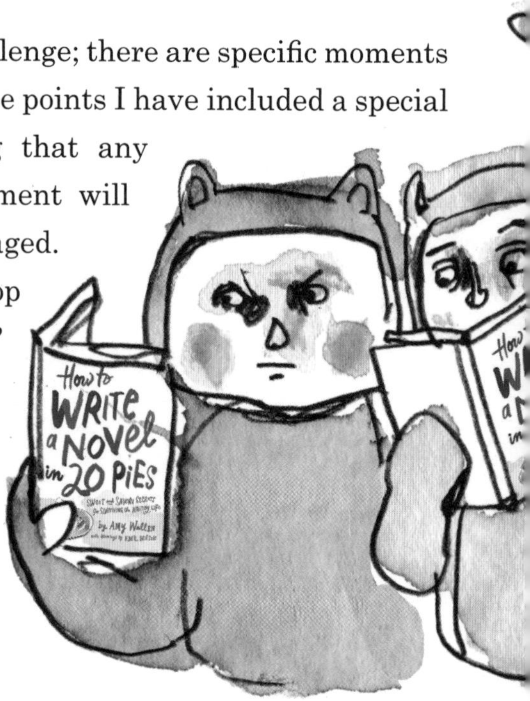
How to
WRITE
a Novel
in 20 PiES

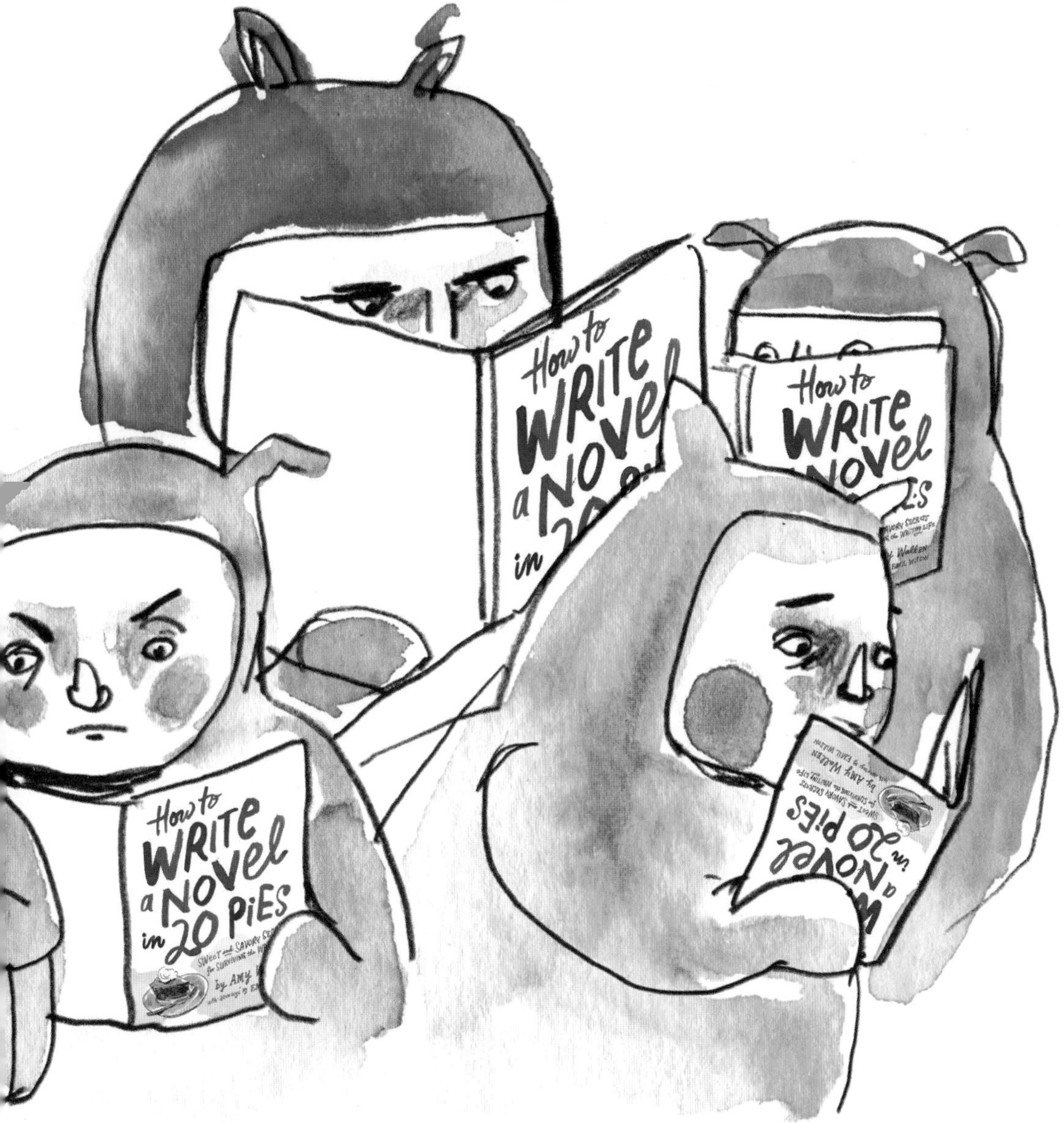
How to WRITE a NOVEL in 20 PIES

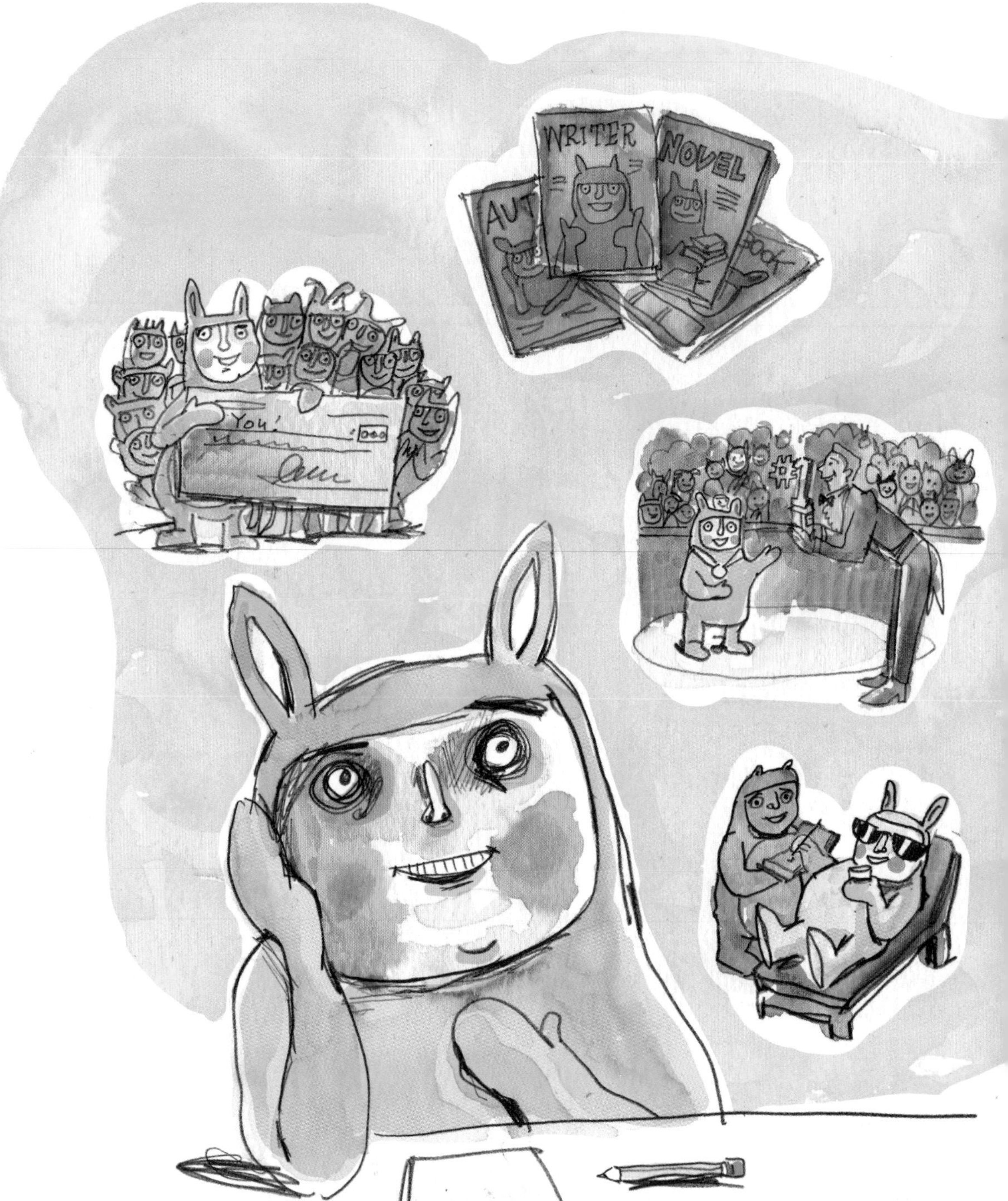
WRITER
NOVEL
You!
#1

Easy as Pie
And other Lies

The first night of Novel Writing class, I stand in front of a roomful of blank stares as the students wait for brilliant stuff to come out of my mouth. Every time my lips move, the students furiously put pen to paper in hopes that I will reveal the secrets to novel writing. Once I do, they plan to go off and publish and be done with me. "Writing a novel," I tell my students in every first class, "may be one of the hardest things you'll ever do." The stares twitch a little. Their pencils quit moving. I know what some of them are thinking, *Hard? Nope. Not for me. Now hurry up and get on with the secrets.* I know this is what they are thinking because, like all teachers and moms, I am a mind reader. Actually, I know this because inevitably at the end of the first class I will have at least one student come up to me and say, quietly so as not to reveal how far ahead they are and thus stir up jealous rage among their classmates, "How do I get an agent?"

"Have you finished your book?" I ask. Often this student hasn't written a word, but they have a to-die-for idea. They don't usually want to tell me the idea for fear I will steal it. "Don't worry," I tell them, "I can't steal it because that would mean I'd have to write and finish the novel before you do, and I'd have to want to write a novel about whatever that idea is in the first place." They hem and haw that the idea is so good, that I'll want to write about it. "Okay, don't tell me your idea, but do write about it," I tell them. "Can you get me an agent?" they persist. "We will talk about publishing and what

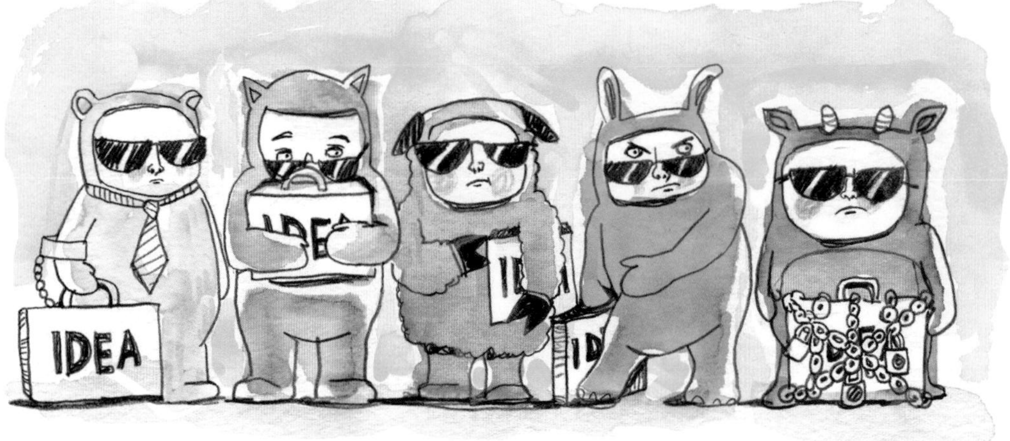
IDEA
IDEA

that looks like on the last class night," I explain. They will have to wait for those secrets, which aren't really secrets at all. "And that's when you'll get me an agent?" they ask. "You have to finish, that's the hard part," I reiterate. The student either hangs their head in supreme disappointment or looks at me like I'm cruel for keeping the key to their fame and fortune from them. *I will go to hell for this*, they think. Either way, they leave, and I know I will get an email soon that says they have dropped the class.

But the rest of the students stay, and I know they have the early symptoms of perseverance. Some will last the first quarter, some will make it all the way through the Advanced Novel Writing classes with me, and some will even email me one day about their two-book deal, and ask, will I come to their book signing? Will I?! Of course. Perseverance must be rewarded.

Okay, okay, you're thinking, hurry up and tell us how to write a novel so I can finish and get to that last part and invite you to my book signing.

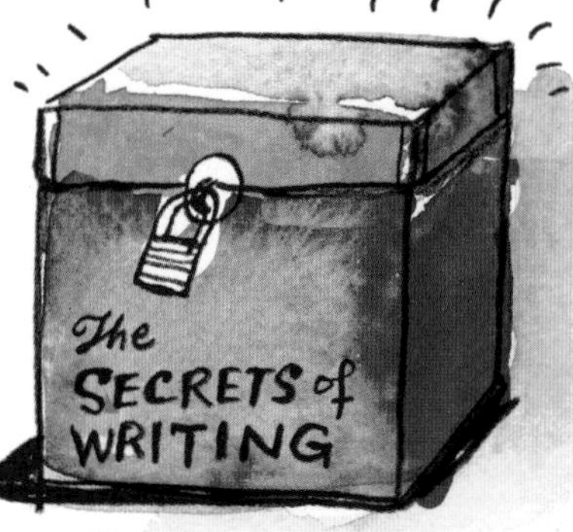
The SECRETS of WRITING

The daunting page count of a novel can elicit the fight-or-flight response in all of us. That first night of class my students share obstacles they face in writing a novel—from the fear of even putting the pen to the page to having no problem getting started, but how do they keep going? The scariest question of all, "Will I ever finish?"

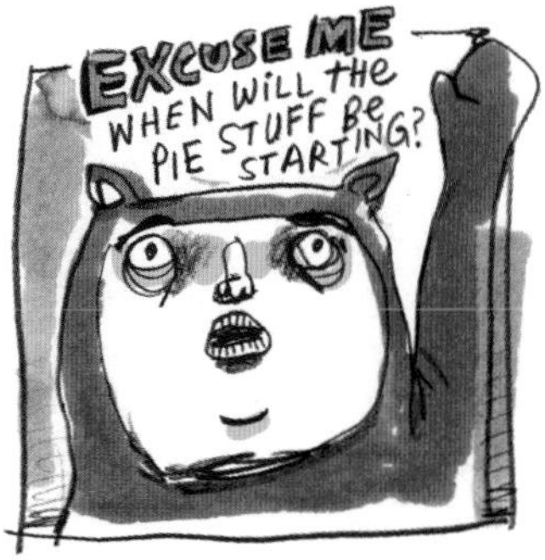
EXCUSE ME
WHEN WILL THE PIE STUFF BE STARTING?

So many surprises jump out at us along the way to The End that it's a wonder we ever do finish, but there must be a means or the bookstores wouldn't be stocked floor to ceiling with bound books.

Maybe that to-die-for idea that I could have possibly stolen doesn't seem so worthy when it hits the page. This happens to all of us: You start writing the story, start telling about this great incident. Your fingers flash over the keyboard, the words spill out—finally! The idea is going to see the light! Then the fingers wane a bit, then hover over the keys, then you notice a hangnail on your left middle finger, then you need a glass of water, but when you get to the kitchen, a whiskey sounds better, and it's only 9:15 a.m. Turns out, that well-guarded idea was just an anecdote, not a full story. It could be a story, but how do you get it there? How will you ever make up two hundred more pages about that same golden nugget? Another reality often surfaces—how do you write a novel when you don't know the first thing about writing a novel?

Here's the first secret: To write a novel, you have to write. But even that includes other secrets, like: To write a novel, you have to write a lot. And, to write a novel, you have to write often. To get a novel right, you have to get past that fear of it not turning out perfect on the first try.

It took me more than a few drafts to figure that out. In fact, I didn't learn it through writing, but through baking. My favorite comfort food since I was old enough to eat a chicken pot pie has been just that—chicken pot pie. Pie helped me get through the trials and tribulations of my first novel, not just the eating (best part), but the baking. But when I decided to start home-baking pies, I couldn't make a crust.

Crusts, like a novel, sound easy to make at first thought. After all, a crust consists of just three basic ingredients—flour, liquid, and fat. Novels from the outside look like they are just an idea, ink, and paper. Getting both a novel and a pie crust right, that takes trial, error, and trial and error, then failing, then trying again, then fine-tuning and finessing—until it not only looks right but also feels right and tastes right.

In the beginning, I had a vision of serving my guests a piping-hot slice of pie with creamy filling spilling out from between two flaky and buttery layers of crust, like you see on TV. Of course, on TV they use glue, Play-Doh, and shellac to get that look. Every crust I attempted barely even made it into a ball of dough, much less the pie pan. My flour and fat mixture turned out dry and crumbly, and that nice round circle of dough that was supposed to be lifted into the pie pan would be brittle and break into a dozen or so pieces. When I'd finish stitching it all back together with wet fingers, I had a Frankenstein crust. I can honestly say I came to tears after multiple attempts. I finally gave up and bought Pillsbury crusts in the refrigerated section of my local grocery. "Easy as pie, that's a lie," I would tell my dinner guests when they asked if I'd made my crust from scratch.

I'll admit, making a crust was scary for me. After so many failures, I had convinced myself that I didn't need a good crust for a good pie. I took the easy way out, and my pies suffered for it. Or they at least weren't as good as I discovered they could be if I just applied a little stick-to-itiveness. Crusts are like a novel in that way—keep working at it, write drafts, take classes to learn the techniques, keep tweaking your manuscript until you know what good writing feels like. Keep adding ink to a scene until you get the consistency you want. Don't be afraid if the manuscript fragments are pieced together like Frankenstein's monster. Even the monster wanted and needed love.

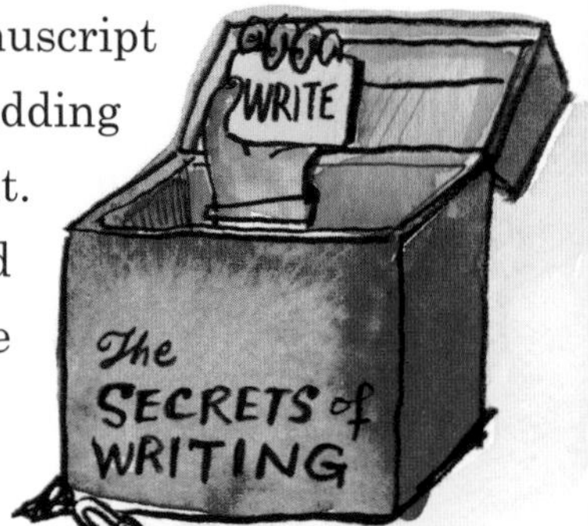
WRITE
The SECRETS of WRITING

Your idea may sound brilliant at first. Then, you watch it crumble on the page and turn into a pile of dry, ragged sentences that don't go anywhere. Maybe you need to add a sense of place; maybe you need practice to know how to get the consistency of description and dialogue right. Maybe your plot is too heavy-handed with characters who are one-dimensional. We will cover craft and character-fillings in more detail later, but taking care to plump up your characters and to let the plot lend itself to those three-dimensional needs will increase your chances at finding the secret to a publishable book.

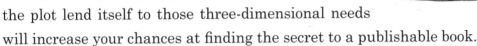

When I took another go at making homemade crusts, I used a combination of Crisco and butter, I used a Cuisinart, and I practiced over and over. The first dough didn't fall apart, but I could tell it would roll out too brittle, so I added a little more water than the recipe suggested. This worked so well that the next time I added more water, and I ended up with a white, slimy mess. Start over and retry. After a few pies, my fingers knew which dough felt right, which dough would not fall apart, which dough wouldn't be tough when baked. I have had many teachers and learned to listen to their

advice and try it on to see what fits for my tastes. I still make mistakes, still am learning better and better ways to make a crust with each pie. But one thing about pie baking that's more satisfying than novel writing—you get to eat your mistakes.

FAMOUS ARTISTS and THEIR PIES

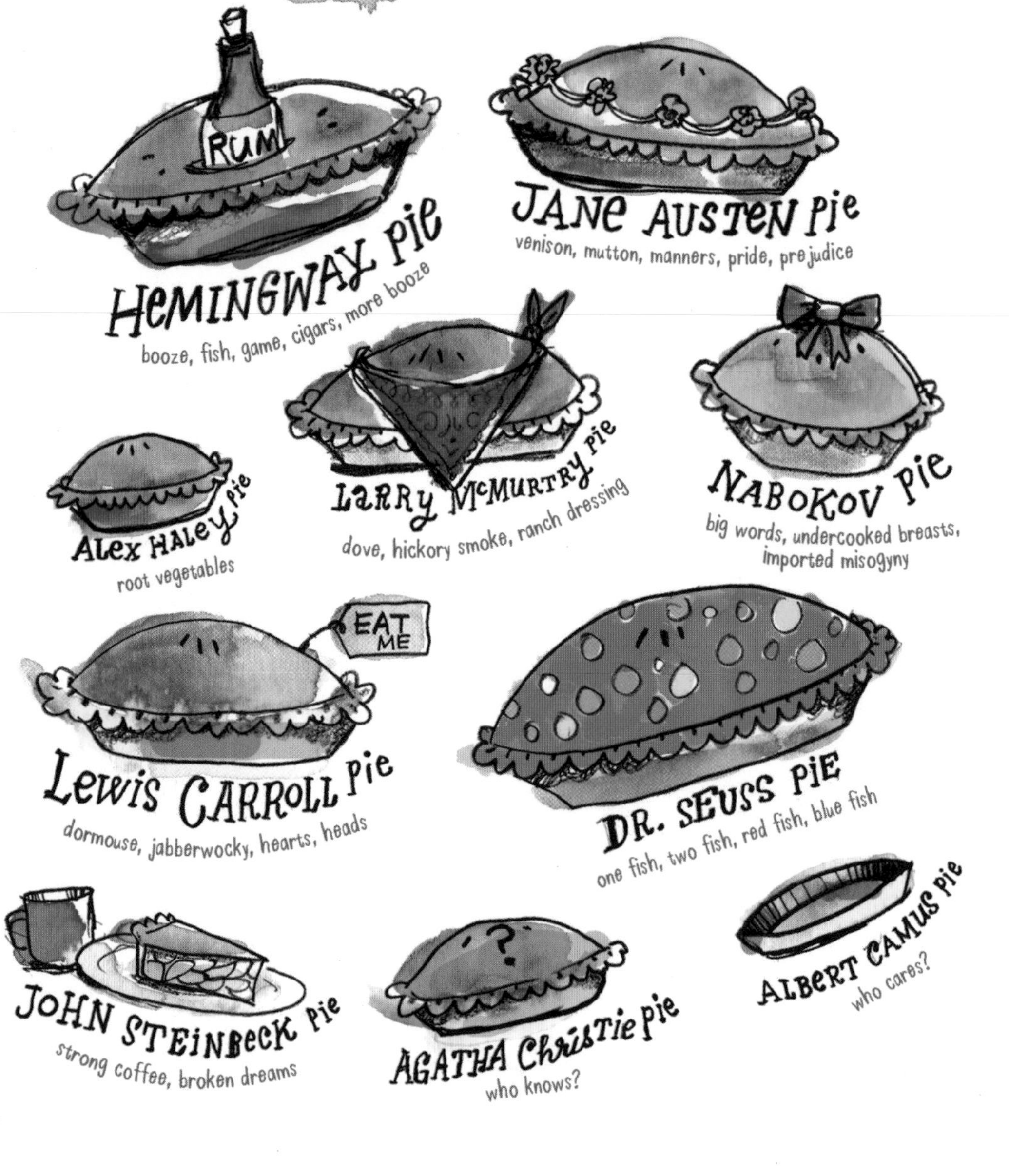
RUM
HEMINGWAY Pie
booze, fish, game, cigars, more booze
JANE AUSTEN Pie
venison, mutton, manners, pride, prejudice
Alex HALEY Pie
root vegetables
LARRY McMURTRY Pie
dove, hickory smoke, ranch dressing
NABOKOV Pie
big words, undercooked breasts, imported misogyny
EAT ME
Lewis CARROLL Pie
dormouse, jabberwocky, hearts, heads
DR. SEUSS PIE
one fish, two fish, red fish, blue fish
JOHN STEINBECK Pie
strong coffee, broken dreams
AGATHA Christie Pie
who knows?
ALBERT CAMUS Pie
who cares?

Basic Pie Crust

Everything should be cold when you make a pie, including your hands. But this is where writers have an advantage—our hands are usually cold from typing away all day. This makes pastry for 1 double-crust pie.

2½ cups all-purpose flour

1 tablespoon granulated sugar

¼ teaspoon salt

8 tablespoons leaf lard

8 tablespoons unsalted butter

½ cup ice water

Place flour in a large bowl. Add sugar (I leave out the sugar when baking a savory pie), and salt. Add leaf lard and butter, both cut up into tablespoon-sized cubes. Drop the cubes into the flour mixture and cover them in flour. This is when your cold hands and warm heart meld the pieces of fat into the flour. With your fingers, break all the pieces of fat into walnut-sized chunks. My first pie teacher outside of a cookbook, Kate McDermott, recommends leaf lard. It changed my pie crusts forever.

Because water has been my nemesis through the whole time I've known pie crust, I measure the ice water, then drop it by tablespoon into the flour and fat mixture, working it all in together until I get the desired consistency, which is somewhere between sloppy and ragged. Test it by squeezing a handful and when it holds together well you have dough. This is the part that takes practice. This is the part where the fine line between too dry and too wet happens.

PIE CRUSTS

TOO SLIMY   TOO DRY   JUST RIGHT

This is the part where I get a little nervous. But you don't have to; in fact, you will probably do just fine, and your crusts will be golden and flaky beauties instead of the beast.

Once the dough forms into a shaggy texture, divide the dough into two flattened balls, one slightly bigger than the other, for your bottom and top crusts, respectively. If you are making a single-crust pie, divide the recipe in half, or save one ball of dough to have for a pie emergency.

Wrap the balls of dough in plastic wrap, and place in the fridge to chill while you prepare the filling.

That's all it takes. If you get it right the first time, then you are a natural and should get back to writing your novel.

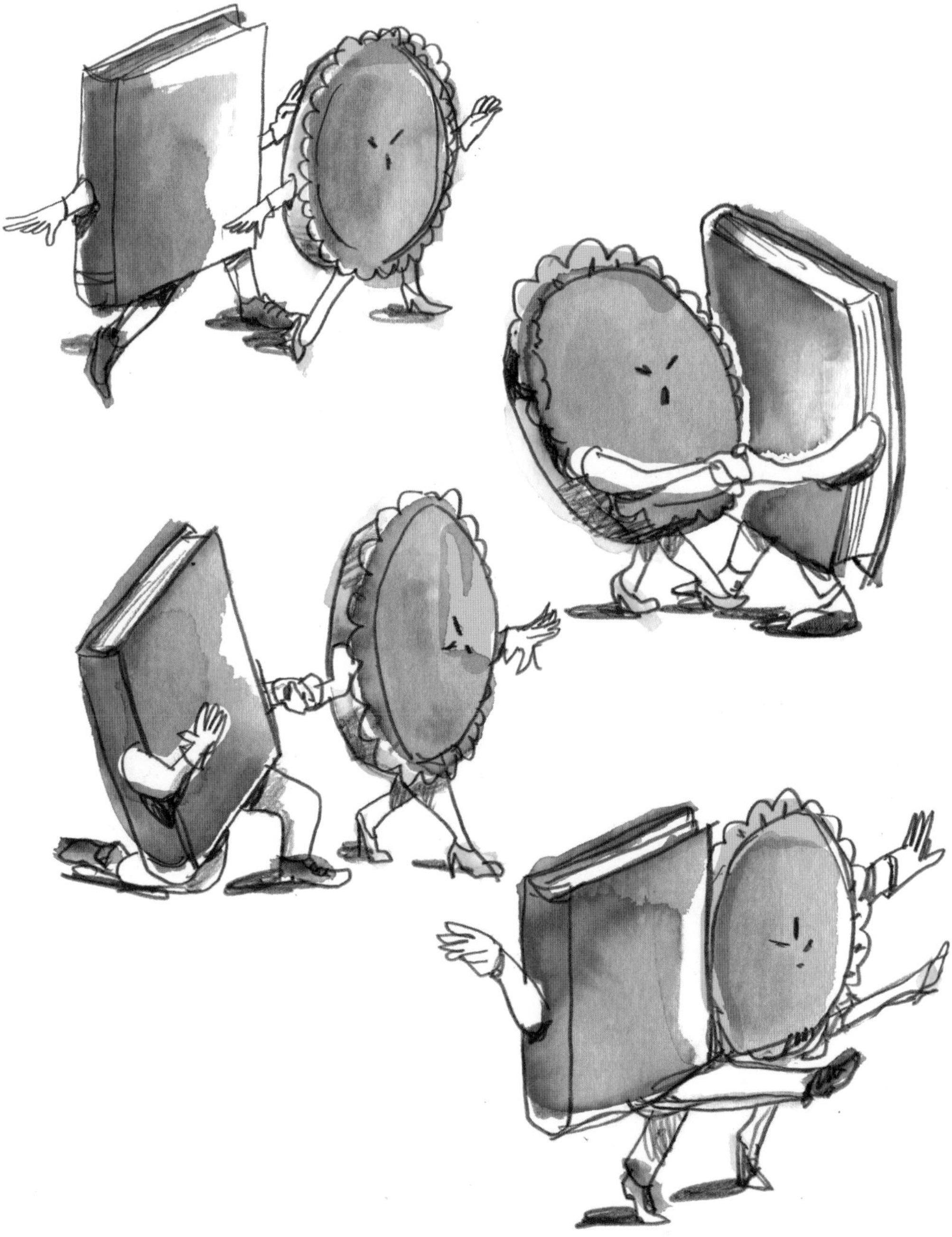

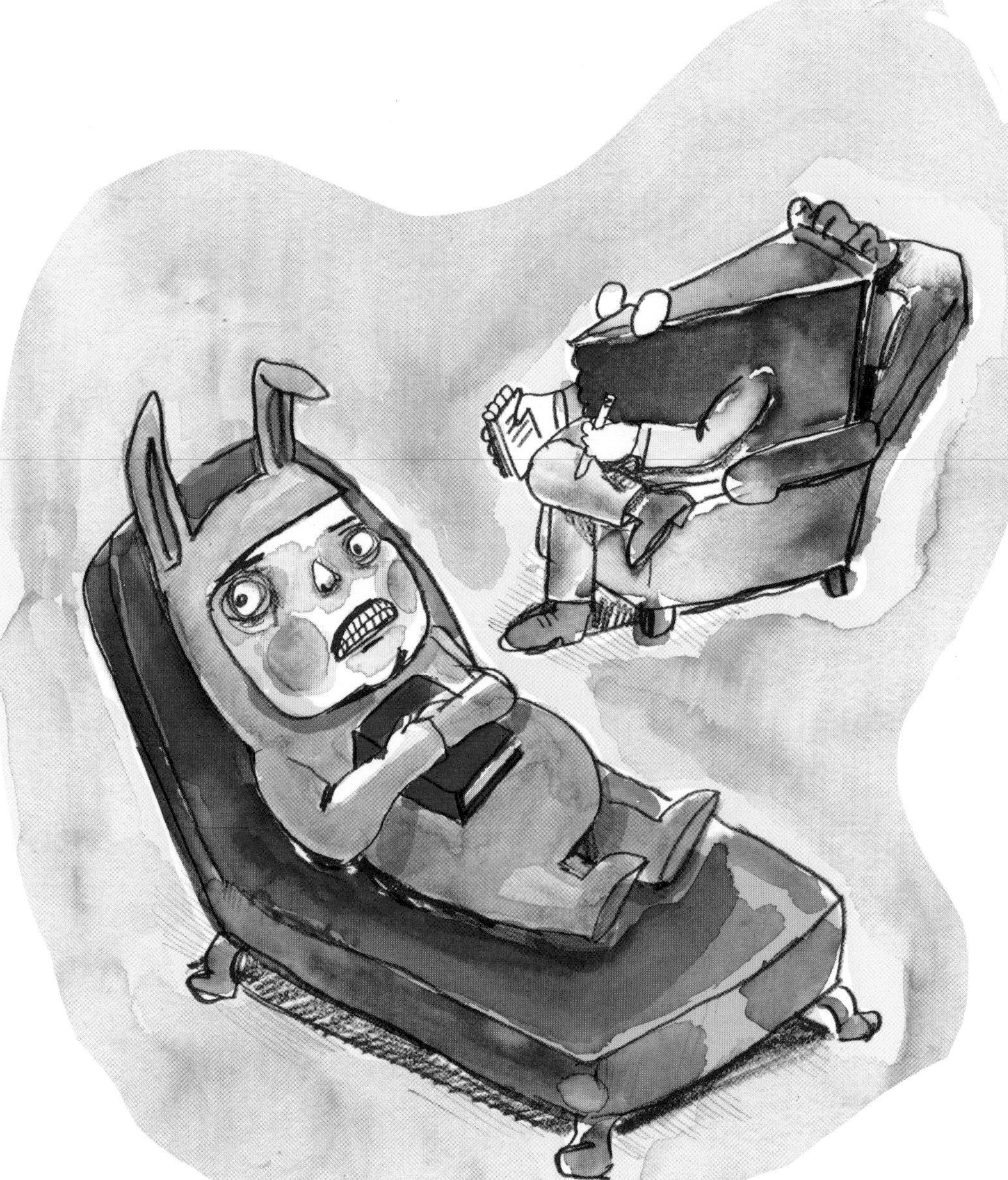

CHAPTER TWO

PiE as SAVing GRace

Some writers start off with a murmur of an idea, some with the bones of a story in their head, and some even have the entire trilogy or mystery series mapped out in their noggins. Some already have their blurbs composed in their imaginations—how they are the love child of Raymond Chandler and Isaac Asimov, which would put them as the nerdiest outcast but probably the true place for a writer to find themselves.

I've seen over and over that writing students who have a character who won't shut up are the writers who will have a finished novel one day. They are the students who show up for every class, the ones who push through all the obstacles in their way, who keep at it until it's done, even if that means never knowing when that will be.

Write what you want to write. Write anything. But write. Then write some more. That is the only way you will get to The End. It's the middle that's the hard part. And the end. And the beginning when you revise. And then the ending since it's changed with the new beginning. *Perseverance* means a steady, persistent course of action, a purpose, in spite of obstacles, discouragement, dogs needing to be walked, children asking to be held, husbands who holler up the stairs, "Where's the milk?" (response: at the grocery store because even the grocery run doesn't interrupt). I stole most of that definition of *perseverance* from Dictionary.com. But if you scroll down further on Dictionary.com you find the theological definition of *perseverance*: "Continuance in a state of grace to the end, leading to eternal salvation."

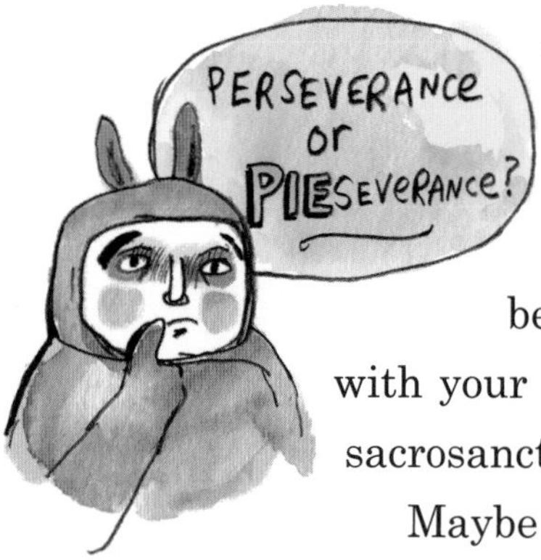
PERSEVERANCE
or
PIESEVERANCE?

Eternal salvation, that sounds so much better than "you're published!" But, in some ways, they are the same. After the long, hard work of living on Earth and writing a novel, when, just before being released to the world, your hardbound book with your name arrives on your doorstep, your novel feels sacrosanct. At least until the critics get hold of it.

Maybe monks writing their memoirs have a consistent sense of grace, but for most, getting through the obstacles along the way can seem more like Dante's nine circles to hell paved with good intentions than a state of grace.

That's where pie comes in. A pie or two for each circle.

For me, pie is grace. That's the secret to getting to The End that worked for me. Pie is a bit of mercy in a delicious, buttery, flaky crust. It is my salvation. I'm not talking about the image of the Virgin Mary in the lattice crust; I'm talking about the making and baking, from preheating the oven to eating the leftovers. That process saves me from giving up every time. Here's why.

Writing a novel can take a long time, and along the way, a lot of people, well-intentioned friends (jerks, if I can be honest), are always asking, "When are you ever going to finish that novel?"

Finish is the key word. Draft after draft, it feels like this could be it, this could be the final draft, this is when I will have all the pieces put together.

I remember the day when pie became my savior: I was so frustrated with my novel, so desiring to be finished, but the concept of The End felt so far away. So far that I couldn't even fathom what it could look like. Not in the story per se, but ever. What would it feel like, what would finished look like, what did *finished* even mean? If I didn't finish, I couldn't publish.

I had heard about E. B. White putting his manuscript in the mailbox to send to his editor, then waiting for the letter carrier so he could take the manuscript back home and make more changes. I could see myself doing this, only with email there's no letter carrier to beg to get your book back. Maybe I was one of those people who starts a million projects and never completes them? I got bug-eyed scared. I craved The End.

The satisfaction of completion had to come into my life soon, or I was going to end up like Jack Torrance in *The Shining*, chasing his family with an axe. I think most novelists would empathize with Jack.

Lucky for me (and my family), instead of an axe, I decided on comfort food to relieve my tortured mind. I baked a savory pie. At the end of the baking process, when I stopped and looked at my finished pie, I recalled what completing a creative endeavor felt like. From the making and rolling out of the dough to inventing and creating the filling—chopping the vegetables, sautéing the chicken, whisking the roux, melding the seasonings and ingredients, adding a dash of this and a dollop of that—I was in that same place I go when I write. I don't know the name of the place, and it doesn't show up on GPS, but it's where the conscious and subconscious converge. I knew, looking at the baked pie, then tasting it, that I had created something, and I had *finished* it. I had renewed hope that I would one day, maybe not soon but not in some infinitely indefinite time in the future, type the words, *The End*. I would get there one pie at a time.

Pie became my salve. When the writing felt daunting, when I needed a space and time to mull the story line, or when I just couldn't bear not being finished any longer, I'd stop to bake a pie. Once I was reassured that I could complete something creative, I'd eat it up, and then I would, and could, get back to work.

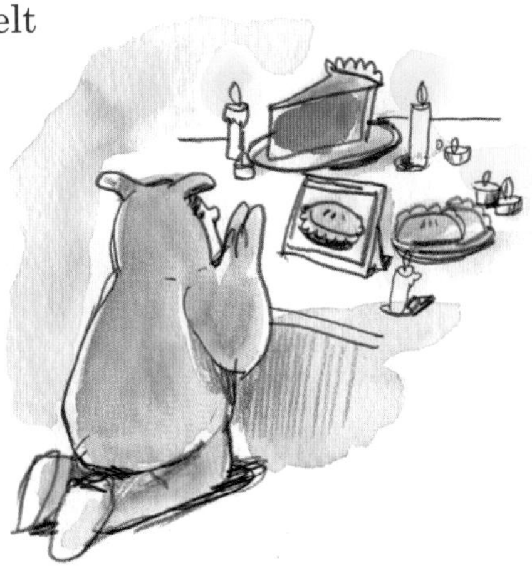

Cliché Chicken Pot Pie

I call it *cliché* because isn't chicken pot pie the first thing that comes to mind when savory pie is mentioned? A *cliché* is something we've heard before, something we are familiar with, and while *cliché* is forbidden in the writing world, in the comfort food world, the most familiar is where we turn to first. The recipe, though, is only as cliché as you want it to be. I always add lima beans to mine, because I love lima beans and they remind me of when I was a kid happily eating store-bought pies. Some people despise lima beans, so I try not to be friends with those people, or at least not invite them to dinner. You can add green beans, I do sometimes. Or mushrooms, which, when they are sautéed in garlic butter, can be such a delight in a pie. But watch out for the water they release, and don't let them make your pie soggy. I learned that the hard way, which seems to be the way I learn everything. Feel free to add your own favorite ingredients, cliché or not. You can find a million and one chicken pie recipes online— try them all! It's a great way to avoid writing.

½ head cauliflower

2 medium-sized carrots

1 cup frozen peas, defrosted

1 cup lima beans

2 tablespoons olive oil

1 6 to 8-ounce chicken breast,
   marinated in white wine

4 tablespoons unsalted butter

4 tablespoons all-purpose flour

1½ cups broth

½ cup half-and-half

1 tablespoon thyme leaves

1 tablespoon Dijon mustard

1 tablespoon sherry

1 cup shredded Gruyère cheese

salt

pepper

SO ORIGINAL.

THAT'S SO OVERDONE.

Preheat the oven to 400°F. Prepare 1 double-crust basic pie pastry.

Cut the cauliflower into bite-size pieces, and peel and cut the carrots into one-inch slices. Steam the cauliflower and carrots for 8-10 minutes, until tender but not too soft. If I have time and am forward-thinking, I marinate a big, fat chicken breast in white wine overnight. I chop this into bite-size pieces then sauté in a medium pan over medium high heat until cooked through. Set aside. If I'm not thinking ahead, I buy a Trader Joe's balsamic chicken breast already roasted, which I chop up.

A roux is like the outline of a story. It's where and when you decide how thick your sauce will be. A tablespoon more or less of flour will make your sauce thicker or thinner. I prefer a thicker sauce that holds the filling in place. Melt the butter in a sauté pan over medium heat. Stir in the flour one tablespoon at a time until thickened and the flour no longer smells like flour. Gradually add the broth and half-and-half until the sauce reaches the desired consistency. Stir in the thyme, mustard, and a tablespoon (or more, who's counting?) of sherry. Those ingredients have been essential to me for chicken pie ever since I came across my first pot pie cookbook.

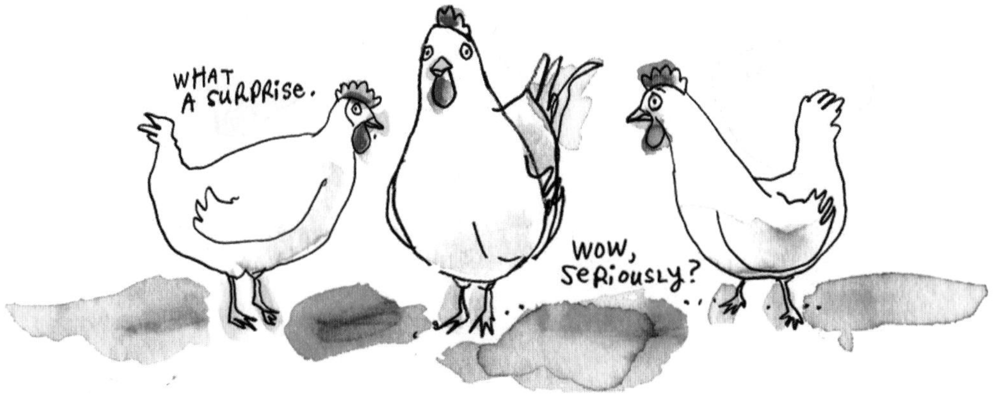
WHAT A SURPRISE.
WOW, SERIOUSLY?

Roll out the bottom crust and place it in the pie pan, then sprinkle the Gruyère cheese on the bottom before piling all the cooked veggies and chicken meat on top. Then, I spoon the sauce over the whole pile before placing the top crust, slicing a few steam vents, and baking for 30 minutes at 425°F, then turning the pan and baking at 350°F for another 25-30 minutes. Check doneness with a knife inserted in the center.

I don't remember the first pie I ate, but many of those little Swanson's boxes and metal pie pans that fill the landfill are mine. I also don't remember the first chicken pie I made, but I do remember the one that made pie baking a way of life for me: A houseguest who I was quite intimidated by asked if I made my crusts myself. This is before I'd conquered the Frankenstein crust. I lied, and told her, yes, I had made the crust myself, at the very same moment she opened the trash can and saw the red Pillsbury box staring up at her. The awkward humiliation turned me from a liar into a homemade crust fanatic.

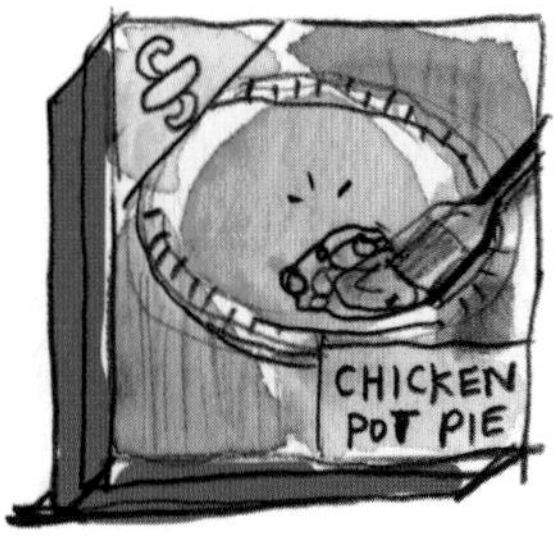
CHICKEN
POT PIE

Think of each pie as a draft for the next one. Oh, and you should add some salt and pepper to the filling ingredients along the way. I should have mentioned that earlier, but I forgot. Next draft.

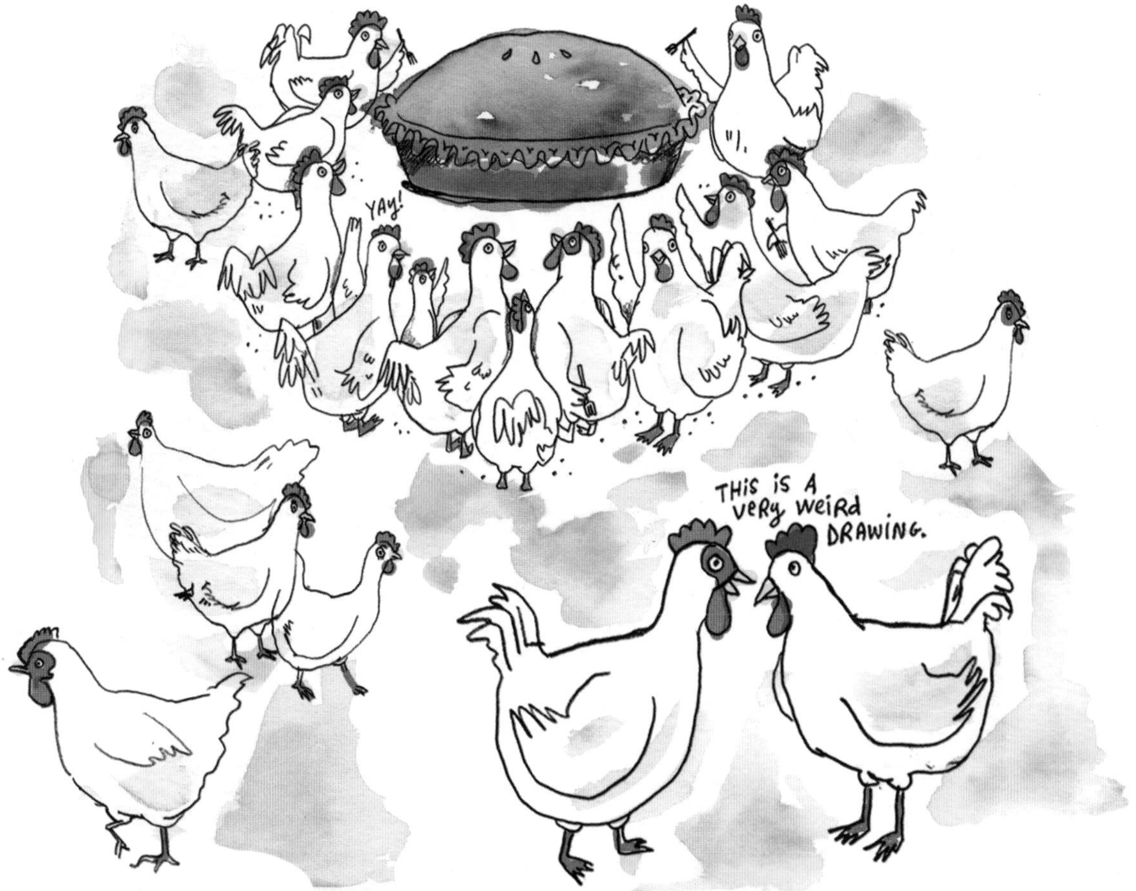
YAY!
THIS IS A VERY WEIRD DRAWING.

MONDAYS
TUESDAYS
WEDNESDAYS
THURSDAYS
FRIDAYS
SATURDAYS
"MOVIE
SUNDAYS
SICK DAYS
BIRTHDAYS
BAD HAIR DAYS
CHRISTMAS DAYS
"I HATE EVERYTHING AND WANT TO SET THE WORLD ON FIRE" DAYS

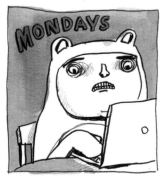

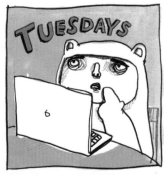

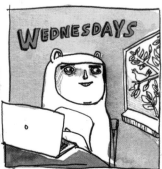

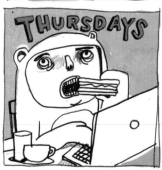

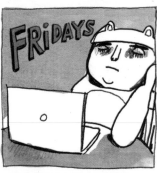

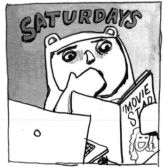

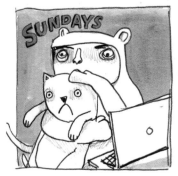

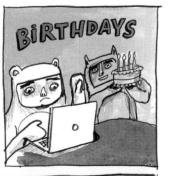

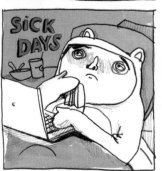

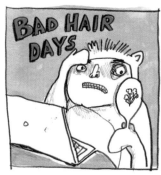

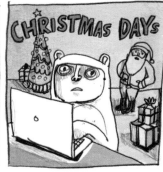

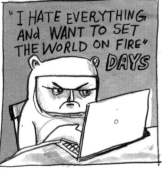

CHAPTER THREE

Pie Butt in Chair

Buckle Up

After I've convinced my students how hard it is to finish a book, I tell them we will all make a commitment to our writing for the entire duration of our class. The commitment-phobes wiggle in their seats. A few eager beavers who usually sit in the front row smile broadly. Reading their minds, I know they think they will win this contest. Although, it's not a contest. Instead, it's creating a habit that will be part of the foundation for getting their book done. It's not about writing the most, it's about writing consistently.

Creating a habit takes three weeks, or so "they" say.

For years, I explained to my students about creating a habit. I would ask the question, "You wouldn't leave your house without brushing your teeth, would you?" With that example of a habit I'd add, "Then don't leave without spending at least the same amount of time writing each day." The amount of time allotted for teeth brushing, about three to five minutes, is long enough to write one page. If you write just one page per day, then that's 365 pages—the length of a novel—in one year. I'd get a ton of blank stares when I mentioned brushing their teeth, but when I said a page a day, I'd get a collective nod.

Then one day, while getting my teeth cleaned, I told my dental hygienist this story. My hygienist loves me because I am an avid brusher. I'm not so great at flossing, but brushing is a bit of an obsession for me. When I finished the analogy of writing and brushing, my hygienist plunged further into my mouth, and said, "That analogy doesn't really work. Now open wider." She went back to taking the tartar off my molars. Through her hand, I garbled, "Waa no?" She explained that, much to my dismay, most people DO leave their house without brushing their teeth! Horrors!

As much as I'd now like to turn this book into an oral care lecture, it will have to suffice to say, "Even if you don't brush every day, at least write every day." But before your book tour, you may want to save up for a set of veneers. And gargle.

Writing every day comes with all those good-intention paving stones on Dante's circles. Sometimes it seems easier to just write when we are inspired, or when we have an idea, or when we have a free weekend, or aren't so tired, or when we don't have to go to the dentist, or right after the refrigerator is cleaned, or the oven after that last pie spilled over. Muses are more often referenced when inspiration and writing are not going so well. Muses are great, when they show up. People often use muses as scapegoats, something to blame when the creativity isn't flowing. I prefer to blame real live human beings. Me, for example. It's my fault I'm not writing. I had to learn HOW to put my writing first, despite my polished teeth.

I was first inspired by Michael Cunningham when I saw him speak at the New York State Summer Writers Institute, where I work as associate director every summer. He described his years of depression and how he

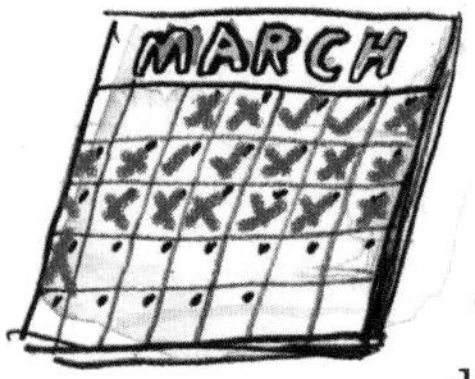
MARCH

wrote through it. I may be paraphrasing him, but what struck me most was how he said he wrote every day, no matter how he felt. Some days he knew he'd written some decent pages, other days he got maybe one good paragraph, and other days—most days he felt—he was pretty certain it was all crap. But he got to the end of the novel that way. The book he was describing was the Pulitzer Prize–winning *The Hours*. In addition to getting to The End, the part of his story that struck me the most, the part that made me realize why my round pie butt needed

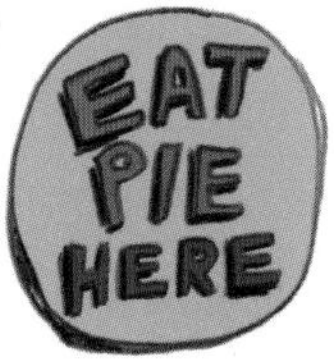
EAT
PIE
HERE

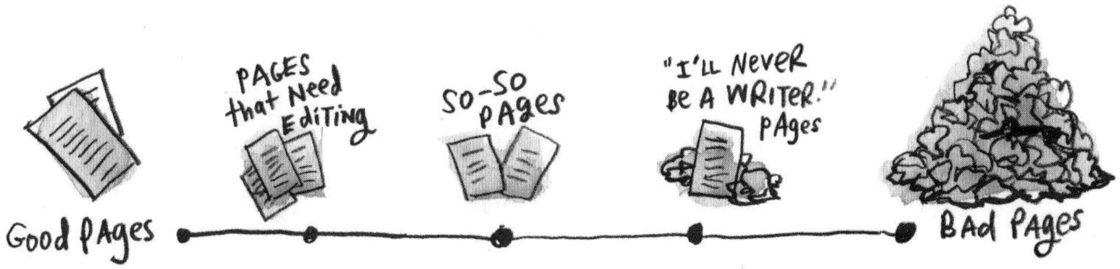
PAGES that Need Editing
SO-SO PAges
"I'LL NeveR Be A WRITER." PAges
Good PAges
BAd PAges

to be in the chair every day, was when he said after the book came out, he couldn't tell which parts were from the good days and which from the bad, it all comes together in The End.

Every novel teacher—hell, every writing teacher—will tell you that you have to write every day. I was told the same thing when I first decided to become a writer. My husband at the time had just gotten a new job, so with the extra money, we thought it would be the right time for me to make writing my career. I hadn't published anything yet, but working a shitty job was holding me back from being a literary genius.

Two hours, I decided, would be enough time to commit to each day. Just to start, then I'd build up from there. I'd read this is what famous writers do. So, the first day of my new "job," I went straight to my office, sat at my IBM Selectric, hit the On button, and was ready to go. I promised myself I would not leave my office under any circumstances. If the house caught on fire, I was going to be found as a charcoal briquette next to my nonflammable typewriter. As my typewriter hummed, I looked at the clock, noting the current time and what time it would be in two hours when I could take a break. I was off and running. Only "running" consisted of staring at the blank paper. Sitting wasn't working. I stood up. I paced the room, the whole ten feet of it, until I stubbed my toe on my desk chair. I checked the clock. About six minutes had passed. This was a time before email, so I couldn't check my messages, nor could I google any strange ailments I'd acquired that week under the guise of research. My husband had left for his new job, so there was no one I could make up an excuse to check on. All my friends were at their jobs, earning money, so I had no one to call. We didn't have a dog, so I couldn't take him for a walk. But I could daydream about having one! He would be a great dog! One that loved long walks! One that was playful and with a slobbery pink tongue! I looked at the clock again. Four more minutes had passed. I had promised myself that I would not leave the room until two whole hours was up, and I would not break that promise. I hadn't come to the typewriter with a particular story in mind, so I thought about what I could write. Nothing. Nothing came to mind.

I could bore you with how the rest of the two hours went, but I'll wrap it up by telling you that I didn't write a word in those two hours, and when the second hand brushed twelve for the second time, I was lying on my back, legs up against the wall, counting fly poop spots on the ceiling. The next day, I started looking for a new job.

I did find a new job, a less crappy one that paid less than my previous job (before my aforementioned non-illustrious one-day writing career), that gave me more satisfaction. I changed my commitment from two hours to

fifteen minutes every day. In those fifteen minutes, at first I still struggled to come up with enough to write about, but I kept my pen to the page. Eventually, those fifteen minutes were not enough, so I changed it to thirty minutes (a pay raise of sorts). Then I couldn't get all the words I wanted down before the thirty minutes was up, and so on, until I was writing two hours every day. I had lessened the pressure and decreased the risk with just fifteen-minute increments. I could write about nothing for fifteen minutes, but soon nothing became something, and something needed more than fifteen minutes.

I had tried to run a marathon without training for even a 5K first. I learned the hard way, but the lesson stuck—I don't force the writing, but I do show up every day for work.

The moral of that tortoise-eats-barbecued-hare story is to give yourself room to grow into the habit. Find what works best for you, and that includes the place, time, and quantity. No one is going to say you aren't a writer if you only write a page a day. They will snicker behind your back if you don't write a word yet call yourself a writer.

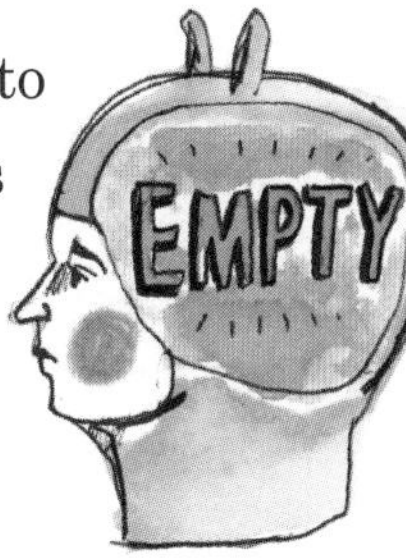
EMPTY

Writing may be the hardest thing you do because it requires commitment. Commitment requires perseverance. Perseverance may mean you have to go at it like a relationship. It requires putting up with the shitty times, getting through the months when the romance has withered with the tedium of work, when one or the other of you wants to bail or give up, the days when you or your partner or your writing don't look so good. Having a relationship means showing up, being patient, and not criticizing every little thing they do. Or every word you write. A long-term commitment means trust, patience, and a lot of grace. And, if I'm honest, I think my husband loves me more because I bake pie.

Commitment to your writing means unconditional love. It means writing anyway, even if you don't feel like it.

Though truly, if I can inspire you to do anything, remember to brush, at least after eating pie.

Side Trips

Let's say you already have the level of commitment that means you're at the page every day. Then I probably also don't need to tell you that there are those days when you show up to the page, but your brain doesn't. Maybe your brain is out there getting its rotors rotated or spark plugs replaced, or it didn't get any of those things done in a timely manner so it's sitting on the side of the road somewhere between bed and desk.

Other days, something scary comes up, and you just don't know how to deal with it. Natalie Goldberg says to keep writing when it gets harder. Go for the jugular, she says.

But how do you know what to write? How do you get around obstacles, stuck spots, hard-to-write-about parts of the novel? How do you tell that jugular what he can do with his plaque buildup and that his mother is a clogged artery without hurting his feelings? The pen may be oh so mightier than the sword, but you have to know how to use both not to get killed. Okay, maybe the pen won't kill you, but the metaphor took that tangent, and that tangent proves my point. Sometimes, the way out of hard spots is to take a sudden turn. Take tangents, try on new angles, swipe at one side, then try the other. What's the worst that can happen? You get a lot of ink on the page. You come up with bad metaphors. And, maybe, you'll hit the vein that spills out the answers, that opens up the heart of your novel.

Remember, when you get to the other side of whatever you are writing that makes your heart whap against your ribs, you can bake and eat a pie safely in your kitchen. But also, remind yourself that when you write through the scary stuff, you come out the other side much more satisfied, much more full.

Driving in the Dark

At the darkest moments, when we don't know where the writing is taking us, we think we don't really want to write that deeper, touchy-feely stuff—why don't we just leave that to other people who want to spend their time on that heartfelt crap. "My book," we say to ourselves, "will be good enough without it. It's funny, it doesn't need to be poignant too." But funny ain't so funny if there isn't pain and suffering to up the ante.

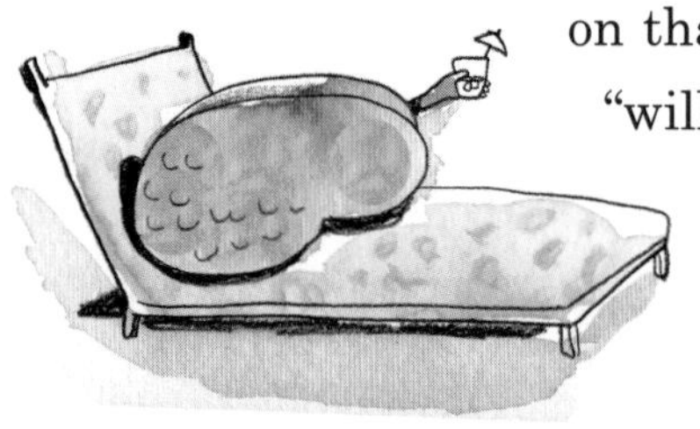

I suspect if someone hooked up a monitoring device to check our heart rate, to see how often we blinked, when our eyes were dilated when we write, we might know from the bells and whistles when we'd hit gold. If the noises weren't so annoying, it might be worth it. We might stay seated longer if we had an inkling when facing something impossibly unsolvable on the page that around the corner on the next page we are going to write something really wonderful, something meaningful that takes the novel to the next deeper level. Beeping lights, a bright neon arrow pointing straight ahead, or even a fierce flagman waving us on—"Keep that pen moving, lady!" Any of these, and maybe we'd ignore the dip in self-confidence, the incongruent ideas, the lack of even a path to get to the end result. It can often seem like a demon awaits us around the corner, or on the next page. Maybe you wonder if repressed memories lurk behind the story your imagination has concocted, and who wants to go there?! Where does this stuff come from, anyway? What is revealed to us can be downright frightening, but that's when we need to be brave and carry on. This is when a pie can come in handy.

Post a sign over your desk that reads, "There will be pie," and keep writing. Stay seated and power through the challenges.

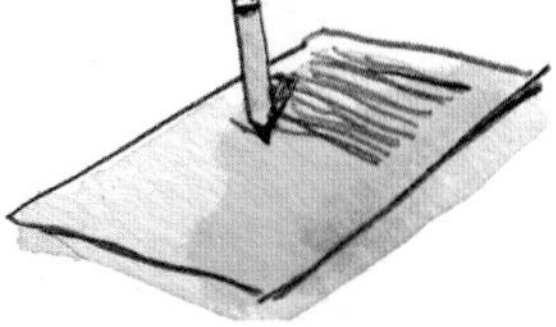

Filling Stations

"But what do I write?" you ask.

Writing practice is the time to allow the accidents and mistakes to happen, to let anything at all onto the page. If you can't come up with anything to write, here's a trick: Write nonsense. Yes, nonsense. It's about letting your imagination take complete control. Throw it all onto the page, anything at all. Sentences that don't make sense, words of any kind, and even made-up words. *Neologism*, the making up of words—one of my favorite words, actually. When you let the words pour out is when something grabs hold,

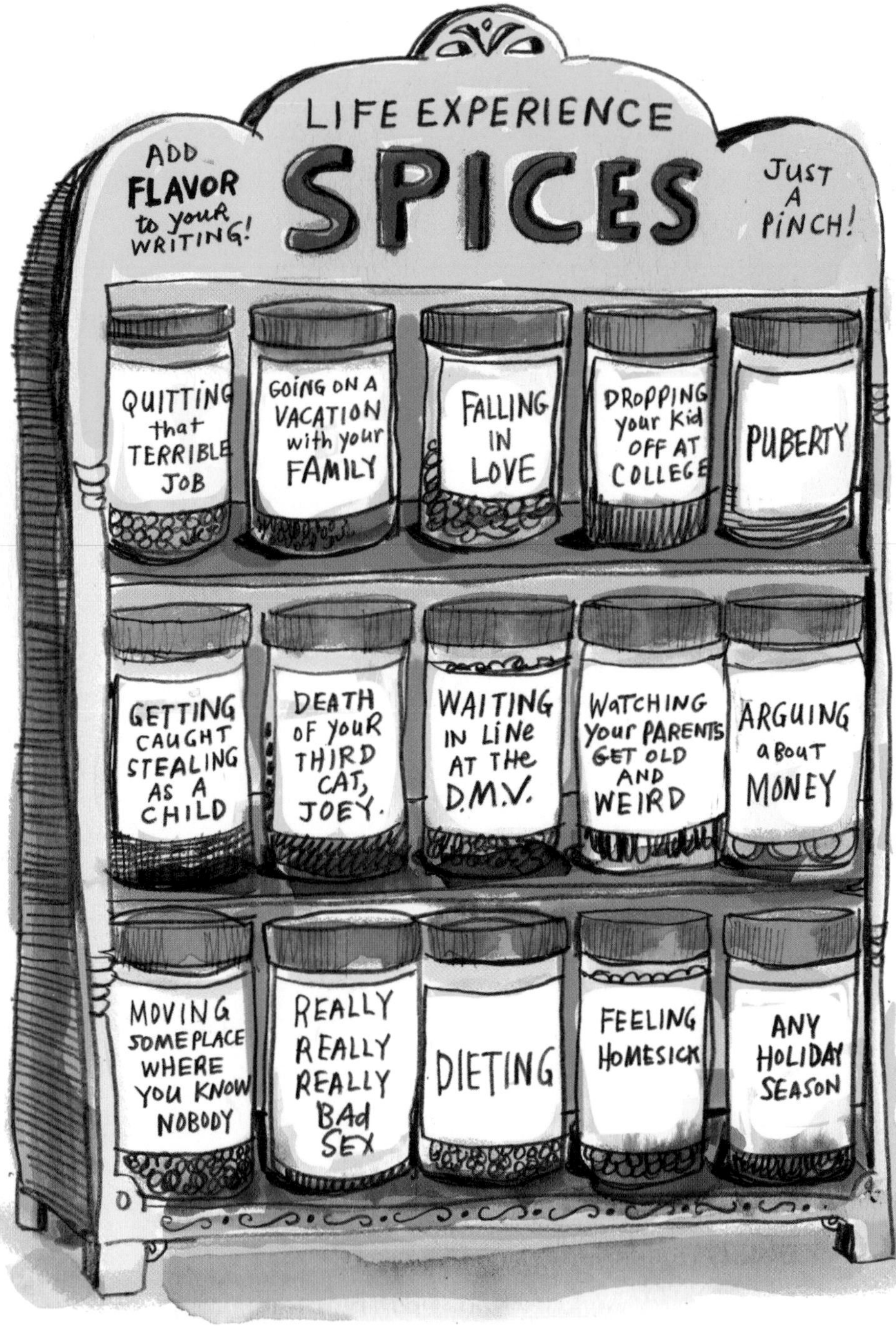
LIFE EXPERIENCE
SPICES
ADD FLAVOR to your WRITING!
JUST A PINCH!
QUITTING that TERRIBLE JOB
GOING ON A VACATION with your FAMILY
FALLING IN LOVE
DROPPING your Kid OFF AT COLLEGE
PUBERTY
GETTING CAUGHT STEALING AS A CHILD
DEATH OF YOUR THIRD CAT, JOEY.
WAITING IN LINE AT THE D.M.V.
WATCHING your PARENTS GET OLD AND WEIRD
ARGUING about MONEY
MOVING SOMEPLACE WHERE YOU KNOW NOBODY
REALLY REALLY REALLY BAD SEX
DIETING
FEELING HOMESICK
ANY HOLIDAY SEASON

some word or sentence or jumble becomes a journey, a trip to a new world, an explanation, or maybe a new direction that you would have missed if you retained control of your imagination and didn't let it drain all over your page. Yes, this counts as writing.

Another clogger of the writing artery is the critic. My pie habit had helped satisfy my need for completion, but it was my pie critic who pestered me about the store-bought crust I used. As writers, we have enough critics in our heads, and a pie critic is especially annoying because she wants to be heard over all the critics. I gave in to her and learned to make a homemade crust, and my pies are all the better for it.

But personal writing critics in our heads can get in the way of our process. How do you shush them? How do you let them say their piece and then get on with your writing? We don't want to completely ignore them, do we? At first, yes, just get that first draft down on the page. When you are in the second draft and beyond, you can listen and learn to sift through the advice. That's another chapter. But right now, in this first draft, learn to put everything on the page, to take tangents to the right and left, try out the weird plot, add in the character who smells bad, and maybe even use a quadratic equation if it comes to you. (I'm not even sure what a quadratic equation is.) Be loose with your ideas and don't hang on to anything too tightly.

Everything PIE

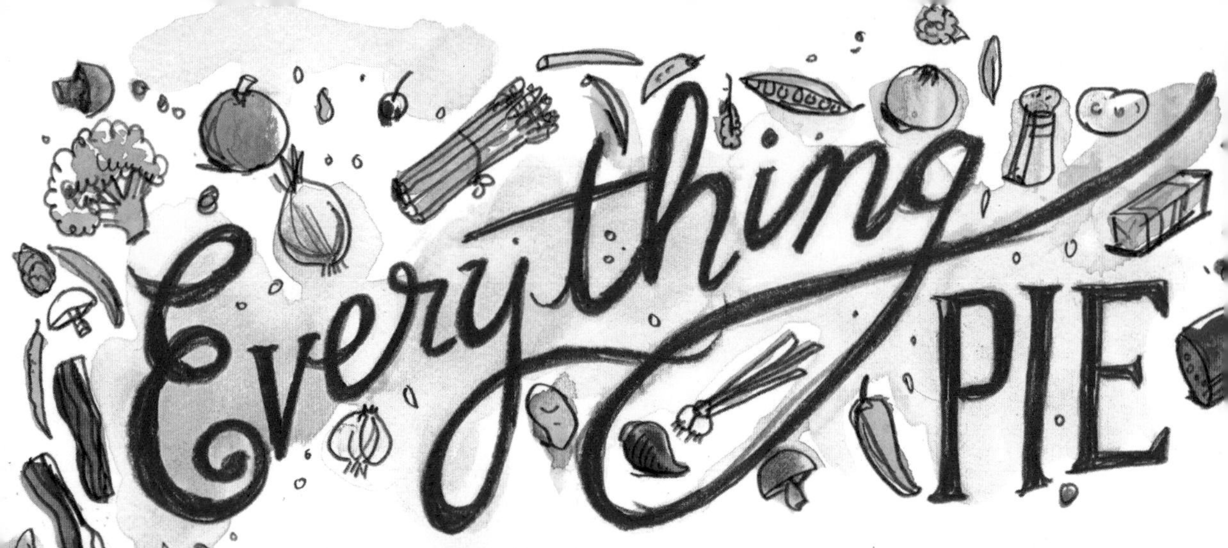

Sometimes, just like the writing, you need an Everything Pie—a pie that just takes any given ingredients from your fridge and pantry.

Sometimes, it's okay to use a store-bought crust. It's not a cardinal sin to use Pillsbury's ready-made crusts. You can even lie if I meet you and ask. I wouldn't know. It's not like there's some embedded tracking device stored inside each purchased book communicating through the internet so I know what rate you read, eat, and pie—yes, *pie* is now a verb.

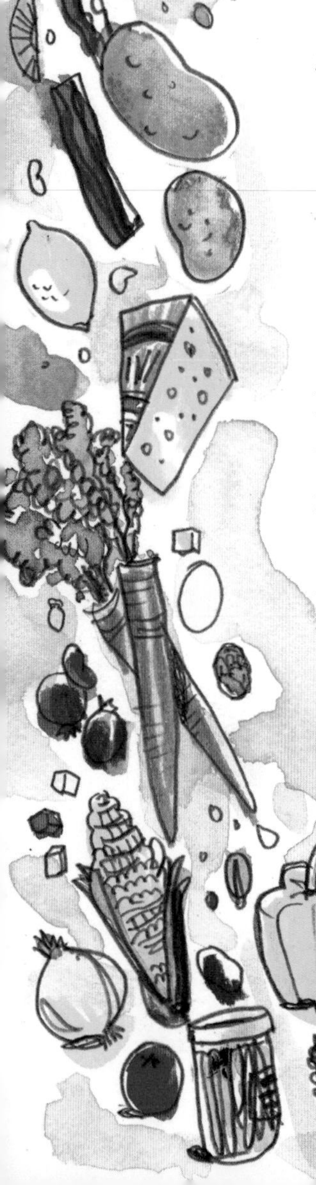

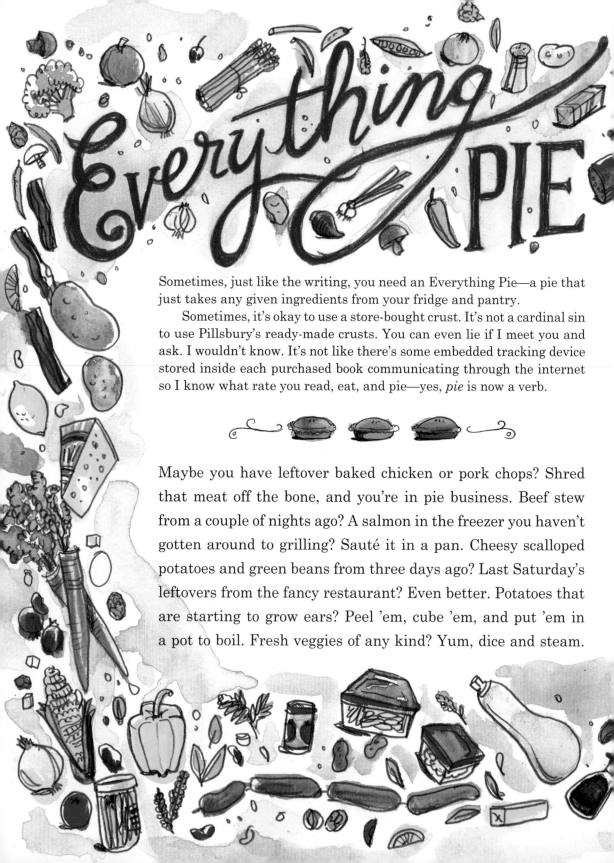

Maybe you have leftover baked chicken or pork chops? Shred that meat off the bone, and you're in pie business. Beef stew from a couple of nights ago? A salmon in the freezer you haven't gotten around to grilling? Sauté it in a pan. Cheesy scalloped potatoes and green beans from three days ago? Last Saturday's leftovers from the fancy restaurant? Even better. Potatoes that are starting to grow ears? Peel 'em, cube 'em, and put 'em in a pot to boil. Fresh veggies of any kind? Yum, dice and steam.

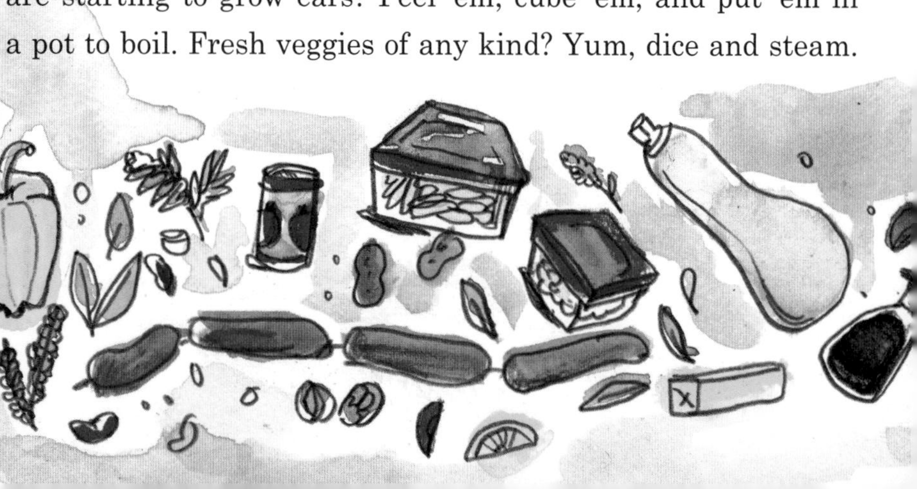

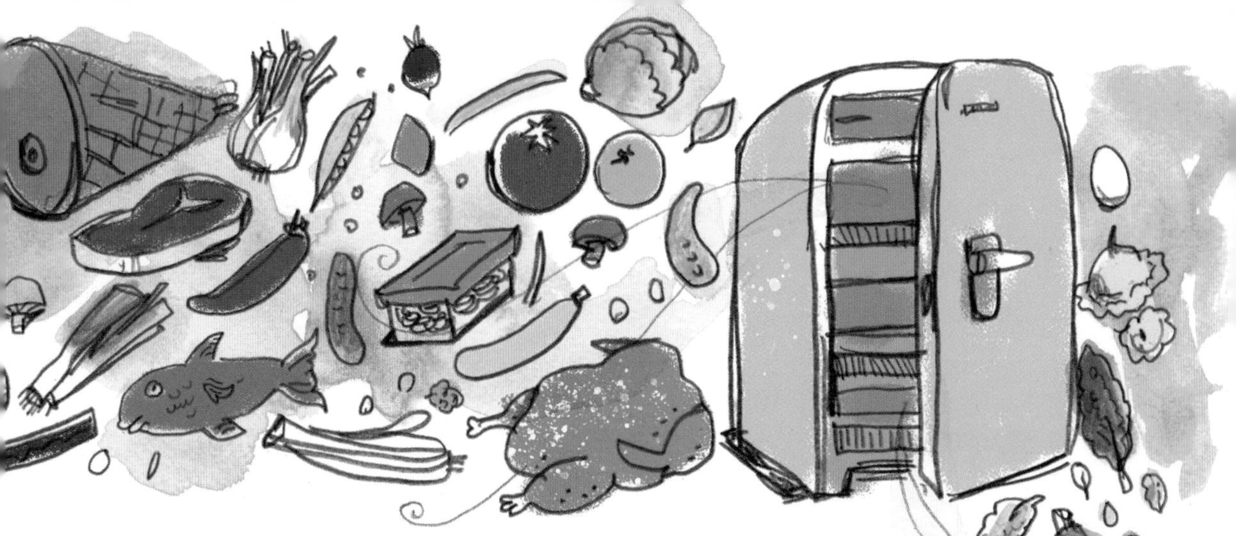

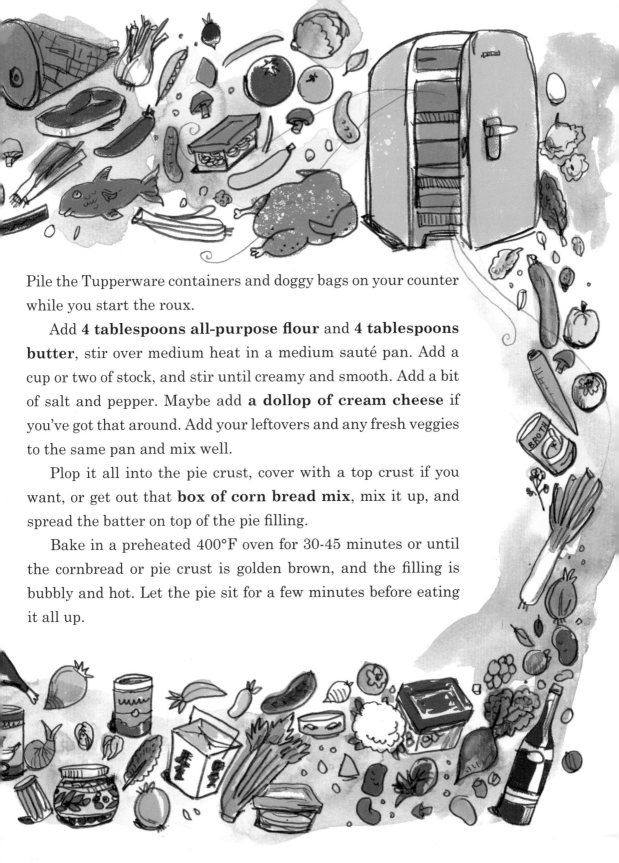

Pile the Tupperware containers and doggy bags on your counter while you start the roux.

Add **4 tablespoons all-purpose flour** and **4 tablespoons butter**, stir over medium heat in a medium sauté pan. Add a cup or two of stock, and stir until creamy and smooth. Add a bit of salt and pepper. Maybe add **a dollop of cream cheese** if you've got that around. Add your leftovers and any fresh veggies to the same pan and mix well.

Plop it all into the pie crust, cover with a top crust if you want, or get out that **box of corn bread mix**, mix it up, and spread the batter on top of the pie filling.

Bake in a preheated 400°F oven for 30-45 minutes or until the cornbread or pie crust is golden brown, and the filling is bubbly and hot. Let the pie sit for a few minutes before eating it all up.

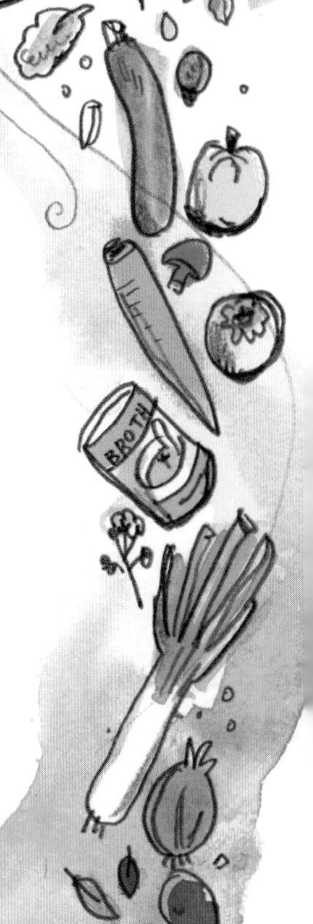
BROTH

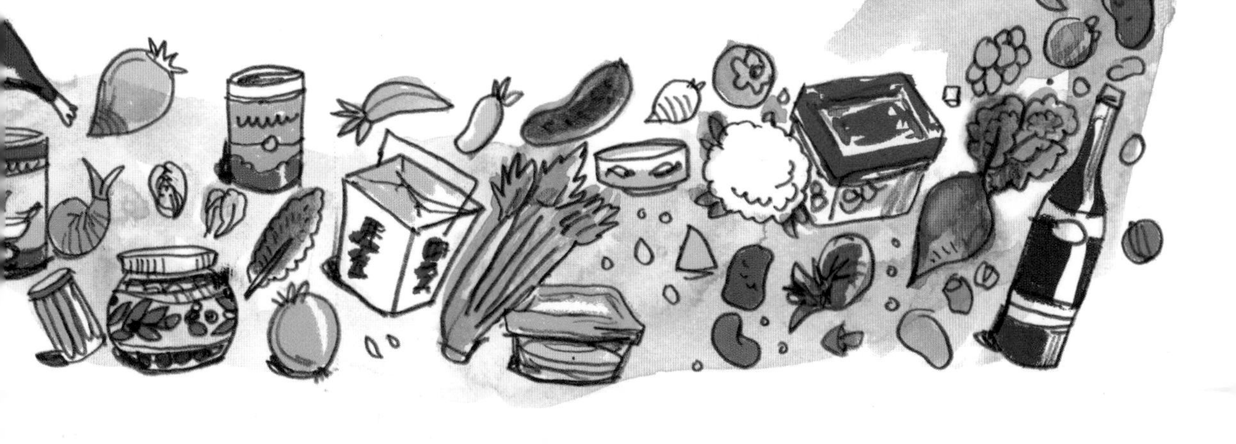

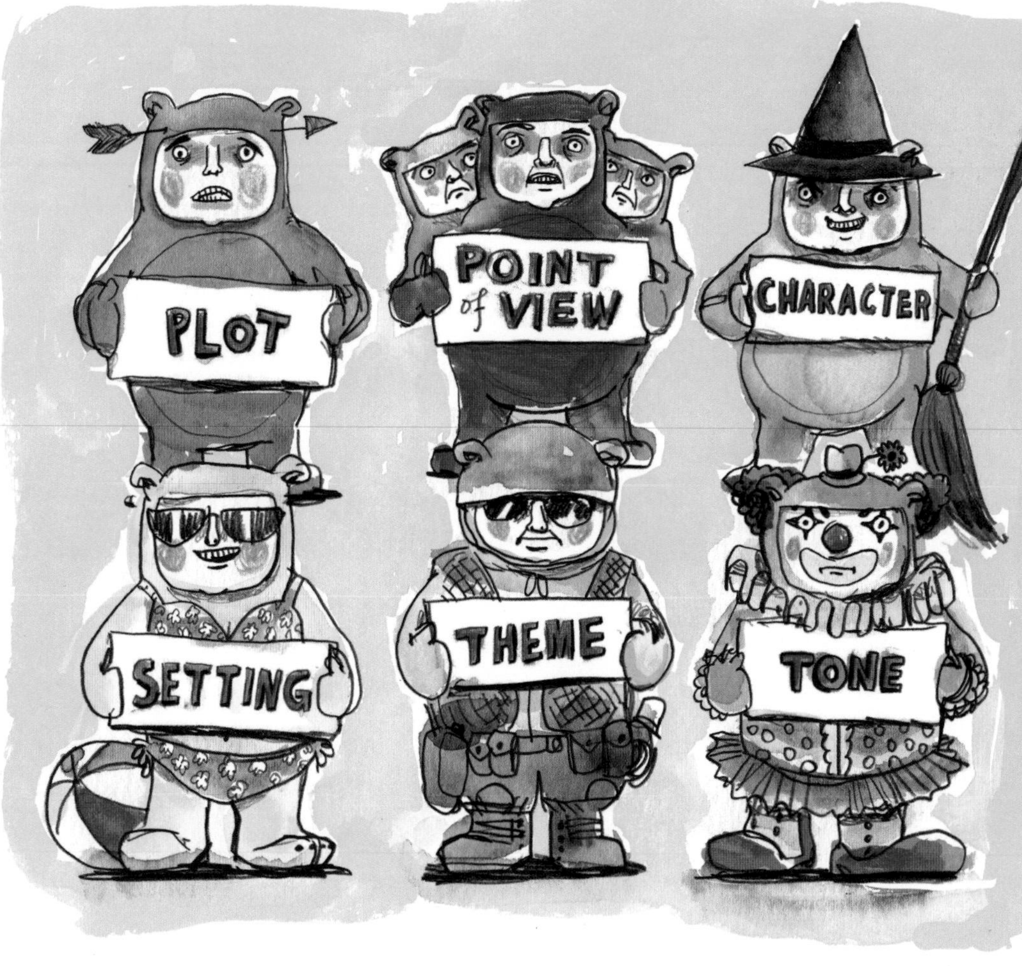
PLOT
POINT of VIEW
CHARACTER
SETTING
THEME
TONE

CHAPTER FOUR

Crafty Craft

If you're writing a memoir, you can skip down to the memoir section in this chapter, but I highly recommend sticking around to see how the other half lives. And same for novel writers: don't think the memoir section has nothing to offer you. I teach a manuscript workshop that is cross-genre, and I repeatedly find that what may, at first glance, seem like it only applies to one or the other, can provide insight into your characters, their stories, and their arcs. Novels aren't just fiction, just as memoirs aren't just facts. Both are about writing the Truth—yours.

Novel Craft

Just like there are only three ingredients in a pie crust—water, fat, and flour—there are only three rules to writing a novel. I stole that from Somerset Maugham—the three rules of writing part, not the pie part (as far as I know, Somerset never baked a pie, but his novel *Cakes and Ale* is a delicious satire). Maugham's actual quote is, "There are three rules for writing a novel. Unfortunately, no one knows what they are." Still, there must be something that pulls a novel all together, right? Novel gluten.

Just as I had to practice before I could successfully make a pie crust by hand, I had to practice the craft of a novel. Character, setting, plot, point of view, tension, suspense, and so on must come together into not just a cohesive state but a faceted story.

I don't particularly care for the word *craft*. It makes novel writing sound like just a quickie weekend glue-stick hobby. But, like a pie without a crust, a novel just runs all over the place without craft elements to hold it together. You need to learn the basics so you can go on to break all three of those rules that no one knows. While *art* is creativity that comes from the heart, *craft* is the technique that is learned through practice. *Craft* is creating a pie that has all the essential ingredients. *Art* is creating a pie that can stand up against all the other pies at the bake-off.

In this chapter, I hope to not only give you a few tools to craft a novel but also to shove you into the artistic side of the endeavor. Because anyone can craft a novel—all they need is a few characters, a plot outline, and at least fifty thousand words. Just look at how many people participate in NaNoWriMo, National Novel Writing Month. Thing is, even with this formula and the ingredients, it's not that easy. You will still need to have an imagination to create a character and something at stake for that character.

This isn't a book on craft, but it does have *how to* in the title, so you might expect me to deliver at least the three rules or ingredients to get you started. So, I'll do that. When I teach my classes, we focus on three things. Maybe they aren't rules, but they do help move the process along. If you practice these three elements over and over, then you may eventually find yourself caught up in the art of the novel. It's practice, isn't it, that gives your mind the strength to pull art from your heart?

Character

Every book needs at least one character. Even if it's a plot-driven novel, like a mystery with a great detective, the character must be three-dimensional. Not just arms and legs, but heart and soul, and faults and warts. In the classroom, I draw a stick figure on the board, and I ask the students to call out characteristics of the person they want to invent. It's a collaborative effort and a messy one. It gets playful, and the excitement ratchets up as we argue about whether this stick figure should be a he with bad acne or a she with bad hair. Should she be an atheist rebelling against her parents who are devout Catholics? "No," someone will shout, "he should be a skateboarder who is a drug addict who loses the world competition." As they throw out ideas, I draw (to the best of my stick figure-cum-dry-erase marker medium ability) the things they shout out.

I ask them to include physical, psychological, and sociological traits. The reader not only wants to know what the character looks like but also what's going inside their conscious and subconscious mind. We want to know all the good gossip about them: who their parents were, where they grew up, what religion they are, how they eat their food, what kind of food (pie, I hope), and how many toes they have, at least in some cases. Because a three-toed Jehovah's Witness is going to have a different view on life than a ten-toed transgender atheist. We also want to know the bad gossip on them: What are their external and internal scars? How do they see and walk in this world? What is their world like? Are they poor, rich, greedy, overgenerous to a fault? Naive or untrusting?

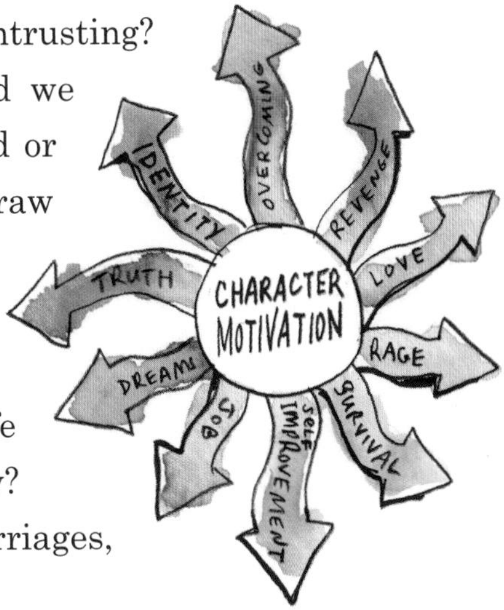
CHARACTER MOTIVATION
IDENTITY
OVERCOMING
REVENGE
LOVE
RAGE
SURVIVAL
SELF IMPROVEMENT
JOB
DREAMS
TRUTH

As the students shout out their ideas, and we discuss which one to keep and which to discard or use for another character, I keep track. I can't draw some of the more ethereal traits, so I list them. But I don't just list everything, we let the character's details come together based on the other details. What events in Stick Figure's life have gone on to make them who they are today? How were they shaped by their childhood, marriages, parents, school, demographics, etc.?

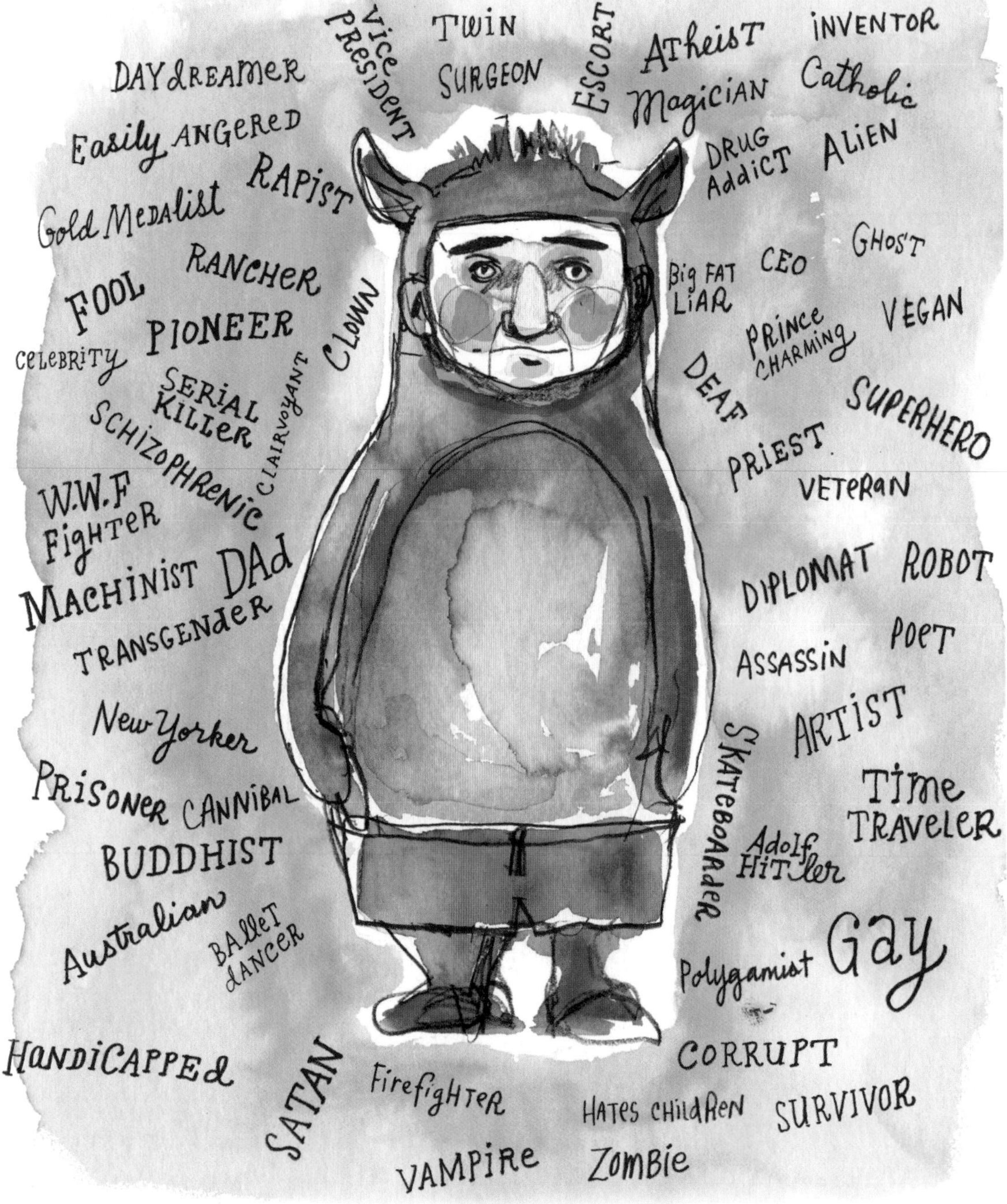

Vice President
Twin
Surgeon
Escort
Atheist
Inventor
Daydreamer
Magician
Catholic
Easily Angered
Drug Addict
Alien
Rapist
Gold Medalist
Ghost
CEO
Rancher
Big Fat Liar
Fool
Clown
Vegan
Pioneer
Prince Charming
Celebrity
Deaf
Serial Killer
Clairvoyant
Superhero
Schizophrenic
Priest
Veteran
W.W.F Fighter
Machinist
Dad
Diplomat
Robot
Transgender
Poet
Assassin
Artist
New Yorker
Skateboarder
Time Traveler
Prisoner
Cannibal
Adolf Hitler
Buddhist
Australian
Ballet Dancer
Gay
Polygamist
Handicapped
Corrupt
Satan
Firefighter
Hates Children
Survivor
Vampire
Zombie

You're going to join a writing group, show your work to friends and eventually an editor, or even your mom might read it, and you're going to be asked, "What is the character's motivation for wanting to climb Kilimanjaro?" You may want to say, "Because it's there," but you can't get away with that for very long (only your mom will accept that answer), so know your character's background. Did having only three toes make hiking a problem for the character living with a family who liked to hike? Did this disability make her resent her goatlike climbing family members, or did it make her so resilient and determined that now she is the inventor of the Goatmobile® and is sitting on a pile of money? In other words, we need to know not just who she is but how and why she came to be who she is. (Goats, by the way, also like to eat everything. A trait I highly admire.) This will not only help the reader understand and appreciate the character's reactions but also it will help you build the story around what a character of this makeup would do or not do when faced with obstacles and other story situations you create. Author Stanley Elkin said he "would never write about someone who is not at the end of his rope." The character has to be ready to take a step into the journey that invites change. This change is where the story builds to an arc.

Plot

What about that story arc? Plot is also an essential ingredient in a novel. Sure, there are novels written without plots. Plenty of them. But let's first learn to make that crust so we can later make a crustless pie. You might even want to create a soufflé. But for our purposes, we are still working on the fat, flour, and liquid. Gluten-free need not apply, yet.

A plot is a road map with many stops and starts along the way. The character is trying to get from Point A to Point Z but doesn't always know that she's traveling, much less what to pack. Along the way from Point A to Z, she hits Obstacles B through Y. In other words, Ms. Stick Figure has a problem that needs to be solved, and with only three toes and overcoming the depression from her strict parents' rants and not winning the skateboarding championship, she's going to have a hard time getting to that end goal. In this way, all novels (with plots) are something of a mystery—how will the main character ever find the way to what they want? The character also discovers they have a need. Need versus want—the main character will gain a deeper meaning, knowledge, or consolation prize by the end of the book as a part of traipsing through the obstacles and learning or losing things along the way. This buildup of change, this overcoming of these obstacles, the growth of the character, this is the character arc. How the events build in intensity, what the character overcomes or fails at, how the suspense grows and the tensions become fraught with anxiety for both character and reader, this is the plot arc. Both character and plot arc eke upward simultaneously heading toward the top of that goat mountain where the climax of both arcs collide. The culmination of the plot arc and character development is what is needed to satisfy the reader.

If only it were that simple. Or maybe that description wasn't all that simple. The textbook I use for my classroom is *The Plot Thickens: 8 Ways to Bring Fiction to Life* by Noah Lukeman. I chose it because it breaks up the novel into the main ingredients: character inner and outer life, journey, suspense, conflict, and context. Noah uses an E. L. Doctorow quote as an epigraph for "The Journey" chapter:

WRITING A BOOK IS *like* DRIVING A CAR AT NIGHT. YOU ONLY SEE AS FAR AS YOUR HEADLIGHTS GO, BUT YOU CAN MAKE THE WHOLE TRIP THAT WAY.

Curtain Up

On or about the second or third night of class, I talk about scene. Not setting particularly, but how to set a scene, how to open the curtain on your play and let us see not only the stage setting, the space, the props, the furniture, the windows with the weather outside but also who is onstage, who enters stage left, and what happens when a new person enters the stage. What props do they pick up, and why? How do they interact with the setting, and with other characters? How does the mood change as one person enters and another leaves, or more enter and no one leaves? What is said, and what is the reaction to that dialogue? What happens between the curtain opening and the curtain closing between scenes?

Remember, you are the director who gets to rule over the whole scene, the whole play—the play being your novel. Just like a stage play, you will need to have characters with specific lines, but you'll also need to write all the stage direction and everything the actors would normally contribute—their reactions to the dialogue, to the other actors' (characters') actions. Every action will have a reaction, which, in turn, will cause an action, and so on and so forth. Write all of that down.

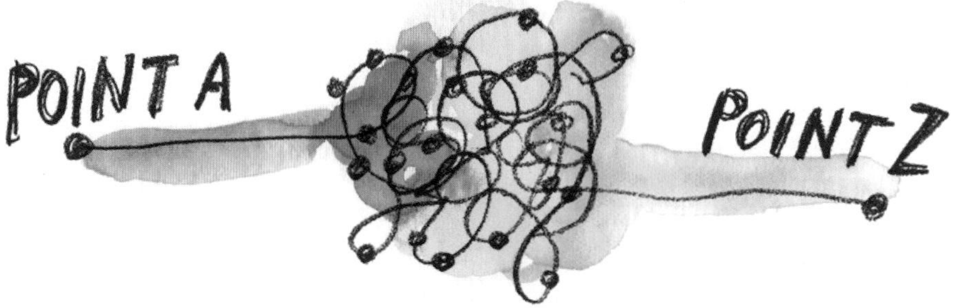
POINT A
POINT Z

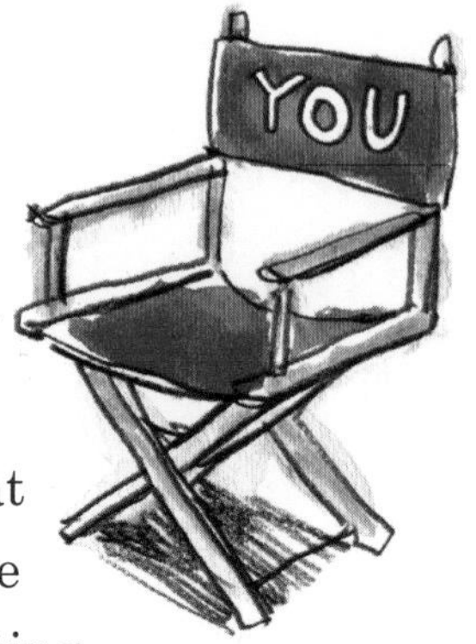
YOU

You have to start someplace, so start with the first action that gets the ball rolling—the inciting incident. The very first page of *MoonPies & Movie Stars* that I wrote was about Ruby sitting in her Barcalounger folding laundry while she watched her soap opera. That was the setting when the curtain rose. That gave me the moment just before the inciting incident. The inciting incident is when the protagonist gets pitched right into oncoming traffic. It's when there is no turning back because after that incident, the main character reacts, and then takes action. In my first draft, for instance, Ruby sat with her feet up folding dishtowels when on the commercial break her runaway daughter goes sashaying across the TV screen in a ButterMaid outfit while hanging out with a cow. What could Ruby do but react with surprise—a mixture of elation and *what-the-hell??* Now she must figure out what to do next. She can't just go on sitting in her Barcalounger for the rest of the novel, not now that she knows where her daughter is. Ruby wants something—to find her daughter, and this is the beginning of the plot.

Memoir Craft

Character

But wait—a memoir already comes prepackaged with its own characters, doesn't it? It does, and just like a novel, everyone needs to be three-dimensional. But memoir has an extra someone special. In memoir we need to see two sides of you. Sue Silverman, the author of *Fearless Confessions*, coined the phrases *Voice of Innocence* and *Voice of Experience.* These are two separate characters, even though they are both you. We see the version of you who is inhabiting the story you are telling. This is the Voice of Innocence. As the story moves forward, the person you are today will show us what has been gleaned from what the earlier you went through—this today-person is the Voice of Experience. How does what happened to you *then* matter to you *now*? The protagonist in memoir is you. You may also be the antagonist if you are getting in your own way of getting what you want. Or maybe someone else is. That distinction is part of the story.

Plot, Not Plot

Mick Jagger was right, "You may not always get what you want, but you just might get what you need." Same is true with plot, whether novel or memoir. But in memoir, you have a situation and a story. Your story can be about almost anything, from living in a tract home in suburbia consuming three squares a day to growing up in a war-torn country so desperate you live on maggots. The situation is that you are there. The story is what you are doing there. What creates the story's trajectory is conflict. A life in suburbia may appear conflict-free, until we learn you want a gritty, more urban life with a faster pace. The story could be how you get out of suburbia into a life of hubbub in Manhattan. The conflict of what you want or need versus the original situation provides the friction out of which the story line emerges.

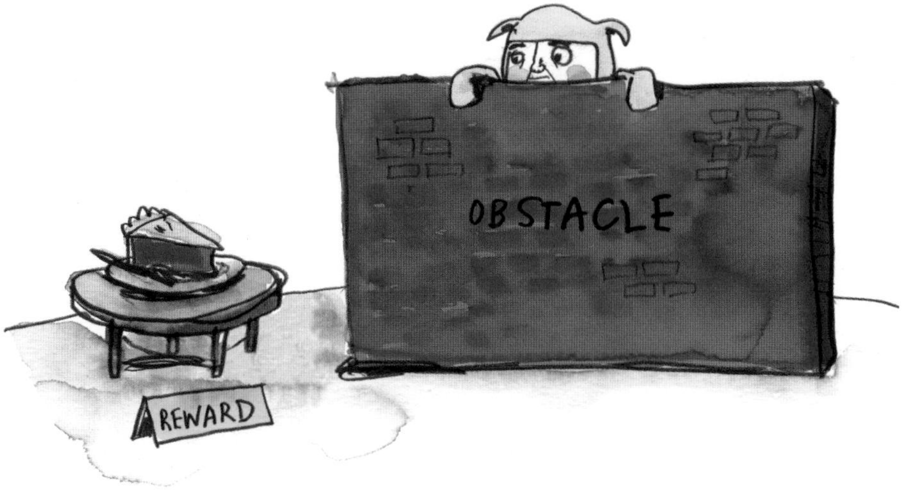
OBSTACLE
REWARD

What Was the Question, Again?

As the author, presenting an overarching question to yourself can provide guideposts on a theme, or how you got from Point A to Point Z or from suburbia to Manhattan, what obstacles you encountered, and how you changed along the way. This question should be self-reflective and pertain to who you were at the beginning and who you are at the end. In my memoir, I used the question, "Are we hideous people?" As my Voice of Experience investigated my family's past, I told the story of myself as a young girl growing up in Africa and South America. My Voice of Innocence was the child witnessing a blue-collar family traipsing around the world pocketing and appropriating cultural artifacts while neglecting little me along the way. My Voice of Experience could explain on the page what my Voice of Innocence didn't understand at the time.

Creative of Creative Nonfiction

Just as a curtain rises on fiction so it does on creative nonfiction—these scenes show the reader how you evolve from the moment you step onstage to when you step off. This is where metaphor based on the world of your memory and your story draws a many-layered picture of what is going on for the Voice of Innocence. Through this metaphorical lens you demonstrate the contrast the Voice of Experience knows but the Voice of Innocence bumps up against. Use your setting's details to show emotional shifts and changes in tone. Dialogue may illustrate one thing being said, another meant. I used a ghost metaphor in my memoir, because my family came and went like ghosts. You never know when a ghost will appear or disappear. The ethereal metaphor illustrated how my family members weren't there for me emotionally.

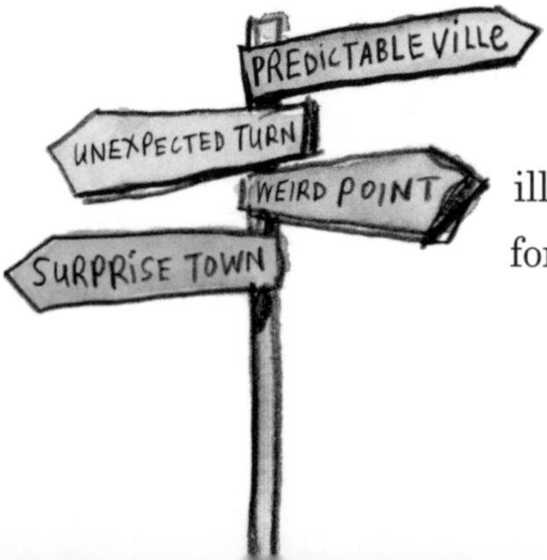
PREDICTABLE VILLE
UNEXPECTED TURN
WEIRD POINT
SURPRISE TOWN

Memory was a theme in my memoir from the beginning as well. Memory, I learned, is not a file cabinet with mislabeled drawers in my head. Memory is created by our imagination. This does not mean it's not real but, instead, means that our memories are constantly being re-created each time we re-remember them. Each time you process a memory by telling it, or imagining it in your head, it is re-created to be more about you. Your story is your story alone and no one else's to tell. That's why it's important to write it. Don't let those naysayers tell you otherwise.

Outliner or Pantser?

Some writers outline the whole plot before they begin. This is perfectly fine, and quite organized. If writing were a race, I'd probably put my money on an outliner to finish first. But just like I prefer not to know the ending when I read a book, I like to write my first draft not knowing where it's going either. I love the element of surprise. I'm a pantser. I write by the seat of my pants. This is where Pie Butt comes in handy. I sit in my chair and start writing what I think will happen next. Without jotting down notes first, I see where the story takes me. My first novel *MoonPies & Movie Stars* spilled out of my pen. My main character, Ruby, had something at stake—she'd just spotted her runaway daughter on a ButterMaid commercial. Ruby knew she had to go find her daughter now that she knew where Violet was. I wrote as fast as I could while trying to keep up with my imagination.

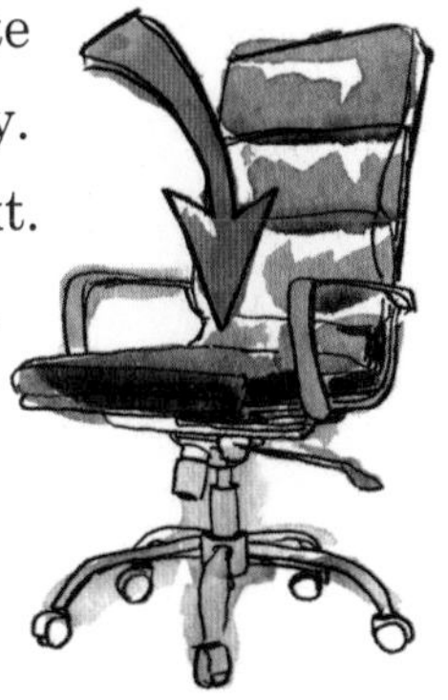

A character showed up in my writerly peripheral vision, so I wrote down what came to me. Yes, many drafts had to be rewritten and revised to reconfigure what changed because of what happened later that didn't mesh with what happened earlier. The process of letting the story just pour out of me, this experience was like reading a book, not knowing how it was going to turn out—a page-turner, only I had to write the next page. I encourage this process with my students because, like the slapping together of three-toed Stick Figure, the imagination gets to be free and loose before the editing voice starts tidying up the pages. I wrote my whole novel without knowing where it was going. At times, I felt discombobulated—not knowing if I was doing the right thing, if it made any sense, or even if maybe I'd disappeared inside some fiction and was really just one of those ladies who had voices inside her head who baked pie. I probably am, but the voices had some good ideas. I followed the tangents but reeled my imagination back in when I got too far off course. At most I plotted out the next day's scenes in my head before falling asleep and typed them up in the morning. I never knew exactly where I was going to go, but that was okay, because you know what? No one was going to die from it.

As I've said before, sometimes I felt I might never be finished. Often along the way, I worried my plot and I had taken a wrong turn and ended up on some back alley in a town that had nothing to do with where we were supposed to be headed. How would I find my way back? At these junctures, I would jot down an outline of where I had been. From that list, I could jot a few more lines of what scenes would likely come next. This was an outline of sorts. An outline of what I had so far, and what was on the horizon. Any type of outline, one written from the starting line or one written while I'm driving by my headlights alone, needs to be held loosely while the macadam is being laid.

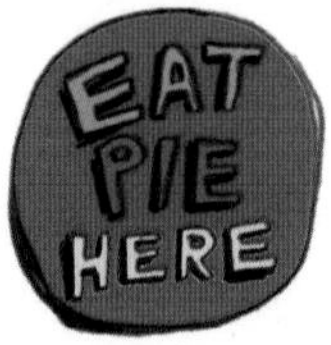
EAT
PIE
HERE

It may feel like a waste of time not to know where you are going, but instead, you may discover new story lines that you never would have thought of if you'd stuck to the safe road. Think of it this way: you don't need a map; you are the mapmaker, and you get to draw the roads and all the bumps along the way. Writing can be an adventure.

What you need to start this journey is a character who has something at stake. This can be fiction or you. Pack them a bag that includes conflict, suspense, tension, and context, and bring along an antagonist to sit shotgun, and be sure to bring a spare bag to load up on some unexpected surprises.

Easier said than done, you say?

This is where I say, just write, because that's the only way you are going to find out what happens at The End. That's where perseverance comes in.

Here are the three rules no one knows, but I'll tell just you:

RULE #1 — CREATE —A— CHARACTER

RULE #2 — TAKE Them on a JOURNEY, ONE SCENE at a TIME.

RULE #3 — STOP AT REST STOPS and EAT Pie.

SCABBard Apple PiE

I spend my summers in upstate New York in a small town called Saratoga Springs. It's known for its racetrack, but also for the jazz, dance, and writers institutes. As associate director of the New York State Summer Writers Institutes, I spend most of my time working with the faculty and students. I'm in New York for work, so not much pie baking gets done, but one summer, I decided that shouldn't be the case anymore. I have a nice kitchen in Saratoga, much nicer than my kitchen in San Diego, so why didn't I just carve out a bit of pie time? Besides, I owed an author friend, an avid pie lover, a favor.

That Saturday at the farmers market, I went to the apple lady's stall. As a Californian, I'm always surprised how the apple booth has so many varieties of apples—in July!

I mentioned to the apple lady that I was making a pie, so I wanted two pounds of Granny Smiths, a couple of honeycrisps, and two pounds of McIntosh.

"For pie?" she said, "you don't want McIntosh for pie. It won't hold its shape."

"I love the flavor of McIntosh," I replied.

The apple lady is rather abrupt and rarely friendly, but I'm used to her, so I stood my ground.

"McIntosh is sweet but becomes mush," she says. "You don't want."

"Yes, I do want," I said. I rarely can tell an authority what to do, and an apple lady is surely an apple authority.

The woman in line behind me agreed with apple lady. "You'll get mush if you use the McIntosh."

"I get a lot of compliments on my pie being not too sweet and just the right texture pie filling," I tell both, a little dismayed, but prepared to stand up for my apple pie. "The Granny Smith holds its shape and provides a nice tart flavor, and the McIntosh fills out the filling with a nice sweetness and gives the texture of the filling more thickness since I don't add much sugar like most people."

"I make a lot of pies," the lady in line tells me. "You'll regret it." As though I couldn't possibly know what she knows.

"I make a lot of pies," I say, looking at her two pints of cherries she has in her hands. She'd drawn her scabbard first.

"I make many cherry pies," she said. "I put in a pint of sour and two pints of sweet cherries."

"Three pints, that's all?" I said. If I didn't let out a haughty laugh, it was certainly sitting in my craw. I gave her a once-over from her tiny pints to her mealy eyes. "I use three *pounds* of cherries in each pie, and I pit all of them by hand." I thrust my sword, pulled it out slowly, then I sacked my Grannies and McIntoshes, and paid the apple lady who had a smile on her face, as I'm sure she knew I'd be back to buy more cherries to make a pie tomorrow too.

Here's why I tell you that story—an apple pie is an apple pie, but you have to know the basics of an apple pie to know what to add to make it your own. The craft is simple—apples, some sugar, some spice, and throw it in a crust. What you decide to add to it, how you spice it up, how you make it the pie you want to eat with the texture you like and the details that make it unique, that's how you write the book you'd want to read, because ultimately, you're the first reader/eater.

Here I share my apple pie recipe. Later, I'll share The Best Cherry Pie. Scabbards and swords not included.

FAMOUS LITERARY APPLES

POISONED

Heroic

GOLDEN

FORBIDDEN

NEWTON'S

NEW YORK CITY

6 to 8 apples

⅔ cup plus 1 tablespoon granulated sugar, divided

1 tablespoon lemon juice

Zest from 1 lemon

¼ teaspoon salt

1 teaspoon ground cinnamon

3 to 4 tablespoons coarsely chopped crystallized ginger

1 egg yolk

1 tablespoon milk

Preheat the oven to 425°F.

Core and thinly slice all those apples, 6 to 8 should be plenty. Please use any variety you want. I made one at Kate McDermott's, author of *Pie Camp*, Pie Cottage and we used eight different apples plus part of a quince—delightful. I don't peel my apples, but that's up to you. All the apple slices go in a big mixing bowl, add ⅔ cup of the sugar, lemon juice, lemon zest, salt, cinnamon, and crystallized ginger. Toss until well combined. Put them all in a crust (all-butter is my fave, and complements the apples), brush on a mixture of egg yolk and milk, then sprinkle on the remaining tablespoon of sugar. Bake for 30 minutes at 425°F, then turn the oven down to 375°F and spin the pie around to bake evenly on the other side for another 25 to 30 minutes.

Oh, and that lady behind me at the farmers market—she also claimed she made somewhere near SIX pies a year. Only six? I hope she spends her free time reading good books.

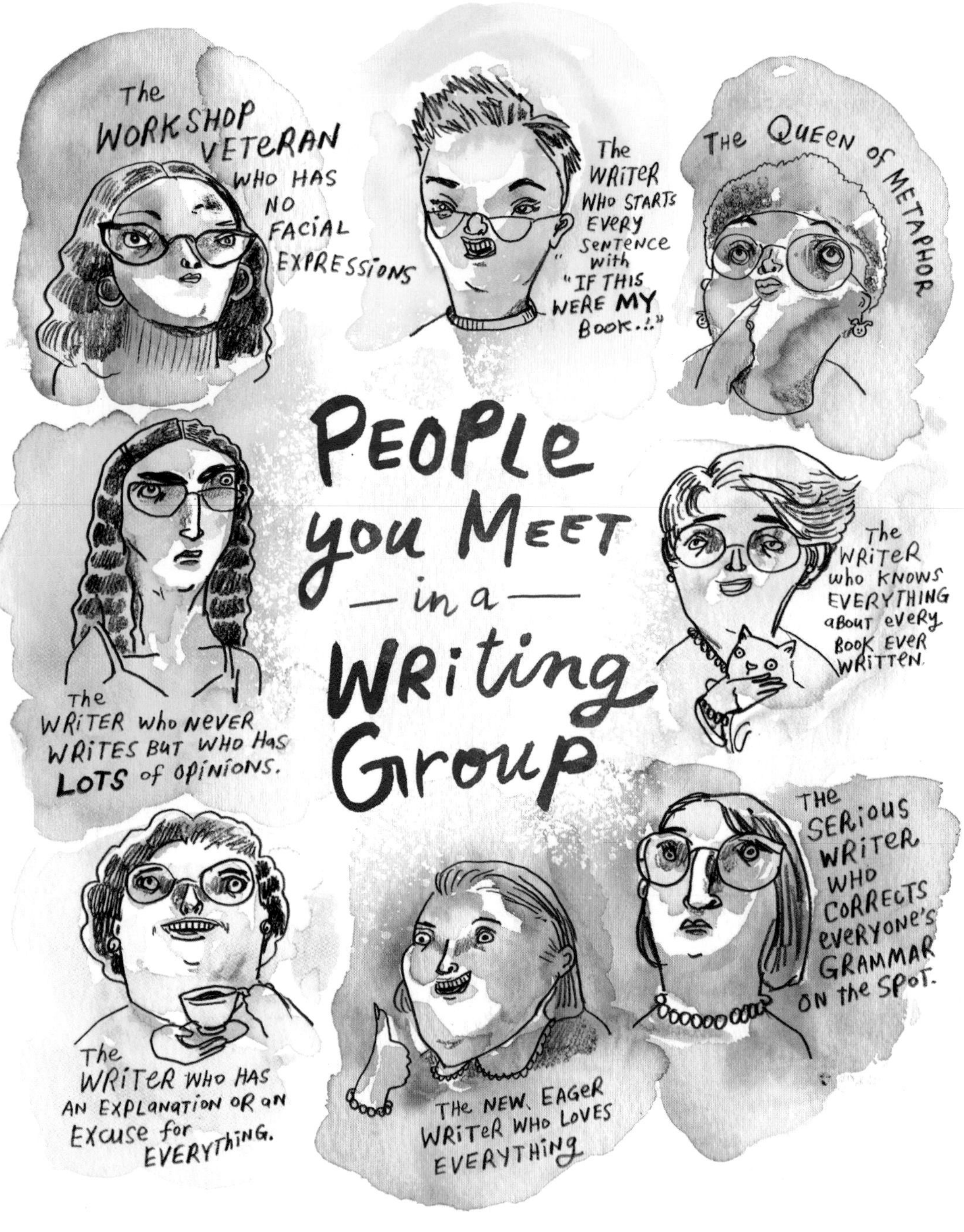
People you Meet in a Writing Group
The WORKSHOP VETERAN WHO HAS NO FACIAL EXPRESSIONS
The WRITER WHO STARTS EVERY SENTENCE with "IF THIS WERE MY BOOK..."
THE QUEEN OF METAPHOR
The WRITER who NEVER WRITES BUT WHO HAS LOTS of opinions.
The WRITER who KNOWS EVERYTHING about every BOOK EVER WRITTEN.
The WRITER WHO HAS AN EXPLANATION OR AN EXCUSE for EVERYTHING.
The NEW, EAGER WRITER WHO LOVES EVERYTHING
THE SERIOUS WRITER WHO CORRECTS EVERYONE'S GRAMMAR ON THE SPOT.

CHAPTER FIVE

Wrangling Writing Groups

The Gut

I was something of a writing group whore while writing my novel. I don't mean I slept with everyone in my group. Trust me, most groups are filled with middle-aged women, and we don't show up to group in anything that doesn't have elastic waistbands, and we usually leave crying and craving comfort food—not the sexiest. What I mean by *whore* is that I joined every single group that I could find. I wanted feedback galore on my pages. So I tried them all. Sometimes I belonged to two, even three, simultaneously. And this was the most whorish thing of all: I did everything they told me to do.

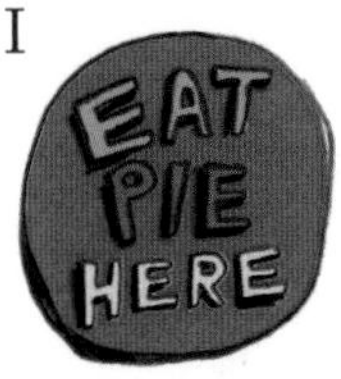
EAT
PIE
HERE

One group in particular I called my Power Group because they were all women (plus one man) who made things happen in the world. That is, if the world were Hollywood. They consisted of, among others, a movie star's publicist, an already famous author, a TV star from a hit '70s sitcom, and an advertising copywriter for all those cool ads you were watching in the early 2000s. The leader was no less than Janet Fitch, writer extraordinaire, author of *White Oleander*, an Oprah's Book Club selection, back before 2.0. In fact, I joined right after Janet made that club and received instant bestseller status. I was there to witness when her books started selling and Janet bought new bathroom towels, then a new coffee table, and we watched as Oprah changed her life. I was completely devoted to this group because they were obviously better, smarter, and richer than I was.

Some people have issues with authority, but not me; I have no problem with authority figures—I do whatever they tell me to do, and we are all happy.

When the group critiqued my pages, I was ready to take whatever they gave me. When these women (plus one man) told me to get rid of the churchy lady in my novel, I did it. When Janet suggested I switch from first person to third, I did it. The switch worked brilliantly: it gave me more peripheral vision for a character who was leaning, or rather lying flat out toward one-dimensional. When they told me the dialect wasn't working except in the dialogue, out it went. My metaphors, they said, needed to be more focused toward the Southern and on-the-road environment. Ah! I get it, and I worked that out. "Give Ruby a job," Janet said of my protagonist, and off to bowling alleys I went to research Ruby's new self-employment. Soon Ruby had more substance and verve. Those perverted truckers that show up in chapter 8—stricken from the story. Ruby should sock the mother-in-law in the face, I was told. Check. (Although, I did this reluctantly.) The stops in New Mexico and Arizona—gone. The Hells Angels scene with no purpose, deleted. When Janet one day told me that the era feels more '70s, I had to laugh—my TV references were from the '70s, all the clothing was straight from a '70s Sears catalog, and I had been resisting everything I knew about the bicentennial, but Janet was spot on. So 1976, here I come. Stir in some Hollywood grunge—I'm on it.

I'd race home from Los Angeles, where the group was held in Janet's living room, to my house in San Diego on a junk food high from the snacks we always brought. At my desk, I'd toss, rewrite, delete, change up, add, revise, edit, like a dog in a garbage pail digging for the chicken skin at the bottom.

That group took my novel to places I never could have gone on my own. I benefited from the input, and I could see my book changing shape. My writing changed drastically.

When I had the fifth draft under my belt, I sat down to read the whole thing through. When I finished, I cried. Not tears of joy that I had a Pulitzer Prize winner or that Oprah would be calling soon. I cried because I couldn't tell if my book was about a woman selling rattlesnakes on the roadside, a soap opera star who ate MoonPies, or a one-armed petunia vendor in Albuquerque. I had a mulligatawny stew. I no longer knew what this novel was about. Okay, maybe I never really knew what it was about, but I at least had some sense where my characters and I were headed.

It became clear to me that I had taken on everything without considering what I wanted the book to be. Not just *about*, but *be*, as in the heart and soul of the book. I had done just what I was told. I hadn't kept the part that was true with a capital *T*. I had listened to all the wonderful women (and one man) in the group, all to a certain degree of success, but I had never listened to me, or my gut. I hadn't listened to my instinct—whatever that was. Maybe I spent too much time brushing my teeth and not enough time considering how the rest of the world, or at least my group's advice, should be taken in the context with which it was delivered.

When the group had said the Hells Angels scene wasn't adding anything to the narrative, they were right, as far as how that scene was unfolding in the manuscript. But if I'd listened to my gut, I'd have heard it ask me, "Okay, what does the scene need to make it work in the context of the novel? Because these badass guys didn't show up on your page unless they had something to say."

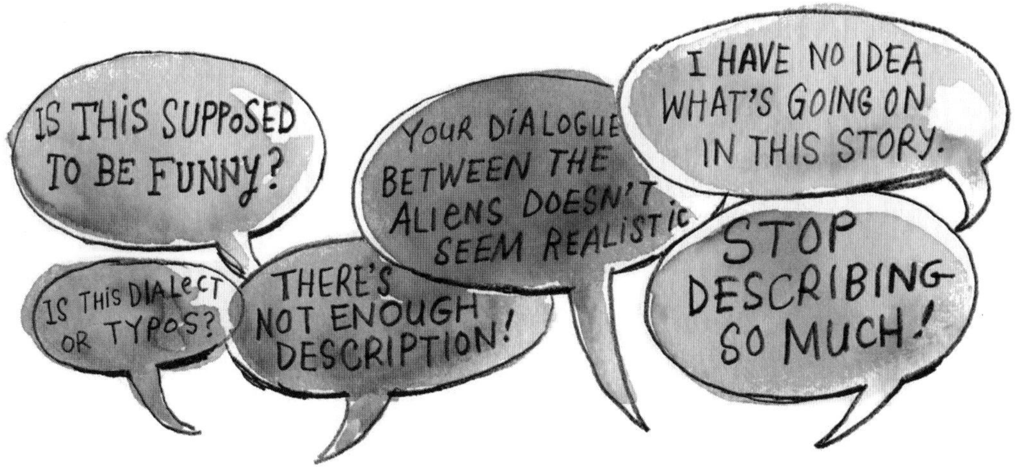
IS THIS SUPPOSED TO BE FUNNY?
YOUR DIALOGUE BETWEEN THE ALIENS DOESN'T SEEM REALISTIC
I HAVE NO IDEA WHAT'S GOING ON IN THIS STORY.
IS THIS DIALECT OR TYPOS?
THERE'S NOT ENOUGH DESCRIPTION!
STOP DESCRIBING SO MUCH!

While I sat at my fiberboard desk shoved into a corner of my ten-by-ten bedroom, I stared at the pages where the scene used to be. Somewhere between Lordsburg, New Mexico, and Phoenix, Arizona. As I continued to stare at the space that had held the missing scene, my gut, my intuition, my subconscious, my tiny inner writer whispered to me. A whisper so quiet I had to say, "What?" And she still whispered, so I kept saying, "What? What was that?" I needed this voice to speak up. What did she know that I didn't know?

The voice wasn't used to speaking, so it gurgled a phlegmy whisper that said: The Hells Angel named Burl, the one revving his motor, would have firsthand knowledge about being abandoned by a mother. He'd tell Ruby what she should expect when she got to California, whether she wanted to believe him or not. This advice would be something Ruby could take with her for the rest of the trip, gnawing at her and adding tension. As it turns out, what that Hells Angel had to say was not good news, but it was the truth that was needed at that moment in the story.

But it was also the inclusion of this scene, in its revision, that was important to the narrative as a whole. The scene was a Truth to the spirit of the novel. While the group was right when they said the scene wasn't working, that didn't mean—given a little reworking and a whole lot of tuning in to that whispering inner writing woman—it didn't still belong.

I continued to look to my group for feedback—after all, they were still smarter and better looking than I was—but this time I arrived each week with specific questions in mind, questions regarding what I was stumped on in a particular scene. I prefaced each piece with what I wanted from them, what I felt might be missing, or asked what they thought was missing. As they told me what I needed, I listened to the group, but this time I fully searched their feedback to determine what resonated within me, what I felt was in line with the intentions of the story. And in this way, in only five

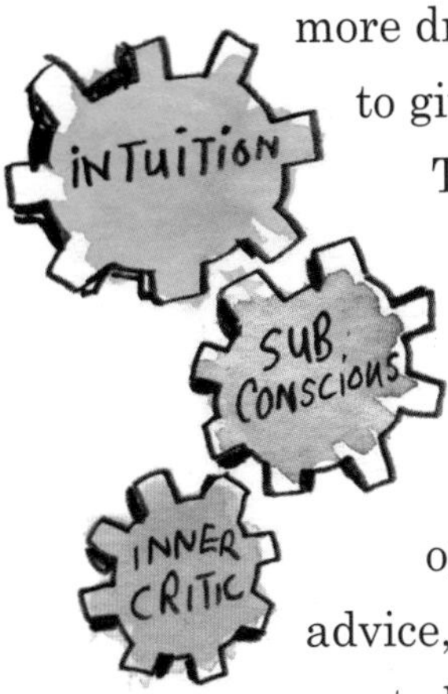
INTUITION
SUB-CONSCIOUS
INNER CRITIC
more drafts, I got to The End. I'm a slow learner and reluctant to give up wanting to be told what to do.

This is my experience, but writing groups are a different experience for everyone. I have one friend who, when I asked her what her biggest obstacle was, replied, "ego." She said she had to learn to take in what the group or individual readers said. She had to learn to listen the opposite of how I did. She didn't want to take any of their advice, but learned the hard way, like I did, that their input was to be considered within the context of the story.

Having readers review a work in progress is scary and dangerous, but a group provides many other levels of support in this lonely world of writing. You can't write in a vacuum. Okay, maybe you can, but how will you know if your work resonates or is just the contents of a vacuum cleaner bag? Maybe you don't care if you're writing about amorphous dust bunnies and skeins of hair. Even if you're the guy who stares at his fingernails while the group gives constructive critique, a writing group also provides a deadline. Being accountable, knowing that biweekly someone expects strong writing and not just drivel, is what drove me to The End. Deadlines are how daily newspapers get written, and many a novel. Even the books with dust bunnies as main characters.

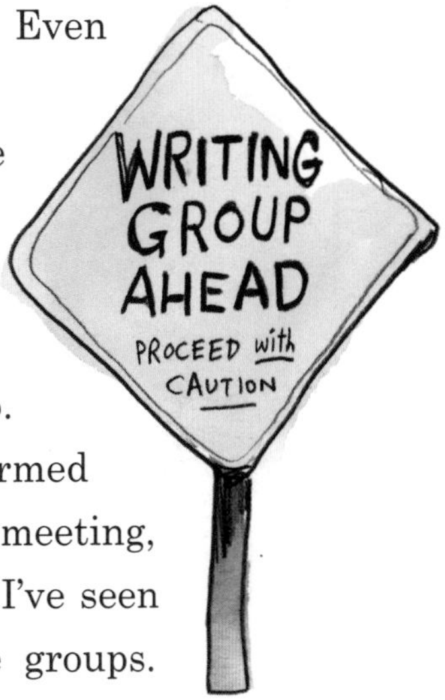
WRITING GROUP AHEAD
PROCEED with CAUTION

I couldn't have written my novel without those women (plus one man). The camaraderie, the food we consumed during the meetings, the input, which was often spot on, was invaluable. I may have been a slut, but I birthed a happy bouncing baby book with their help.

How do you find a group? Many writing groups are formed at the end of my classes. The class decides to continue meeting, and they carry on after the school quarter has ended. I've seen more than a few published novels come from these groups.

BENEfits of BEINg IN a WRITING GROUP

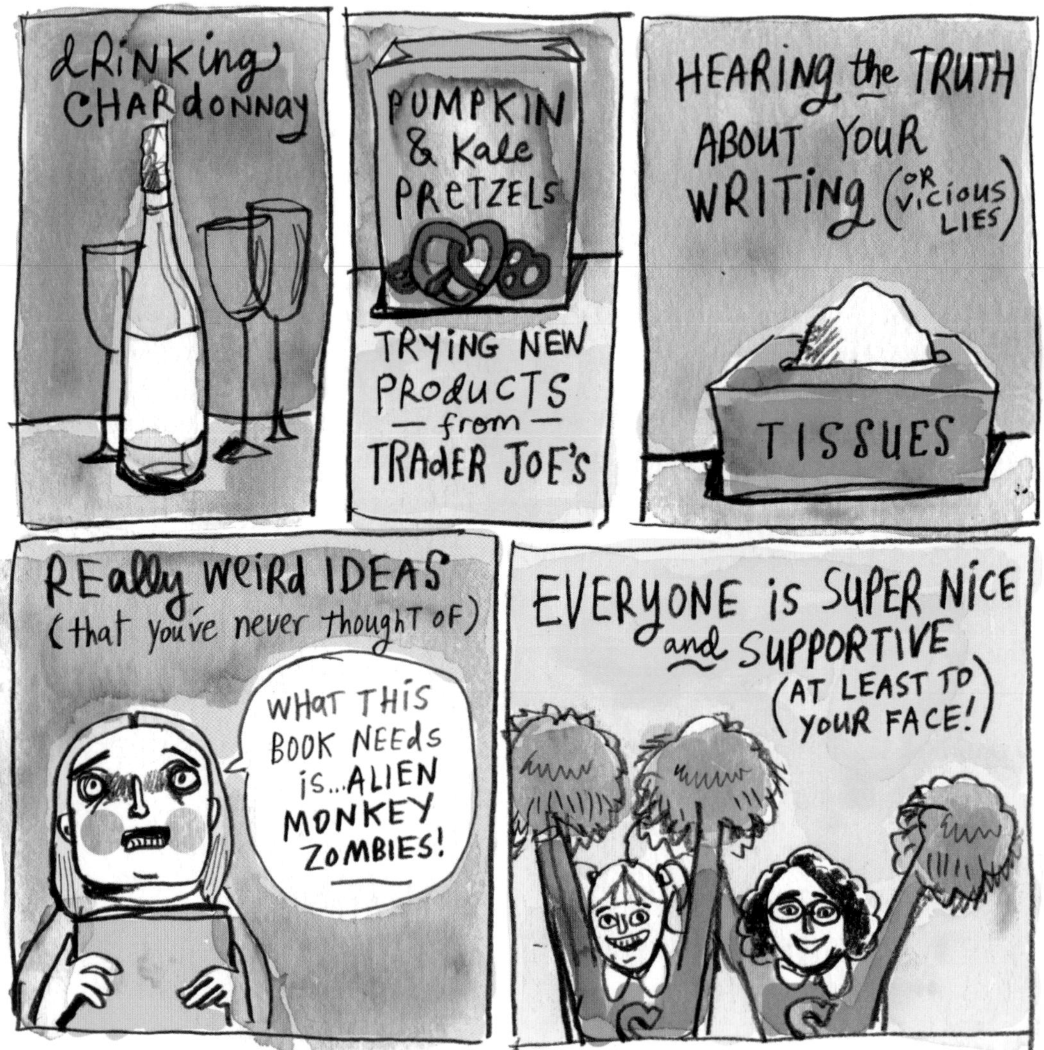

dRiNKing CHARdoNNay
PUMPKIN & Kale PRETZELS
TRYING NEW PRODUCTS — from — TRAdER JOE'S
HEARING the TRUTH ABOUT YOUR WRITING (OR VICIOUS LIES)
TISSUES
REally WeiRd IDEAS (that you've never thought of)
WHAT THIS BOOK NEEdS is...ALIEN MONKEY ZOMBIES!
EVERYONE is SUPER NICE and SUPPORTIVE (AT LEAST TO YOUR FACE!)

Also many friendships, if you're into that kind of thing. Many cities have writing centers where they offer read-and-critique groups for a fee. Teacher-led groups often help avoid the blind-leading-the-blind syndrome, but peer groups also provide the support and, if a well-read group, they know as readers what they want and need in a story. Try to avoid asking your mom or your spouse to be your reader. This is the age-old issue because we want feedback, and they really want to help (or know what you've been up to behind closed doors), but you need constructive criticism. Sure, you think your husband's input is constructive, and he's always honest with you, but don't rely on just him unless he's Franz Kafka or Jack Kerouac. If he is Franz or Jack, you probably have other relationship issues anyway. In the end, you'll want more than one set of eyes on your pages, and you'll want to find a good strong reader or two or eight.

I wasn't making pies when I first joined a writing group. It took years before I had the kind of confidence where I could share a pie with my group. But, boy, did we eat a lot of comfort food in Janet's living room, and how I wish I could have shared pie with them. Maybe all our books would be better for it.

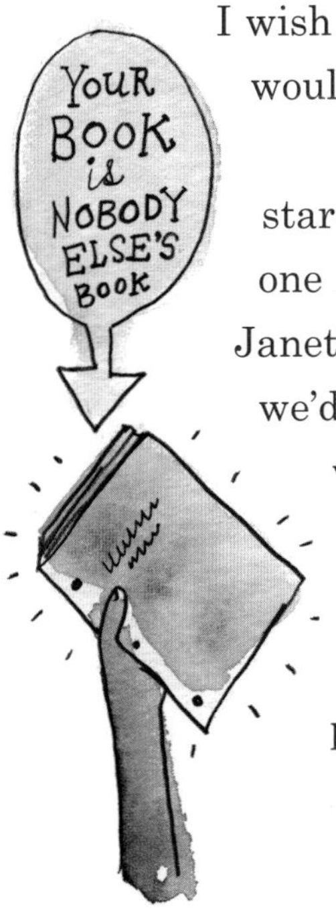
YOUR BOOK is NOBODY ELSE'S BOOK

Comfort food was definitely a part of the experience. I started taking the train up to LA and Emil Wilson (my plus-one man) would pick me up at the train station to take me to Janet's group, where he was a member too. After the workshop, we'd go back to his house where he'd have baked a pie, which we'd eat, and then we'd lie on his living room floor, our stomachs protruding, while we reflected on the day's critiques and contemplated the virtues of eating both savory pie for dinner and sweet pie for dessert. Was it possible to have too much pie? No, was the conclusion.

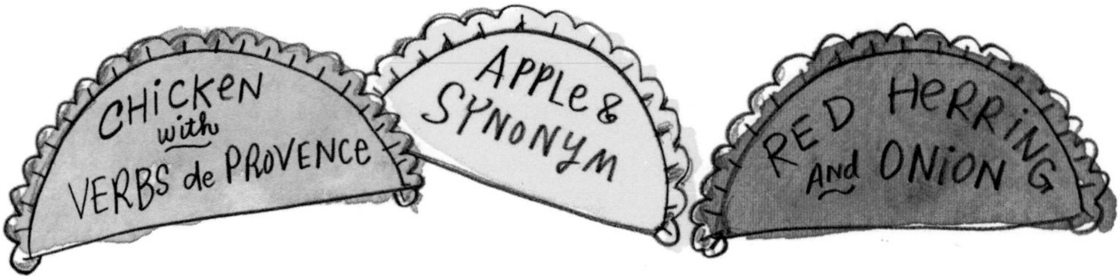
CHICKEN with VERBS de PROVENCE
APPLE & SYNONYM
RED HERRING AND ONION

Sharing Pies

If you have the inclination to take pie to your group, or if you want to start a group, I suggest hand pies to share. Any of the recipes in this book can be made into shareable pies. Just chop the ingredients finer and increase your double-crust pie dough recipe by about one-third. If you want to make more than six hand pies, then double, triple, or even quadruple your recipe and do the same with your pastry. Hand pies are simple, and who doesn't love a warm sweet or savory pie in their hand headed right toward their mouth? Your group will want to give you nothing but kudos on your pies and your writing.

Here are the deets on six mini-pies:

Chill the dough in much smaller flattened disks, maybe 5 or 6 instead of 2. Roll out 1 disk at a time and cut out 2 to 3 5-inch circles. Fill one half of the circle with the filling of your choice. Fold over the empty side and crimp the edges to make half-moons. These don't take as long to bake as a full-sized pie; check them after 20 minutes, and expect to cook them for 30 minutes at 400°F.

Or use muffin tins or ramekins. Again, these can be filled to any level and can have a top crust or not. I often use the mini-muffin pans to make itty-bitty pies for appetizer-sized bites. With these you can pop as many as you want in your mouth while arguing the importance of metaphor for character development, and no one will be the wiser as to how many you ate.

MUSHRooM Hand Pies

In this recipe, I use muffin tins. A single pie crust pastry will make 6 mini pies with tops.

1 single crust dough

FILLING

1 tablespoon olive oil

1 large shallot, chopped

6 ounces mushrooms of your choice, chopped

1 tablespoon finely chopped fresh thyme

1 tablespoon finely chopped fresh rosemary

1 tablespoon tomato paste

1 tablespoon soy sauce

2 tablespoons all-purpose flour

1 cup broth, beef or chicken or vegetable

¼ cup ricotta cheese, skim is fine

½ cup shredded sharp cheddar cheese

Preheat the oven to 400°F.

Heat the oil in a sauté pan, then add the shallots, mushrooms, and herbs. Sauté until softened and mushrooms have released their water. Add the tomato paste and soy sauce and stir until a nice crust begins to form on the mushrooms. Add the flour, stirring until well distributed. Pour in the broth in ¼ cup increments until the flour and broth begin to make a sauce. Stir in the ricotta. The mushroom filling should be smooth and creamy. You can make it whatever consistency you prefer.

Roll out your dough, and cut out six 4-inch circles. Line each muffin tin with dough, with a little extra spilling out around the edges. Sprinkle the shredded cheddar cheese evenly on the bottoms of each lined tin. Chill while you roll out the tops. You may need to roll out the scraps of dough once to have enough dough to make the lids. Cut the remaining dough into six 3-inch circles for the tops of the mini-pies.

Fill the dough-lined tins with 2 tablespoons of the mushroom mixture. Moisten the edges of the dough both for the bottoms and tops of the pies. Place each 3-inch circle over the filled tins. Crimp the edges, or flatten with a fork. Cut vent slots on the top of each pastry.

Bake for 25 to 30 minutes. Allow to cool for a few minutes before removing. Using a dull knife, slide the blade around the edge of each pie, then lift from the tins.

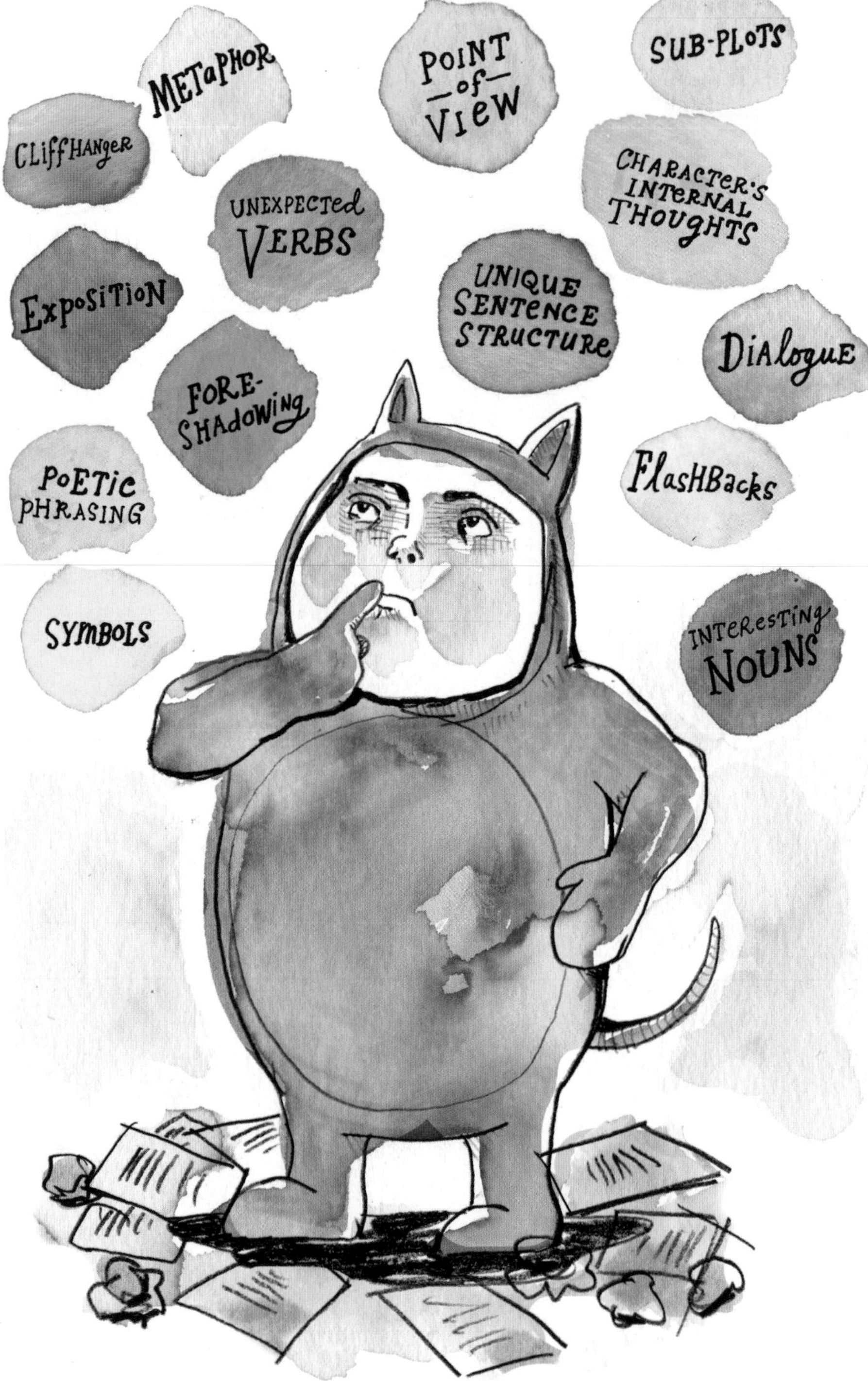

METAPHOR
POINT of VIEW
SUB-PLOTS
CLIFFHANGER
CHARACTER'S INTERNAL THOUGHTS
UNEXPECTED VERBS
EXPOSITION
UNIQUE SENTENCE STRUCTURE
DIALOGUE
FORE-SHADOWING
POETIC PHRASING
FLASHBACKS
SYMBOLS
INTERESTING NOUNS

CHAPTER SIX

Reading, Writing & Hitchhiking

The title of this chapter should be "Studying with the Masters." But that's boring. So I've broken it up into three seemingly disconnected subtitles that are all about how the stories you read can be your best guides on how to write.

Reading

Read.

That should be all I need to say. But my editor won't let me get away with that. I have a page count due for this project, so it's best I fill in what I mean.

Reading is so important for a writer that it really does deserve its own chapter. There are even whole books on reading like a writer. Reading as a writer is not the same as reading for enjoyment. I usually start the read-and-critique section of class off by giving them a published piece of writing to show how we can always consider each word on a page. How we always should. We dissect the chapter, usually the first chapter of *The Great Gatsby*, to take a look at the author, in this case F. Scott Fitzgerald's noun and verb choice, how he sets up the scene, who he introduces as the narrator (Nick Carraway as opposed to Jay Gatsby), and why did he make this choice?

I do this on purpose to make my students miserable when they read. I do this to make sure they never have fun reading ever again. At least, that's what they try to tell me I've done—how I've punished them. I'm so cruel. My students like to grouse about how I ruined their reading for the rest of their lives when I teach them how to critique, how to edit, how to look at a piece of work up close, to ask questions about every choice the author makes.

Perhaps at first it will feel that way. Stopping mid-sentence to consider the author's word choice or what point of view or psychic distance does to a particular story can be jarring and feel like some sort of CIA torture to make you give up all your secrets. Trust me, I don't want to know your secrets—it's hard enough carrying around my own. But I can promise that while you'll miss the old days when you could completely envelop yourself inside a story and disappear like a warm bath, if you practice reading like a writer, you'll not only disappear even further inside the story but also you'll learn not just the characters' secrets but the author's as well.

What I hope I've done is to teach my students to consider the characters' motivations, to look at how unique verbs can change the tone, how sentence length can slow or speed up the tension, how to listen for the voice of the narration and distinguish it from the characters', even when it is or isn't the same voice.

I've heard that the best way to learn how to write is to be a translator. I've always fantasized about translating great works, but it's on my bucket list waiting for me to get around to it along with studying ballet, owning a pie shop, and traveling to Antarctica, all of which could happen but probably won't since I'm too old to do an arabesque, don't like waiting on people, and don't own a hefty parka. But if you were just translating from English to English (or whatever your first language is), you'd consider each word, each phrase, each sentence, and the structures of all of these animals. You'd want to know why someone is using the subjunctive versus the command of a verb. Are they being sly and manipulative, or just formal in their style? Is their humor sarcastic or slapstick? Let's hope the former, in my opinion.

When you start to read this way, to look at why and how the author wrote the book the way they did, you read slower and more meticulously. At first, this close reading is cumbersome, and you lose track of what was going on on the page—the action narration in your head becomes like a deep voice on slow speed, and you have to rewind or reread to comprehend the whole picture. Eventually, over time and with practice, you don't lose track of the story, and you can hold two things in your head at one time—the character's word choice as he cuts the throat of the villain and see his underlying guilt in his thought process, as well as see the color red not just as blood splatter but as a symbol of their freedom. Okay, that's cheesy, but it gets the point across that everything isn't so literal in literature.

Except when it is. I'll share an anecdote from eons ago. I was watching a late-night show with a novelist as the guest. The host and author chatted about the book, and like most hosts, it was pretty clear they hadn't actually read the book very closely, and the author was trying not to notice. The host was a comedian, and the questions were incongruent, so at some point he asked the author, "In chapter 4 you had a man digging up a potato. I suppose that potato signifies the man is digging deeper inside himself? Or does that potato represent the hard toil of the human race?" The author looked at the host, took a moment, then shook his head. "Nope," he said. "It was just a potato."

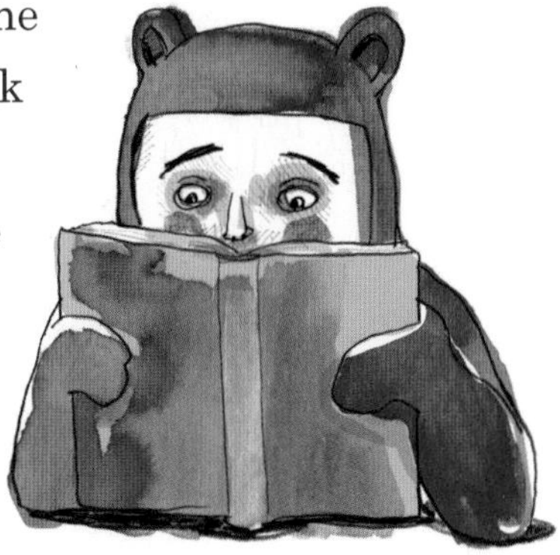

Reading will eventually not only be your favorite pastime as it was before but it will also be the nicest writing teacher because it doesn't require you turn in your homework on time, nor expect you to raise your hand when you have a question. Although it does not bring pie like this teacher.

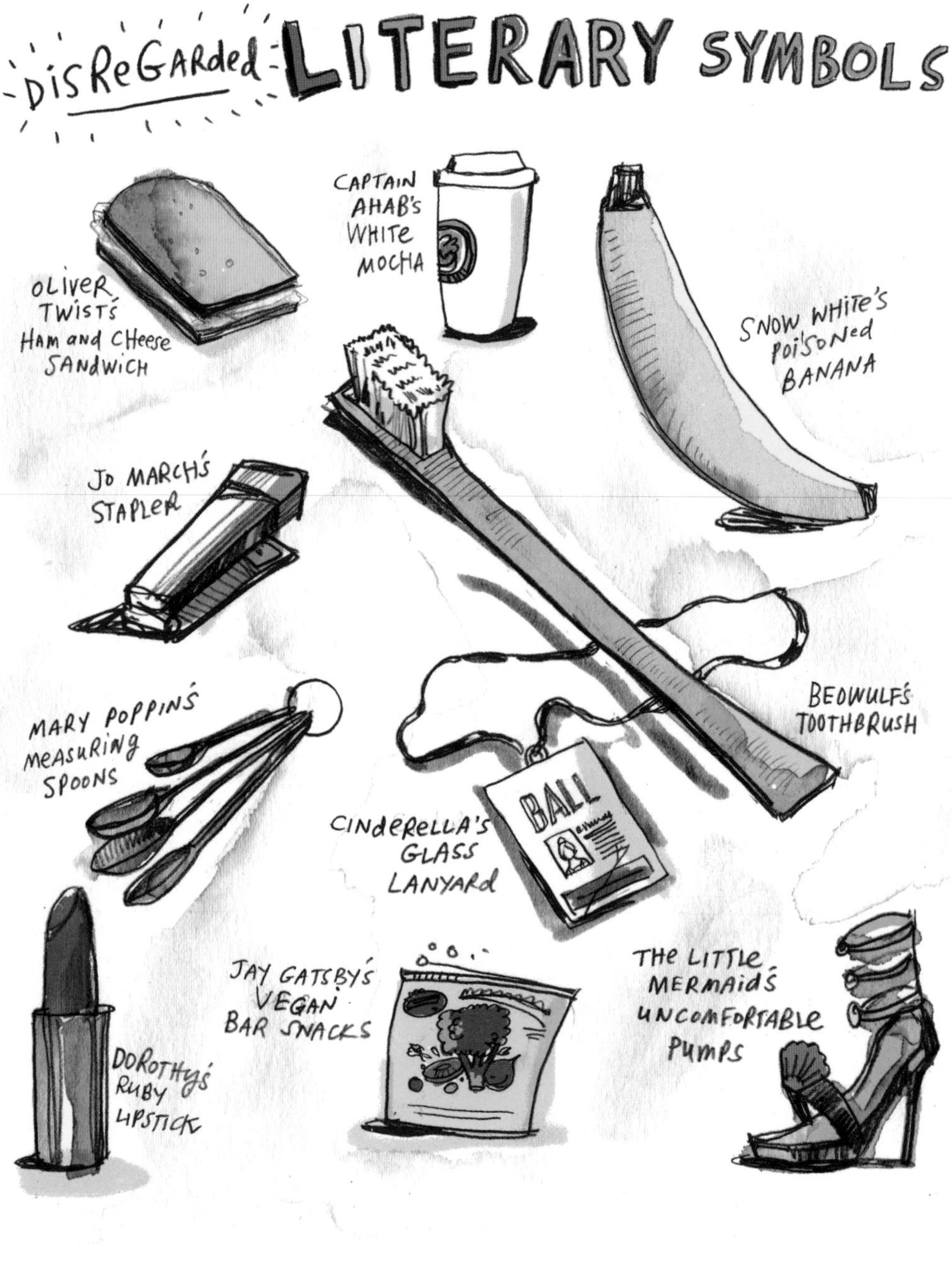

DisReGARded LITERARY SYMBOLS
OLiver TWIST'S HAM and CHeese SANDWICH
CAPTAIN AHAB'S WHITE MOCHA
SNOW WHITE'S POISONed BANANA
JO MARCH'S STAPLER
BEOWULF'S TOOTHBRUSH
MARY POPPIN'S MEASURING SPOONS
CINdeRELLA'S GLASS LANYARD
BALL
DOROTHY'S RUBY LIPSTICK
JAY GATSBY'S VEGAN BAR SNACKS
THE LITTLE MERMAID'S UNCOMFORTABLE PUMPS

Think of reading as an apprenticeship. Only, the master is not just one Picasso, but every master you can find at the library, bookstore, or bookcase anywhere. Even reading this book is an apprenticeship.

Now, go read.

Riding

I bake pie when I need to see a finished creative product, and when I'm craving comfort. But when I want to really mull over a part of my writing, when I want to think about how to get my characters out of jam, or into a jam, and I don't want to be interrupted by measuring ingredients or reading the next step in a recipe, I ride my bike. Reading is an essential part of writing, and so is stepping away from the writing and reading. Sometimes the brain needs fresh air, or a new perspective, or maybe just a new thing to worry about. Many very famous classic authors are known to have written all morning then walked twenty to thirty miles a day, Charles Dickens for one.

Twenty miles on a bike is a lot less than twenty on foot, but it can clear my head and also allow new ideas to float in and out and in again. I often ride the same route and can let my mind wander while my muscle memory takes over the bike riding. For that reason, I think of riding as an extension of my writing. It's where I go to get the endorphins I need to help me get up the hill of writing. My subconscious chatters away on some days. At times like that, my biggest worry is whether I remember every brilliant idea that is jumping out in the road in front of me.

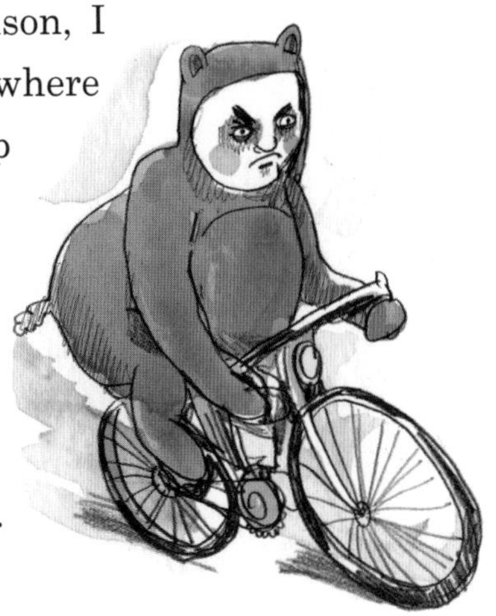

Henry Miller said, "After all, most writing is done away from the typewriter, away from the desk.

I'd say it occurs in the quiet, silent moments, while you're walking or shaving or playing a game or whatever, or even talking to someone you're not vitally interested in."

Bike riding, walking, hiking, gardening, eating chocolate—all of these can be ways to let yourself step away from the page and into an open field where the ideas come to you rather than you chasing them down. Okay, maybe not the chocolate eating, unless that's what you do for exercise. Which, if it is, then I want your metabolism.

I did a little research on why the brain would pop out new ideas when we aren't really trying. I found out a lot more than I expected, like how creative people are more likely to be mentally ill than the average accountant. But the simple answer seemed obvious when I read it. It's basically chaos theory. The brain is self-organizing, and when we are busy thinking, thinking, processing, thinking, it's a mess inside our brains. When we stop to relax, and don't concentrate on one thing, our subconscious is busy taking the opportunity while our conscious mind is out of the house to tidy up. Our unconscious starts matching up our thoughts and experiences and puts them in an order, on the right shelves, and matches the pieces that were scattered on our brain's floor. This is when the *aha!* moments happen.

I'm a nervous bike rider because I ride in the city. I know a car is going to open its door and toss me across three lanes of traffic, or a pedestrian is going to step out in front of me, so I concentrate hard on the path and any obstacles in front of me. This focus on something unrelated to anything except my bodily harm and chug holes allows the rest of my brain that was crunching out a novel earlier to take a rest.

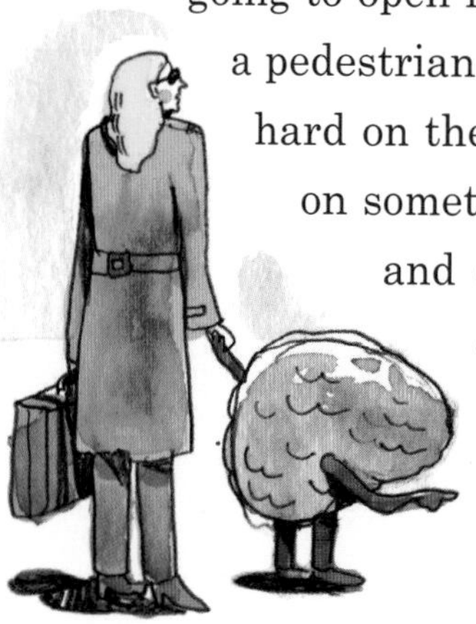

It's not just relaxing but taking your mind off the novel. If I try to relax, I find my mind wanders back over to try to solve an issue in my writing.

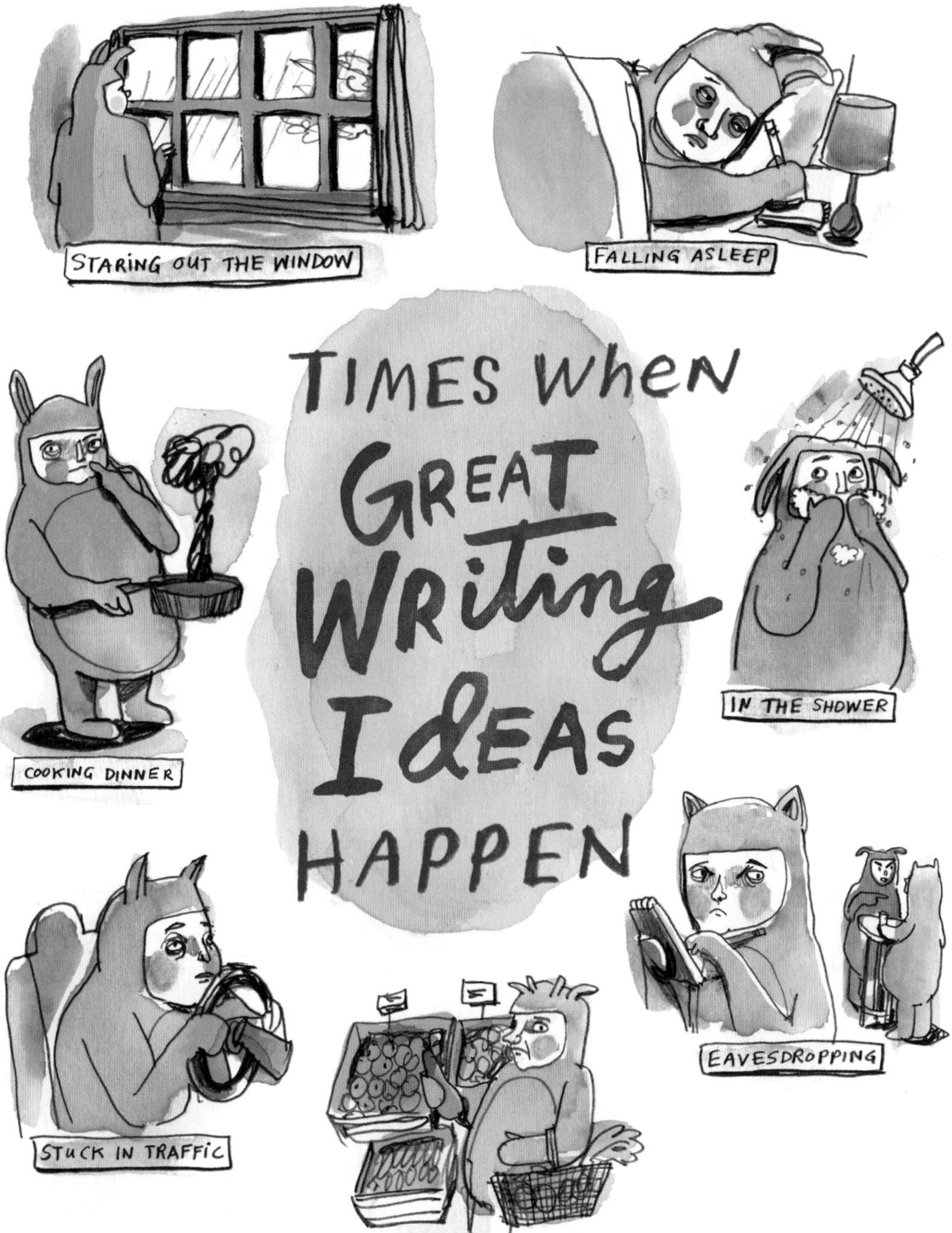
TIMES WHEN GREAT WRITING IDEAS HAPPEN
STARING OUT THE WINDOW
FALLING ASLEEP
COOKING DINNER
IN THE SHOWER
EAVESDROPPING
STUCK IN TRAFFIC
GROCERY SHOPPING

Instead, I take my brain on a journey to someplace else, doing something that isn't problem-solving, but methodical and basic.

Novel writing can often be like an uphill ride, where at the top of the long climb, I need to stop, catch my breath and take a swig of water, eat a granola bar, and look at the vista. In that way, riding is like writing. Stepping away, taking a breather, is when the subconscious can do its work, while the writing muscles get a swig of water to rejuvenate.

Hitchhiking

This subhead is really just a clever play on Reading, Writing, and 'Rithmetic, only I couldn't come up with another *R* word, not that *'Rithmetic* is an *R* word in actuality, nor *Writing* for that matter. But *Hitchhiking* is what I call it when I go for a ride on someone else's writing.

There are days, for *all* of us writers, when the writing just doesn't come. We are doing all of the "things"—showing up at our desk, walking, reading, doodling, whatever our jam is, but still the writing falls flat. What had been a character telling us their story seems like some hollow recording spoken through a tin can. It feels like the voice that was there for us just *poof!*, left us sitting in our desk chair, fingers on the keyboard, waiting for the next words. We type and write, and we try to go down this road with the characters, or we try this direction in the plot, or we read about tension and load up the pages with shorter sentences and direct action rather than avoidance. Every time, it feels like the computer wrote it, not a human. The dialogue is stilted, the interactions are fake, and the attitudes are like cold soup.

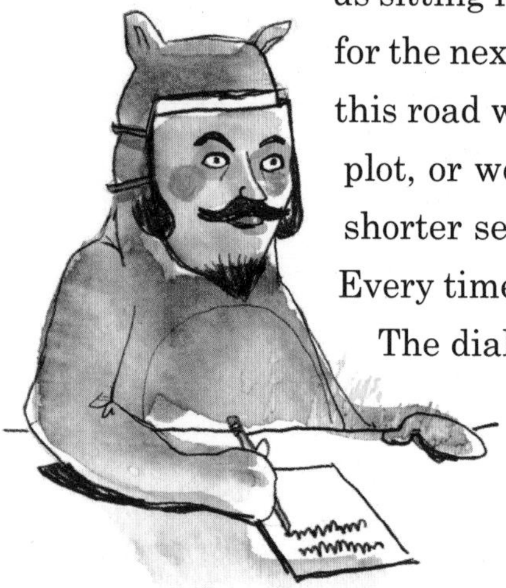

Times like this, I can bake a pie, ride my bike, and nothing helps. When all the attempted ways back into the story don't work, I hitchhike on someone else's writing. I pull out one of my favorite books, one in which I admire the author's writing. It's usually a book that has a similar tone or vibe that I want my story to have. I sit at my desk with pen and paper (yes, those archaic tools) and begin to copy word for word. I suggest pen and paper because some kind of magic happens when you slow down the process and let each word take its time to appear on the page (see chaos theory above). The exercise is not for saving on your computer anyway, as it's just that—an exercise. It's like having a coach teach you how to do a squat properly. It's not that you don't know how to do a squat (other than you don't want to do one), it's that you need to be reminded of the nuances, the tiny movements, like stick your butt out more, bend those knees—more, no more, even more, more than that. You may need to be reminded of better verbs, no, even better verbs, even better than those.

Over a couple of days to a week, I will copy a chapter or two. It doesn't usually take the place of my writing that day, but sometimes it does, depending on how far outside of my story I've drifted, and how badly I need to get inside the workings of words that connect to make meaningful sentences. Like those squats, I soon can do them without coaching. I can stick my butt out so far that I'm like a sumo wrestler. In more ways than one, thanks to pie.

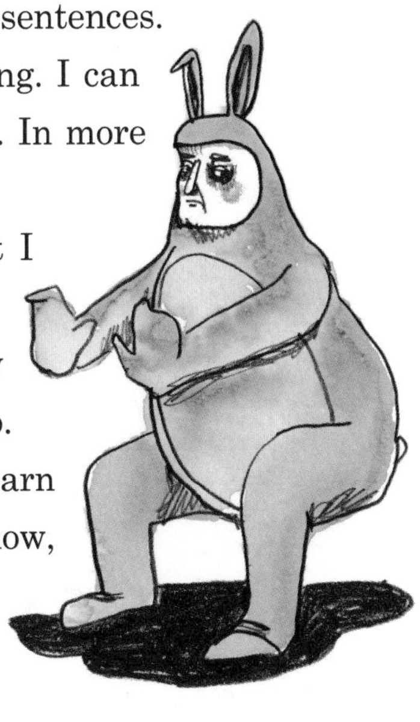

I hitchhike on someone else's writing at first, but I don't take the whole trip that way. I get off when I can tell I'm capable of walking the rest of the way on my own, usually only a few pages or maybe a chapter or two. Like any good hitchhiking experience, along the way I learn some new tricks, I am reminded of what I already know, I'm careful not to accept rides from creeps, and I take leave when the song from their stereo is in my head.

Lemon Meringue Pie
à la Kate McDermott

I have never been able to make meringue. I even find ways to avoid making any kind of pie that requires it, like lemon meringue pie. But who doesn't love lemon meringue pie?! I do, but I don't like the meringue. If someone serves it to me, I enjoy every tangy bite of the lemon filling and leave the gooey white stuff on the side. But everyone asks me to make lemon meringue pie, and I wanted to learn but didn't have the wherewithal to follow a recipe for something that I wasn't going to feel confident would even taste good. I had also seen a lot of failed meringues—watery, pulled-away-from-the-sides, flat brown sticky messes—and who wants to start a pie that has a high chance of failure? All other pies I've created either off the top of my head or from my own variations of a recipe. I couldn't get my head around how to make a meringue. I would read a recipe, shrug, then make a coconut cream with swirls of whipped cream with toasted coconut on top, or a Shaker lemon with a whole wheat double crust. Avoidance is easy when it comes to pie. Another reason to like pie!

But maybe if I could have someone show me how, step-by-sticky-step, I wouldn't be so afraid of it?

When the 2020 pandemic hit, Kate McDermott, my favorite pie guru and author of *Pie Camp*, *Art of the Pie*, and other delightful cookbooks, started online classes. A couple of years before, I'd been to her Pie Camp in Port Angeles, Washington, making the long trip north to spend a day making pies with others—who knew heaven was this little cottage in the Northwest that smelled of fresh-baked pie? But for this online class, I would be in my own kitchen and Kate would be in hers, as would the many others taking the Zoom class. I used my own mixing bowls, hand mixer, spoons, and pie pans. Kate walked us through each of those sticky steps. In an hour, I had made my first lemon meringue pie. My meringue was tall and stiff and just like I'd seen in pictures. I was so elated with the thrill of making a meringue that was successful, and easily so, that as soon as the Zoom call was over, I made a second one. And then a third! And I gave them all away because I still don't like meringue, but now I like making it.

Here's Kate's recipe from the Zoom class. And I highly recommend her online classes, but to get a whiff of her Pie Cottage is to die happy.

Kate suggests preparing either a prebaked single crust or a press-in crust. I make it with a gingersnap crust, which I find delightful with the lemon. I'll share my version for you here.

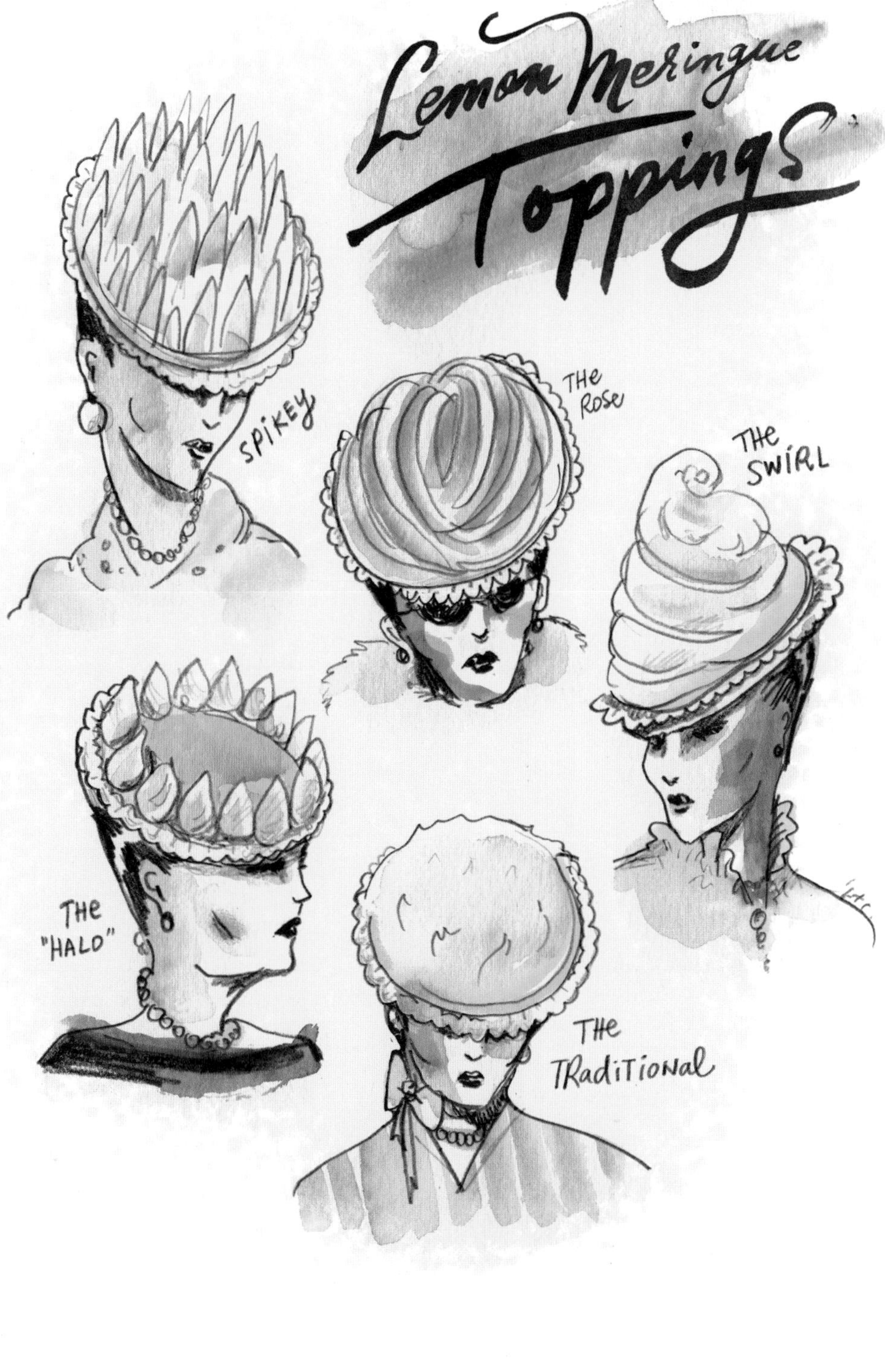
Lemon Meringue Toppings
SPIKEY
THE ROSE
THE SWIRL
THE "HALO"
THE TRADITIONAL

GINGERSNAP CRUST

1¾ cups gingersnap crumbs, or about 15 gingersnap cookies

2 tablespoons granulated sugar

4 tablespoons melted butter

Preheat the oven to 350°F. Put about 15 gingersnaps in a food processor and pulse until like sand. Place the crumbs into a bowl with the sugar and melted butter and combine with a fork. If they aren't sticking together well, you can add 1 tablespoon of water.

Dump the mixture into a pie pan and spread it out evenly over the bottom and up the sides. Using your fingers, spread the crumbs evenly and smoothly. Place in the fridge for 10 minutes. Bake for 7 minutes. Place in a cool place while you make the lemon filling.

LEMON FILLING

4 egg yolks, beaten with fork

1 cup granulated sugar

⅓ cup cornstarch

Pinch of salt

1¼ cups warm water

2 tablespoons butter

Zest of 1 large lemon

½ cup lemon juice

Place the egg yolks in a medium bowl.

Separately, combine the sugar, cornstarch, salt, and water in a saucepan over high heat. While constantly stirring with a whisk, bring the mixture to a boil. Reduce the heat and cook for 2 more minutes while continuing to whisk. Don't be afraid to whisk vigorously as it gets thicker. Take about ½ cup of the hot mixture and stir it into the egg yolks. Return this mixture to the saucepan and cook at a full boil while stirring constantly for 2 minutes more until the mixture is thick. On Zoom, Kate gave us a special note that I wrote on my copy of the recipe, so I'll add it here for you, too, because I made a lemon filling another time, and it was a watery mess. I have a feeling I didn't do this: make sure to boil and whisk *all* of this time, because it will separate otherwise.

Stir in the butter, lemon zest, and lemon juice and cook for another minute. Immediately pour into pre-baked pie crust.

Now comes the part where I changed my attitude about meringue.

MERINGUE TOPPING

½ teaspoon cream of tartar

¼ cup plus 2 tablespoons granulated or superfine sugar

5 egg whites

½ teaspoon vanilla extract (optional)

Preheat the oven to 375°F.

Mix the cream of tartar and sugar together and set aside.

In a squeaky-clean bowl, place the egg whites and vanilla extract, if using. With an electric handheld beater or stand mixer, beat them on low for a minute. Increase the speed to medium and continue to beat until you see soft peaks when you lift the beaters.

Sprinkle in 2 tablespoons of the sugar mixture and continue to beat on medium.

Turn the beater to high and add the remainder of the sugar mixture 2 tablespoons at a time. Mix until soft peaks are formed. Lift out the beaters.

With a flexible rubber spatula, turn the meringue onto the top of the pie near the edges (my copy is underlined, so she must have emphasized this) to set a seal, and lightly and evenly spread it toward the center. Make sure (underlined again) the meringue reaches all the way to the edge of the crust and that there are no gaps. Use the backside of the edge of a spoon to make some peaks and valleys in the meringue.

To brown the meringue, place in the preheated oven for 6 to 10 minutes until the peaks turn brown. Or use a blowtorch. I think she meant use the kind of blowtorch used for crème brûlée, not the kind a welder uses.

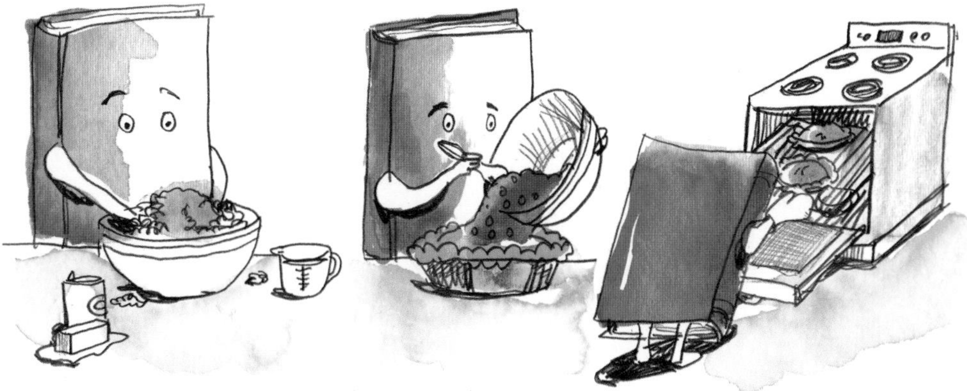

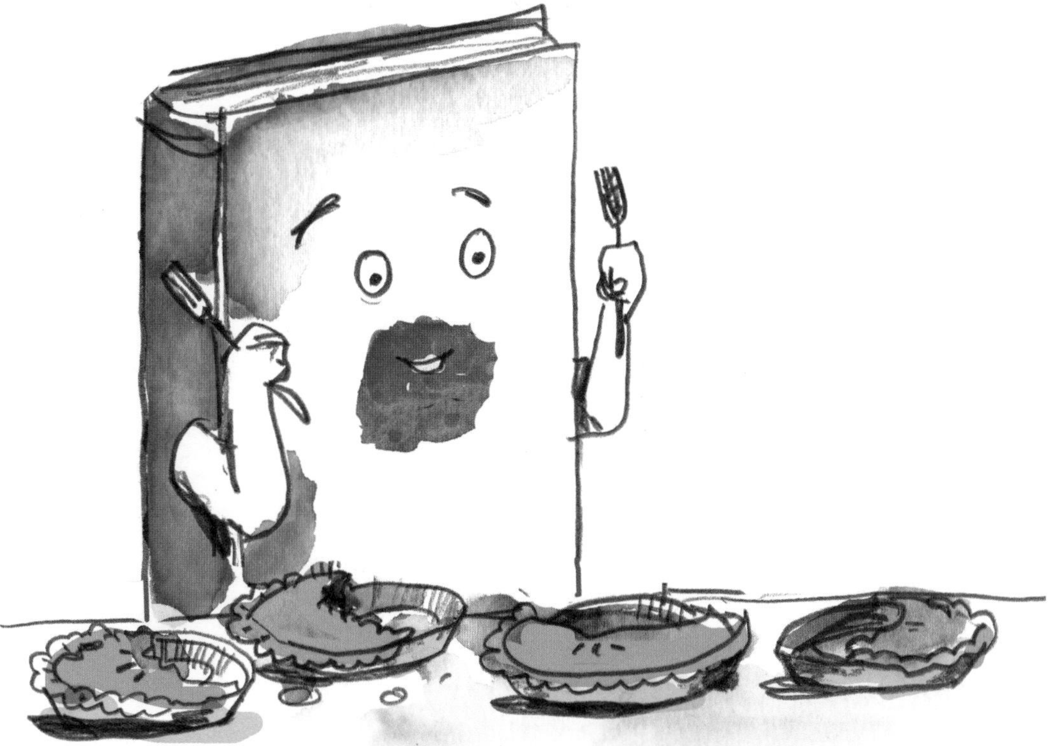

NO GUARANTEE PEACH PIE

Sometimes you see a peach that has a rosy, art-directed blush and a fragrance sent from heaven. You think, this is the perfect peach. It will be juicy and summery and change my life in the way that only a fresh peach can. You can either immediately begin eating that peach or you can double down and use it in this pie.

This pie is a bit of a gamble. Just like anything having to do with writing or publishing, you'll follow the recipe perfectly but nothing is guaranteed.

The crust is a magical cookie, made with almonds, coconut, butter, and sugar. There's no flour to mess things up. Once it's baked, you lay sweetened creme fraiche or honey-flavored Greek yogurt in the shell followed by peaches. It's topped with whipped cream. Sounds perfect, right? You followed the steps perfectly. Then what could make this pie taste terrible? The answer: NATURE.

WHICH is the GOOD PEACH?

SOMETIMES A PEACH WILL LOOK PERFECT ON THE OUTSIDE BUT TASTE TERRIBLE. AND FOR THIS PIE, YOU MIGHT NOT KNOW THAT UNTIL YOU'RE EATING IT.

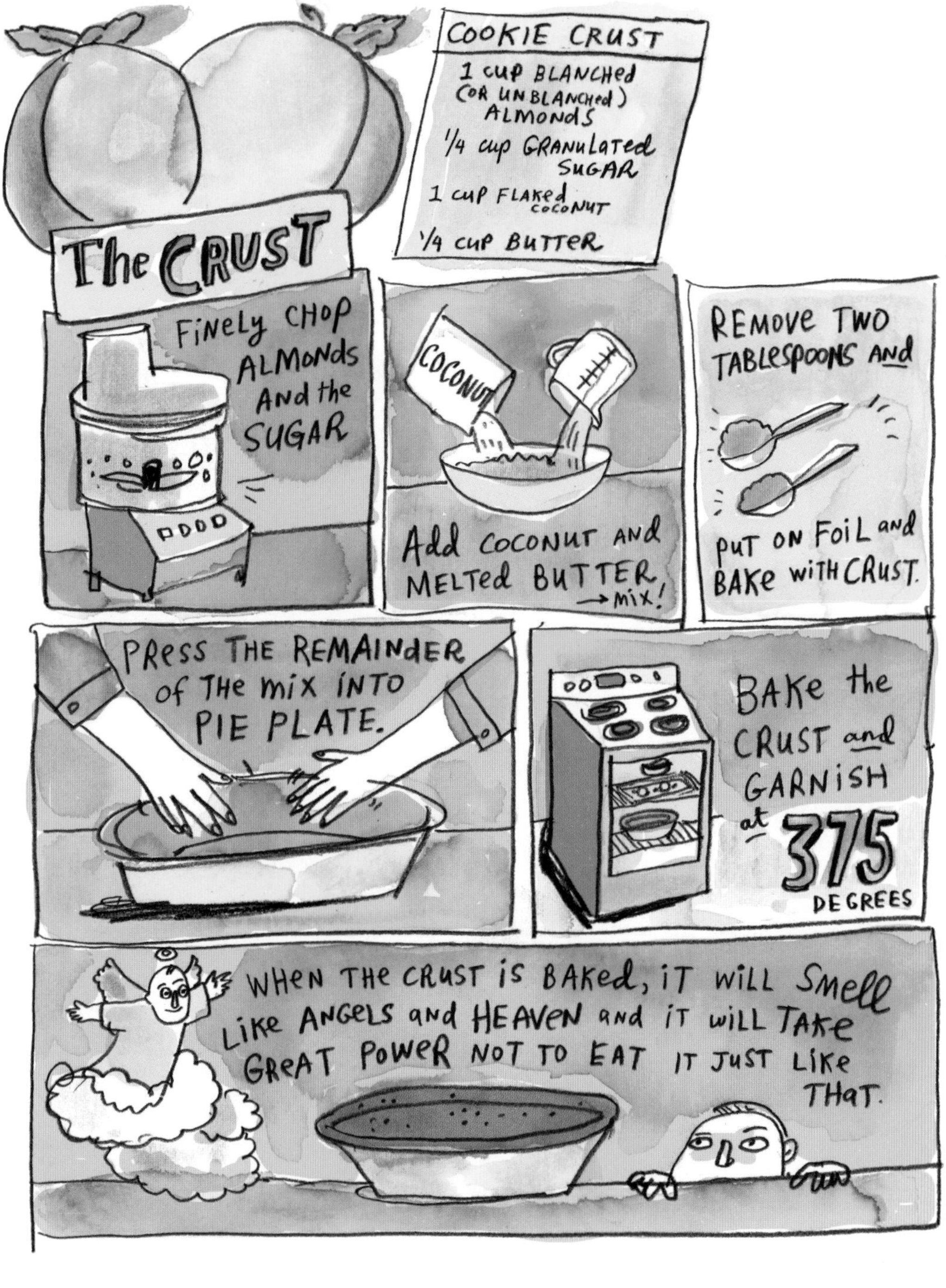
The CRUST
COOKIE CRUST
1 cup BLANCHED (OR UNBLANCHED) ALMONDS
1/4 cup GRANULATED SUGAR
1 cup FLAKED COCONUT
1/4 cup BUTTER
FINELY CHOP ALMONDS AND the SUGAR
COCONUT
Add COCONUT AND MELTED BUTTER → MIX!
REMOVE TWO TABLESPOONS AND
PUT ON FOIL AND BAKE WITH CRUST.
PRESS THE REMAINDER OF THE MIX INTO PIE PLATE.
BAKE the CRUST and GARNISH at 375 DEGREES
WHEN THE CRUST IS BAKED, IT WILL SMELL LIKE ANGELS AND HEAVEN AND IT WILL TAKE GREAT POWER NOT TO EAT IT JUST LIKE THAT.

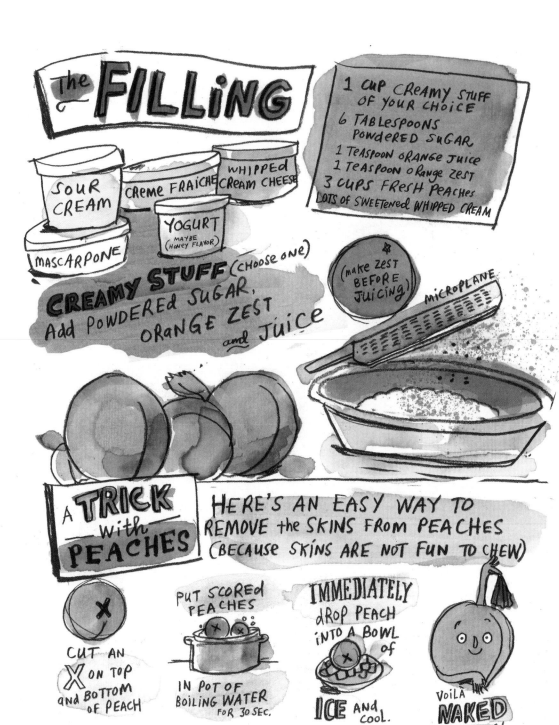

the FILLING

1 CUP CREAMY STUFF OF YOUR CHOICE
6 TABLESPOONS POWDERED SUGAR
1 TEASPOON ORANGE JUICE
1 TEASPOON ORANGE ZEST
3 CUPS FRESH PEACHES
LOTS OF SWEETENED WHIPPED CREAM

SOUR CREAM

CREME FRAICHE

WHIPPED CREAM CHEESE

YOGURT (MAYBE HONEY FLAVOR)

MASCARPONE

CREAMY STUFF (CHOOSE ONE)
Add POWDERED SUGAR, ORANGE ZEST and JUICE

(make zest BEFORE juicing)

MICROPLANE

A TRICK with PEACHES

HERE'S AN EASY WAY TO REMOVE the SKINS FROM PEACHES (BECAUSE SKINS ARE NOT FUN TO CHEW)

CUT AN X ON TOP and BOTTOM OF PEACH

PUT SCORED PEACHES IN POT OF BOILING WATER FOR 30 SEC.

IMMEDIATELY dROP PEACH INTO A BOWL of ICE AND COOL.

VOILÀ **NAKED** PEACHES!

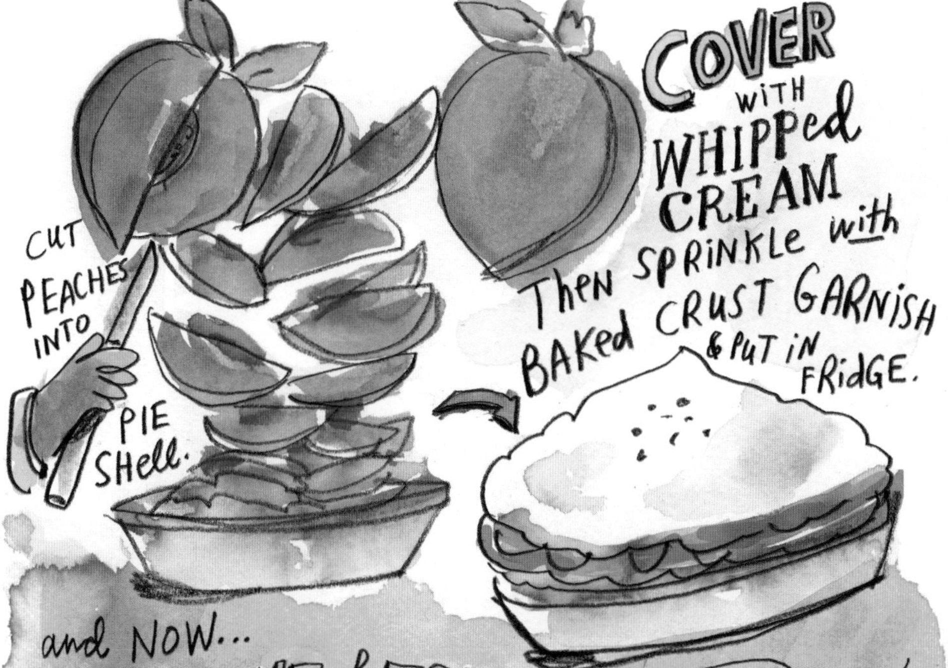
CUT PEACHES INTO PIE SHELL.
COVER WITH WHIPPED CREAM
Then SPRINKLE with BAKED CRUST GARNISH
& PUT IN FRIDGE.

and NOW... THE MOMENT of TRUTH

You took a risk and it paid off. This peach pie is the single-best forkful of dessert you've had in your life. You now contemplate buying a lottery ticket and sending your book to the top literary agent.

Those delicious-looking peaches are in fact disgusting and tasetless. After two bites, your faith in nature is ruined. You consider never eating pie again. Instead of writing a novel, you will raise goldfish.

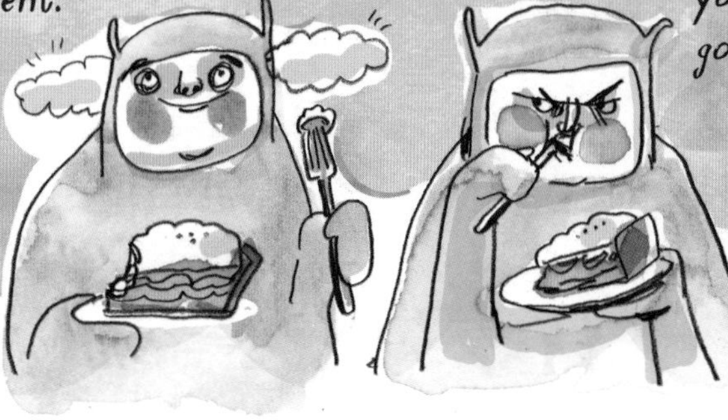

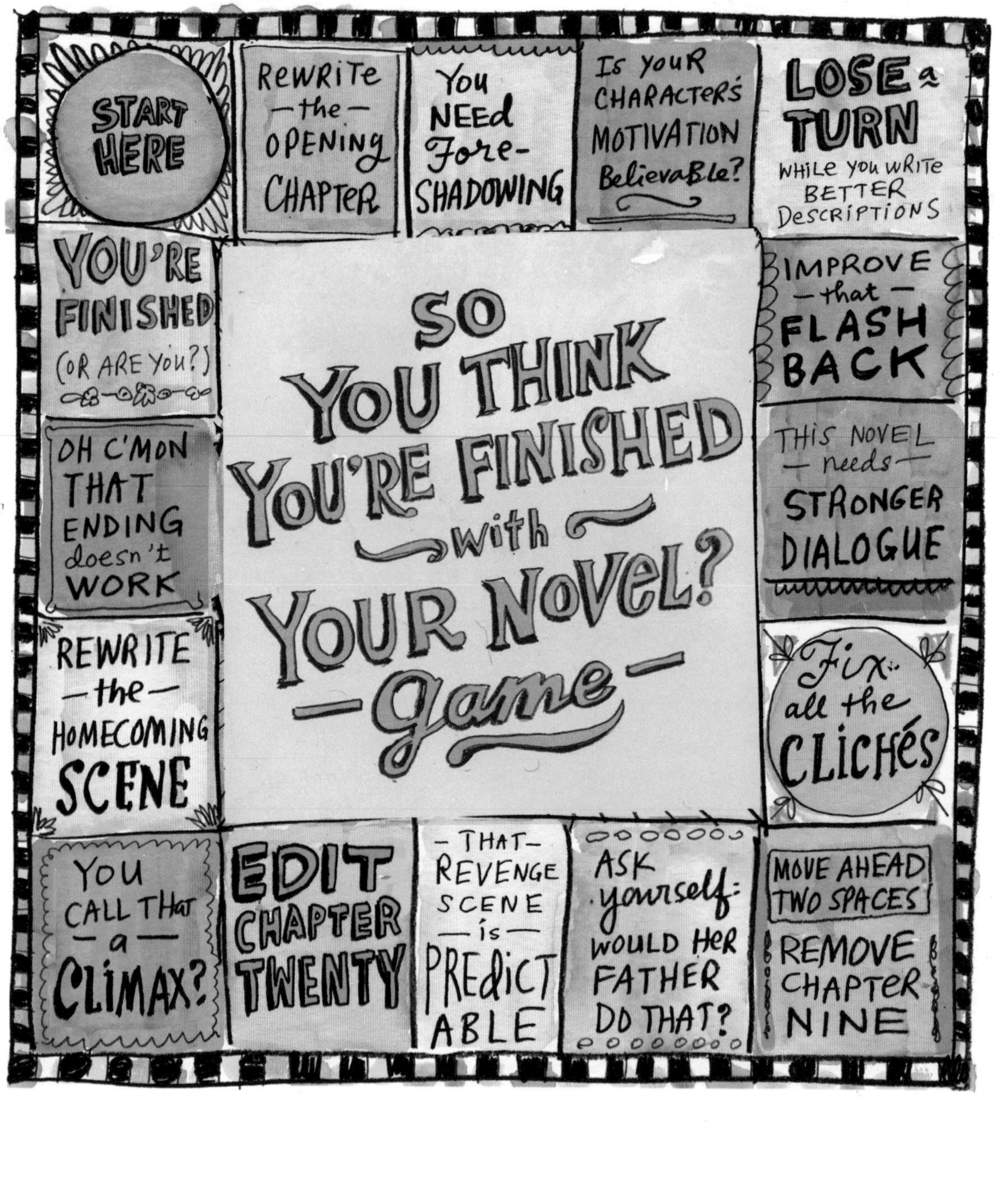
SO YOU THINK YOU'RE FINISHED with YOUR NOVEL? game
START HERE
REWRITE the OPENING CHAPTER
YOU NEED FORE-SHADOWING
IS YOUR CHARACTER'S MOTIVATION BELIEVABLE?
LOSE a TURN WHILE YOU WRITE BETTER DESCRIPTIONS
IMPROVE that FLASH BACK
THIS NOVEL needs STRONGER DIALOGUE
Fix all the CLICHÉS
MOVE AHEAD TWO SPACES
REMOVE CHAPTER NINE
ASK yourself: WOULD HER FATHER DO THAT?
THAT REVENGE SCENE is PREDICTABLE
EDIT CHAPTER TWENTY
YOU CALL THAT a CLIMAX?
REWRITE the HOMECOMING SCENE
OH C'MON THAT ENDING doesn't WORK
YOU'RE FINISHED (OR ARE YOU?)

CHAPTER SEVEN

Revising, Rewriting, Reimagining

I recently finished a rewrite of a novel. This novel has been through so many variations. The book has more issues than an over-moist pastry. First of all, it's a mystery, and I've never written a mystery. Most importantly, it has a main character who isn't originally mine, but someone else's. I'll explain in a bit. But it is a book I want to write and can't seem to quit writing. It's a book that may or may not see the light of day, but I'm going to keep revising until I know I've exhausted all possible directions. Then I'm going to pursue submission to agents and editors to see if my bookchild is viable. All these possible ways it can be rejected, why would I set myself up for that in advance? One, I believe perseverance can get you through most anything. Two, revising, rewriting, and reimagining can—and often does—bring about a more satisfying end result.

Revising

I taught a creative writing workshop at UCLA Extension, and each nightly session was three hours long. One of the issues the students listed at the beginning of the class was that they didn't have enough time to write. Where and how could they carve out enough time to get their writing done? they pleaded for the answer. If it takes a year to write a novel, then can that year be made up of five-minute increments? I reminded them, and I have to remind myself over and over, that five minutes or a page here and there still keeps you in the game and keeps the writing flow going. You don't have to carve out a year, or even a month. In fact, you don't have to carve, or drill, or even dig. Think of it as a massage of time. A nice rub here and there. Yes, some days, it's a total marathon that gives you plantar fasciitis, but it doesn't always have to be.

Because I am a benevolent dictator of a teacher, I provided a fifteen-minute free writing exercise during the weekly UCLA class. I offered a prompt, set my timer, and told them to keep their pens to the page until I let them know when the time is up. It's an old Natalie Goldberg *Writing Down the Bones* writing trick, and it works wonders. Just put down what comes into your mind. Let that first draft be shitty, as Anne Lamott says. This first night of class, at about minute seven of the fifteen-minute exercise, I looked up from my own page (I usually try to take advantage of the writing time too), and I noticed about half the class was on their phones texting.

I stopped the writing assignment early and asked why they weren't taking advantage of the time I had offered them. One guy, who I will refrain from calling arrogant, replied, "Because I finished."

"You finished?" I asked. "But then why not keep going, or go back over it and see what you could revise?"

He replied, without a hint of sarcasm, "Because it was perfect."

"Perfect?"

"Yeah."

Wow. I'm rarely at a loss for words, and this time I could think of nothing to say for a moment. The rest of the class, I could tell, was clearly jealous. They wanted to write something brilliant in seven minutes. Don't we all! [eye roll emoji goes here]

If he was that brilliant, I wanted to say but didn't, why was he taking a class? I couldn't read what he had written, and if he read it out loud when I offered the opportunity to share their work with the class, I don't remember it, so I doubt it was that brilliant. Or even edible.

He's probably a bestseller by now. Or a CPA.

The point of this anecdote is that brilliance does show up, but even brilliance needs to be honed and polished. Even though I wrote twelve drafts of my first novel, none of it was brilliant. I learned how to write a novel by writing a novel. Each draft, I learned more about what not just my novel, but any novel, needed. I had to keep figuring out what I was doing.

"Who's ready to have their manuscript ripped apart?"

Rewriting

In the early days after I returned home from my writing group, I would start with a clean page and rewrite the pages again from memory with the changes I wanted to implement. When I think about that now, I shake my head at my (1) youthfulness at feeling like I had all the time in the world, (2) youthfulness that I could remember what the scene was even about, (3) naivete that I had to start over every time I wrote a new draft.

While I had a much better memory back then, my computer did not. I had an Apple portable laptop the size of a shirt box that weighed more than a bag of sugar. Despite being big for "portable," the RAM couldn't hold a whole novel, not to mention all the drafts I was creating, so I organized my novel by chapter and eventually upgraded my computer.

My process was tedious. Each draft, each chapter, I came at it from a new perspective. But each time I went deeper. Draft four I found the heart of my story. Draft six or so I found its soul. Draft ten I finally figured out what the story was even about.

I no longer write by hand, so I don't start fresh, but I do a Save As of the original document and then go through from the beginning and read it as though it's my first time to read the pages, and I make revisions as I go. I clean up the prose, revise the sentence structure, and tackle the order of the paragraphs to clarify the narrative. Rewriting may include changing point of view or an intention, or maybe even a complete overhaul of the story the main character stars in. In early drafts of *MoonPies*, the main character Ruby sat in a Barcalounger in the inciting incident. When I made her the proud owner of a six-lane bowling alley, the story took on a whole new bent with a busy career woman at the helm. This required a rewrite—a deep rewrite.

Reimagining

In my current novel-in-progress, I had to ditch the main character altogether and make the story someone else's. I had this idea that had pestered me for years—how was Nancy Drew, Girl Detective, coping with middle age? She'd had the perfect high school life, so how did she handle midlife? Had she continued her perfect life or had that idyllic growing up set her up for some rougher times once she hit that stage of life where we look back and evaluate what we've done so far? I finally sat down and wrote the novel I wanted to read. I had a hilarious time. I used all the old Nancy tropes: Nancy and her blue convertible, now dented; her attorney father now had dementia; and Nancy and the old housekeeper now had substitute-mother issues. Basically, an out-of-shape, depressed woman who can't run and would rather be drinking wine and eating Peanut M&Ms than solving a mystery. But a mystery she solves nonetheless.

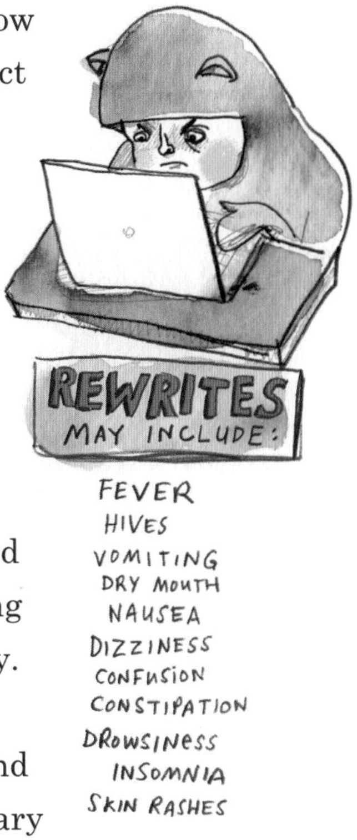
REWRITES
MAY INCLUDE:
FEVER
HIVES
VOMITING
DRY MOUTH
NAUSEA
DIZZINESS
CONFUSION
CONSTIPATION
DROWSINESS
INSOMNIA
SKIN RASHES

A big obstacle stood in between my final draft and The End. A biggy. To be able to use another literary character, they must be in the public domain. I knew from my first draft that public domain would never happen with Nancy because the author, Carolyn Keene, is immortal—she's a pseudonym, but I had stubbornly proceeded to write the novel I wanted to write anyway. I was having too much fun to stop and consider the book wouldn't happen as I had originally imagined it.

A literary attorney gave me the same advice as any good therapist. Nancy wasn't Nancy. She must be delusional. She needed to *think* she was Nancy. I would not be deterred. I started over yet again. I created a character who, as a young girl, had aspired to be Nancy to the extent that she imitated everything about Nancy's life in the books.

Voilà, I had the premise for my story. *The Case of the Missing Life* was solved over Peanut M&Ms and cabernet. When I rewrote this draft, making the necessary shifts from someone else's fictional character to my own fictional character who wanted to be someone else, I had more periphery to see what took her to new places on a personal level. At the end of that draft, I had a better story.

Reimagining requires both revising and rewriting. Reimagining begins in that moment when you realize something central to your story is missing. To find that something central, you need to reconsider the entire story. Turning things on their heads can often shake loose many new ideas that only improve the big picture. Never be afraid to reimagine a story if it just doesn't to want to head in the direction you keep trying to make it go. Yes, this will require rewriting, and more revising, but writing the best story you possibly can—this is when you'll feel the satisfaction of eating a pie of your own creation. Or go mad trying.

These are my definitions of *revising*, *rewriting*, and *reimagining*. Maybe there are some legitimate ones out there and these match or don't, but this is how I get my head around each one. I'll probably revise this chapter umpteen times, but for now, I'm going to move on.

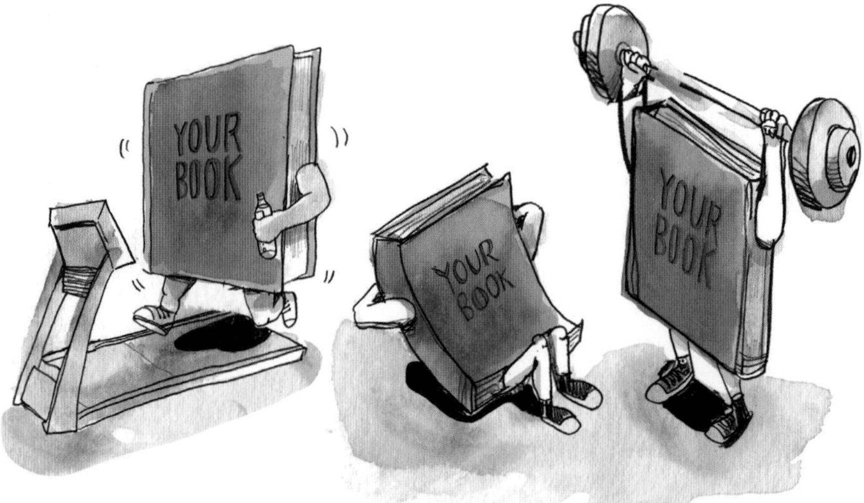
YOUR BOOK
YOUR BOOK
YOUR BOOK

Final note: there is an exception to reworking something too much—pie dough. Reworking pie pastry too much, kneading and rolling it out more than once or twice, can make the dough tough and elastic. When you roll it out, it starts to spring back, and when it's baked it's chewy instead of flaky. In the same way that this is the exception, this is also the perfect example of learning how to find that sweet spot of when your work, whether pie or writing, is just right—when to stop, and when to add more. The best way to learn this sweet spot is to practice, to take it too far, then have to start over and try again. It's never a waste when you are learning and persevering.

Reimagining Pie

My family called my great-aunt *Sister*. What I remember about Sister was her pie. I don't remember her serving it, or eating it at her house, but I remember having it every single Christmas dinner growing up. It was this dark (and I mean DARK) chocolate pecan pie, which Mom called *Sister's Pie*. The recipe was on a stained 3 x 5 card in Sister's old-fashioned script. By pecan pie I don't mean the treacly Karo Corn Syrup pecan pie, but instead a thick, rich dark chocolate custard filled with jillions of pecans. I would get to lick the pot, scraping out every last drop of that chocolate custard. In addition to not being skilled at meringue, Mom used an already-in-the-tin-breaking-apart, frozen, store-bought crust, and the custard was usually curdled. I loved that pie. I should say, I loved the filling chock-full of pecans surrounded by deep, dark chocolate cream. I did not care for the meringue, which, Mom forgive me, was watery and flat and just a sticky, gooey marshmallow. We all wept over her weepy meringue. The crust, well, frozen and store-bought. 'Nuf said.

True confession: my mom always made two pies. One year when I was about sixteen, my siblings had come home from college, and we'd had

Christmas, including pie. When they left, there was still one pie remaining. I sat in the kitchen when everyone was gone and no one could see me, and I shoved the meringue to the side and devoured that entire pie by myself. I did not regret one sweet bite.

I never attempted to make the pie myself until I was well into adulthood. When I mentioned to my brother that I missed that pie and was going to try to make it with a graham cracker crust and no meringue, he said he had a better custard recipe for the chocolate.

I have two recipes now, three really if you count the one where I added my own graham cracker crust, and four if you count Sister's original note card that she wrote for Mom. All are covered in chocolate thumbprints, egg yolk goo, and what looks like smeared cinnamon stains. The older recipe is handwritten with both mine and my mom's handwriting on the back of a page torn from an old to-do notepad. The other recipe is a printed email from my brother. He explains that his version of Sister's pie recipe isn't changed so much other than to use chocolate instead of cocoa, except that I notice the original called for canned milk and water, and even flour. Then he goes on to explain that Guitard is even better than Ghirardelli chocolate. So, you can see where this is going—this is going to be the chocolatiest of rewrites.

Brother/Sister Chocolate Pecan Pie
in a Pecan-Graham Crust

CRUST

8 cinnamon graham crackers

½ cup pecans

⅓ cup brown sugar

1½ teaspoons ground cinnamon

½ cup (1 stick) melted butter

½ teaspoon salt

First, and this is my part, start by making a pecan–graham cracker crust. Inspired by Ken Haedrich's "Nutty Graham Cracker Crust" in his book *Pie*, he offers a recipe that can use any nut. Preheat the oven to 350°F. Crush the graham crackers (the kind kids love) in the food processor. Add the pecans and pulse a few more times until it's not too much crumb, not too much powder. Pour the crushed grahams and nuts into a big bowl. Add the brown sugar and cinnamon. (I added this ingredient because who doesn't love cinnamon with their chocolate?) Pour in the melted butter. Oh, and don't forget to add salt to the dry bits. Mix with a big fork until well blended. Pour into a 9-inch pie pan and smooth around the bottom and up the sides. Did I tell you to grease the pan? You should do that first. Chill in fridge for 10 minutes, then bake for 7 minutes. I could say 5 to 10, but 7 seems to be the magic number. Remove from the oven and place in a cool, dry location while you prepare the filling.

FILLING

3 whole eggs

3 egg yolks

⅓ cup granulated sugar

1 teaspoon vanilla extract

1 cup milk

1 cup heavy cream

3 ounces dark chocolate

2 cups broken pecans

For the filling, beat together the whole eggs, yolks (Sister called them "yellows"), granulated sugar, and vanilla.

Then, in a double boiler, simmer the milk, heavy cream, and dark chocolate. I use 85 percent dark, but choose your level of a rich chocolate like Guitard.

Add ¼ cup of the milk and chocolate mixture to the egg mixture and stir to acclimate the eggs. Then, gradually pour this acclimated egg mixture into the chocolate mixture in the pot, a small bit at a time, stirring continually until this thickens well. (My brother writes: "Don't stop for anything, even if the prize control knocks at the door with one of those giant cardboard checks.") Use an electric whisk, if you have one, but a wooden spoon works well too. This may take a long time but is what makes a custard smooth and creamy. Don't be tempted to turn up the heat, as this may scramble the eggs. Just keep stirring, and stirring, and stirring, until eventually you have a rich, thick, creamy, chocolately custard.

Add the broken pecans. Yes, two cups. You may chop them, but I like the pecans almost whole for the crunch.

Pour the filling into your prepared graham cracker crust. I decorate the top with pecan halves, but you can also top with whipping cream. Or, if you must, meringue is an option. Place in the fridge to chill for 2 to 3 hours.

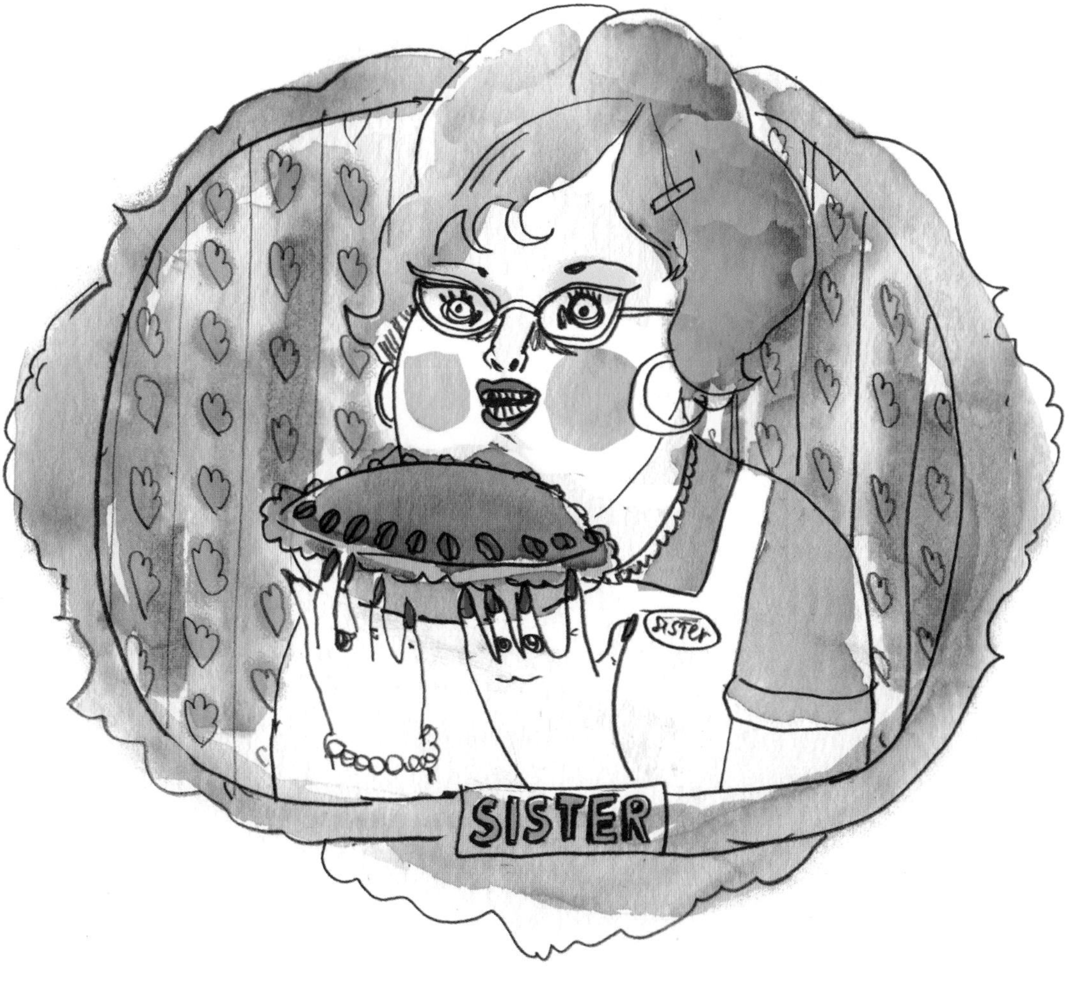
Sister
SISTER

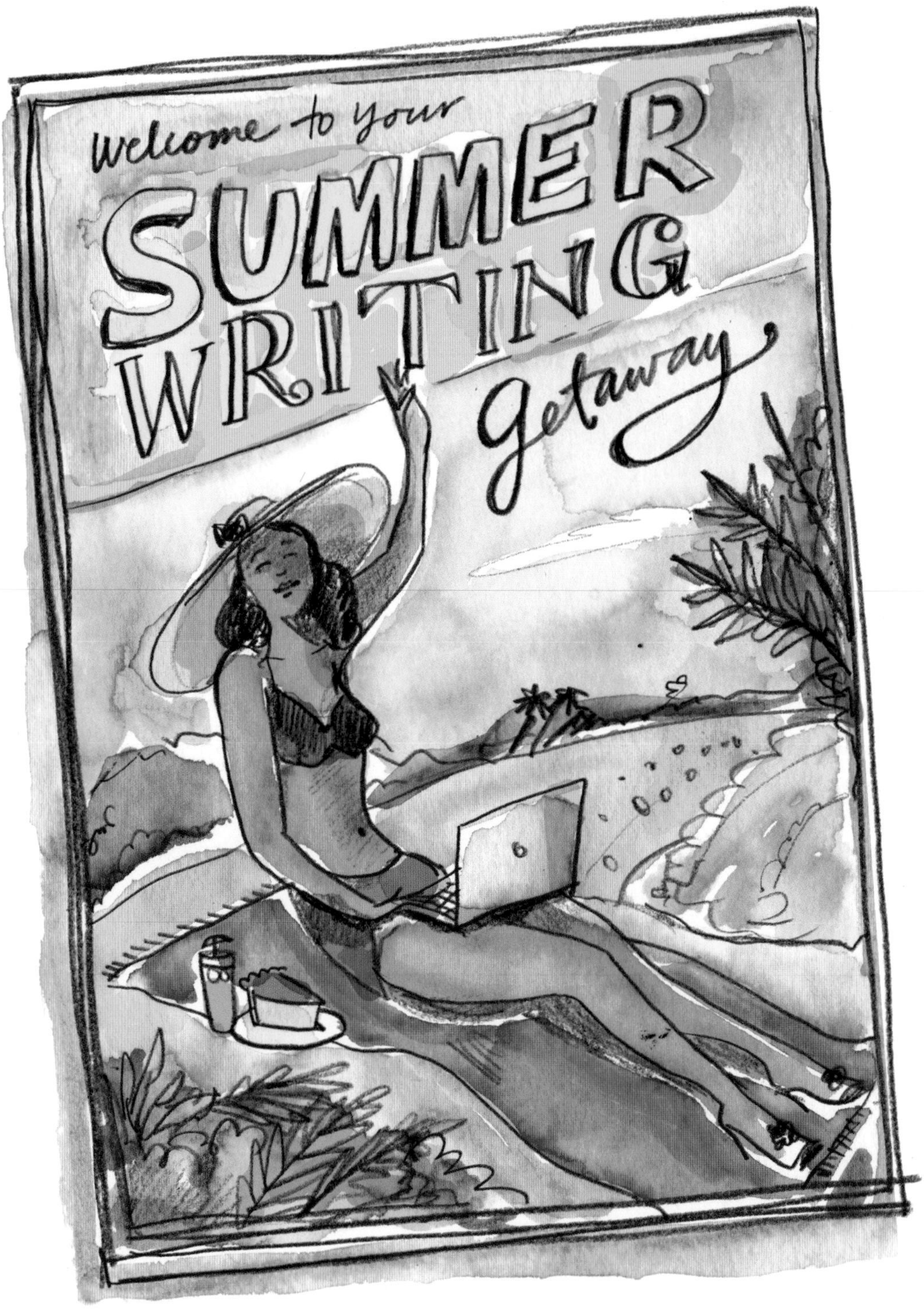
Welcome to your
SUMMER
WRITING
Getaway

CHAPTER EIGHT

WORkSHops, STRaNgers, and BUddHists, OH my!

I was out riding my bike while thinking about this chapter. Getting out, moving, walking away from the page for a while—this we've talked about before, why it can be necessary. But we usually think of these times away from the desk as solitary. There is no band to get together when you need to practice, it's just you, yourself, and the story.

Community is part of humanity, though. Sometimes after looking at enough silly memes on Facebook, I think I'd be fine without humans, especially strangers. While biking and thinking of this chapter, I remembered the summer when interacting with strangers was exactly what I did. An entire summer, all for the sake of writing.

When I went through my divorce, I had heard about so many people who backpacked across Europe, or hiked Kilimanjaro, or ate 226 pounds of chocolate just to get away and get perspective on their new life. Okay, maybe the chocolate-gorging they did because they felt immense despair. I didn't want to do any of those things, but I did want to get that new perspective. If I wasn't going to have a marriage, I at least wanted a writing career. I was determined I was going to make a living as a writer, or at least try. I needed to learn everything I possibly could in one summer.

It should be pretty obvious that that wasn't reality. Not much is focused on reality when going through a divorce. It's more of a combination of sorrow, grief, relief, vengeance, and madness, with moments of erratic elation sprayed on top with a power hose. In the midst of my own personal craziness, I decided that my escape would be a summer of writers' workshops.

I lined up all the conferences I had ever wanted to attend, organized them by date, and began applying. I had been to conferences and retreats before, but usually just one or two weeks a year. This would be two months' worth. Two months of wallowing in writing!

The Iowa Summer Writers Festival was my first stop. I signed up for a weekend workshop on humor writing. Our first assignment was to write about a time you made a fool of yourself. *That was easy*, I thought. I had so many embarrassing moments to choose from, but I knew immediately which instance I would write first. I set my pen to scribbling about a time early in my marriage when my husband had asked me to be a guest speaker on Buddhism for the Religion and the Environment class he cotaught with a woman who will remain nameless to protect the not-so-innocent. The only experience I really had with Buddhism was that I had spent a month in Nepal about a year before we were married. My exposure to Buddhism was no more than when I stayed in a guesthouse outside Tengboche Monastery and awoke to the sound of the dung chen trumpets bellowing at sunrise before hiking toward the Everest Base Camp (a hike I undertook completely unprepared and also could be counted as a time I made a fool of myself).

Initially, when my husband-at-the-time asked if I could teach a class on Buddhism, I told him I wasn't experienced enough. But he had a way of talking me into things—like marrying him. I agreed to do the lecture, researched my subject matter, wrote out little three-by-five note cards, and practiced my talk until I felt confident that I could recite what the encyclopedia said.

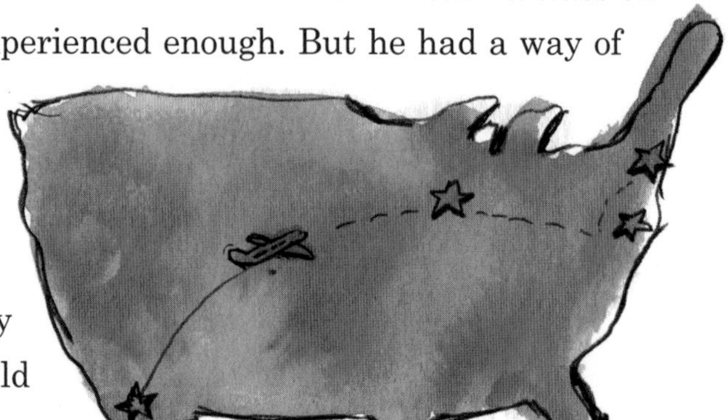

The night of my guest speakerdom, I was both nervous and excited that I could be conquering my fear of public speaking. As I stood in front of the room of college students, I reminded myself that my husband had said these students were naive and wouldn't even know if I made any mistakes in my lecture. I relayed the basic history of how the Buddhist philosophy traveled from India to China then Japan, how the philosophy evolved as it traversed Asia—all information easily found in my generation's Google— *Encyclopedia Britannica*. Then I opened my talk up to Q&A. The first student asked me, "If a mosquito bites a Buddhist, would they swat it and kill it?" I didn't know the answer but made a joke about how it depended on how devout the Buddhist was.

This next part is when I thought my humor essay got to the fool-making part. I read it out loud to my Iowa Summer Workshop class with a light voice, building as I got to the really funny part, rather the part *I* thought was funny:

Two young guys sat in the back with their heads down, arms crossed, and I assumed, sleeping through my lecture. As the other students asked questions, and I stumbled over the answers, the boys lifted their heads. One politely raised his hand, so I called on him. The young Asian man asked me in a soft, gentle voice, "Are you familiar with Deer Park Buddhist Monastery in Escondido?" Escondido is a suburb about twenty minutes away from San Diego. I was not familiar with the monastery and said so.

"We are Buddhist monks from that monastery," he told me, as he and his friend pulled gold amulets out from inside their white T-shirts.

Instead of melting into a puddle of idiot goo, I suggested the monks answer their fellow students' questions that I didn't know. I felt the fool, but hopefully recovered as best I could.

Flash forward to Iowa, when I finished reading my draft essay out loud, even though no one was laughing, I sat up proud and certain the teacher

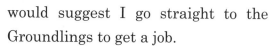

would suggest I go straight to the Groundlings to get a job.

Instead, he turned to me and said, "You knew it was a setup, right?"

"What? Setup???"

"Your husband had to know those boys were Buddhists. Teachers know about their students."

No, the answer was a resounding "No." I did not know it was a setup. My "How I Made a Fool of Myself" story just added an extra fool. One in my past, and one in my present.

I barely made it through the class, as my throat swelled with the lump I tried to shove back down into my left ventricle to staunch the bleeding. I had no Buddhists who came to save me in this classroom in the middle of the cornfields. The Iowa City Sheraton probably had to get a wet-vac to clean my room as I cried the whole weekend.

Years later, maybe even as I write this chapter, I came to realize that the Buddhists taught me numerous things:

1. Teachers are not always at the front of the classroom.
2. Perspective can become clearer with time.
3. The input of strangers on our work is often the most truthful.

Honesty can be hard, and sometimes brutal, but it's important to see what is below the surface of what you are writing. Both fiction and creative nonfiction have layers and layers of what our subconscious is putting on the page while we innocently think we are saying something else.

The next week of my writing sojourn was better. No writing was required, at least not personal. I took one of my all-time favorite classes on reading. We read five novels before arrival and discussed one a day over the next five days. Reading . . . ah, a writer's salve.

I left Iowa and headed to upstate New York, where I was enrolled in the monthlong residency at the New York State Summer Writers Institute where I workshopped both fiction and nonfiction. When I asked my fiction teacher if I needed an MFA to create a Writing Life, she said, "Write, then publish. That's what a writer does."

Next stop: Fine Arts Work Center in Provincetown, Massachusetts. I traveled to the tip of the Cape Cod peninsula for Pam Houston's short story workshop. Pam does this thing where, when the student reads their work aloud, she closes her eyes. I thought for sure she had fallen asleep while I was reading. But, like the Buddhist monks, she was listening. Something else I needed to learn, and am still learning.

Eventually, I had to go home. As I sat in my little writer's cottage in Provincetown, I asked myself if I had all I needed to prepare for a new life when I returned. A writer's life. I had set out on this summer of writerly love with lots of questions. I was heading home with a whole set of answers that did not match the questions.

If we want to be published, our writing has to be seen by people we don't know first- or even thirdhand. Putting ourselves out there, for others to see and read, there's a chance something will surprise you, that you may even make a fool of yourself. I'm living proof that you won't die of it, and you'll probably discover more about yourself than just whether or not you're a fool. You may discover you have an even better story beneath the surface. Besides, think of all the strangers who will be reading your book when it's published, so make sure to get the foolish bits out of the way first.

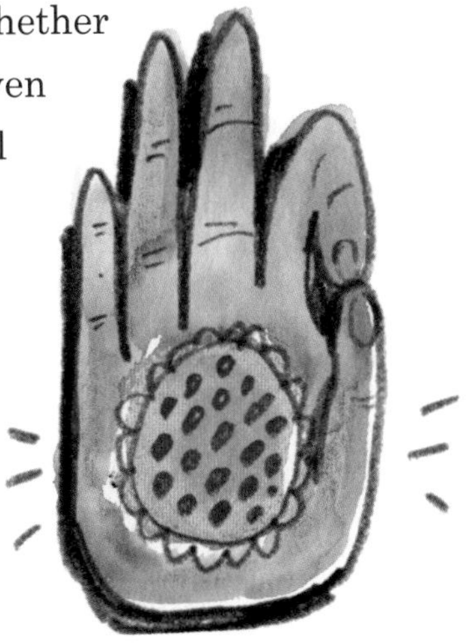

Quite possibly the hardest yet most necessary act in writing is allowing yourself to be vulnerable, to allow your characters in your fiction, or you in your nonfiction, to have weaknesses. And you, the writer, must be willing to be vulnerable to the reader.

Your writing group provides a deadline and camaraderie and regular input on your story, but their familiarity of your work can create prejudice over time. They become used to the foibles and frustrations in your writing and these fall by the wayside. As the saying goes, "When you find a writing group good and true, change not the old one for the new," or something like that. But attending conferences and other workshops can be helpful for fresh input. Finding many teachers and unbiased readers are the strangers who share insight that, like a flashlight, point out the path in the dark.

Some of my students will follow me for years, or many classes and workshops. This is always very flattering. I am invested in my students' work, and I love to watch their progress, but I like to remind them that I only have so much knowledge to impart. Whether they are long-term mentors or weekend workshop instructors who point out your ex-husband was a sneak, it's important to have many teachers. The Buddhists would probably agree with me.

Onion and Cheese Pie

When I chop onions, they make me cry so hard I'm as big of a blubbery mess as I was in my Iowa hotel room. I can't skip the *chop the onions fine* step in many recipes, and none of the tricks to stop the painful process worked: I kept my knives sharper than my tongue, I breathed through my mouth instead of my nose, I held a cracker in my mouth while I chopped (I always ended up eating it before I was done chopping), and nothing worked. I finally found the solution—swim goggles. This pie is both a tribute to my crying weekend and the decadence of that summer of a whole two months of swimming in the Writing Life. This recipe is adapted from a recipe passed to me from someone who passed it from someone else who took it from *The Vegetarian Epicure*, which was a cookbook from 1972 back in the days when vegetarianism was considered *hippy*. It's a classic cookbook still popular today, with many revisions and new editions since the first printing.

4 tablespoons butter

2 large yellow onions, sliced thin

2½ cups shredded Gruyère cheese

1 (3 ounce) bag julienne-cut sundried tomatoes

2 teaspoons basil

2 eggs

¾ cup heavy cream

Prepare pastry for a single crust pie and let rest in the fridge.

Preheat the oven to 350°F.

Melt the butter in a large skillet on medium-low heat.

Sauté the onions in the butter until they soften and start to caramelize, about 20-30 minutes.

Roll out the pastry and place in an 8-inch pie pan.

Spread one-third of the cheese over the bottom of the pastry, then add the onions over the cheese.

Sprinkle the sundried tomatoes and basil over the onions. Cover with the remaining cheese.

In a small bowl, beat the eggs and heavy cream. Pour the mixture over the pie filling.

Bake for 30 to 40 minutes until the top turns that cheesy, crispy golden brown.

The onion pie is a good place to leave some tears. Nothing like a good release to move on from the drama of life. After a good cry, I like to get back to work adding a little drama and excitement to my writing. As I wrote this chapter, all the reminiscing about Nepal gave me a hankering for one of my favorite comfort foods found while trekking. I wanted to make it my own way.

Fried Momo dumplings

Turns out some sects of Buddhists do eat meat (and apparently would swat a mosquito if it tried to bite them). Even the Dalai Lama eats meat. One of his favorite foods is the momo—meat or veggie dumplings.

So many teachers in the form of bakers and cooks gave me lessons for this recipe. This recipe is based on a dumpling filled with all kinds of spices and deliciousness. After attempting to be an authority on Buddhism when, clearly, I was not, I learned my lesson not to just google one source and act an expert. Instead, I asked many teachers for advice on these momos. By teachers, I mean cookbooks and friends. Not sure if this idea of mine—a momo pie—would work, I asked a friend of mine, Madhushree Ghosh, author of *Khabaar: An Immigrant Journey of Food, Memory, and Family*. I told her about my love for momos but explained I didn't know how to make them. She explained that momos are a country food, a comfort food. Yes! I agreed—fools and Buddhists both need comfort.

I appropriated and mixed together every recipe that even came close to what I was trying to create. Both my familiar teachers and strangers were helpful in bringing this together. I am intimidated by fried pies—all that hot grease! I didn't let that fragility get in my way as I learned the difference between fried pie dough and regular pie dough is fat content. My teachers were both Kate McDermott's *Art of the Pie*, and *Handheld Pies* by Sarah Billingsley and Rachel Wharton.

I have a recipe teacher who is a stranger and probably always will be. I'd probably never take a cooking class from her either. I own her cookbook because the photos are gorgeous and the details of the recipes make them sound so delicious that I want to make each pie in the book. But every time I make one of the recipes, it fails. I consider this author a teacher on how to have a goal, but to hold on to it loosely, to accept what may need to be revised, and what may need more experience before it can be achieved. I started taking her ideas and swapping ingredients, adjusting amounts, and finagling the concept. Now I love this book. It's more of an idea book than a cookbook for me. Her masala pasty recipe inspired this pastry, which I switched to a cornmeal recipe.

Here's my end result. I hope you'll learn a little something and go on to create your very own version. Follow your own path.

MAKES 24 DUMPLINGS

CORNMEAL PASTRY

2¼ cups all-purpose flour

½ cup cornmeal

1 teaspoon salt

4 tablespoons butter, cut into pieces

8 tablespoons leaf lard

4 tablespoons sour cream

1 egg, optional

1 tablespoon vinegar, optional

Mix the dry ingredients together well. Scatter butter and lard over the dry ingredients, then, with your fingers, break the butter and lard into the flour until the mess in the bowl resembles pecans in sand. I fold in the sour cream with a spoon first since it gloms onto my fingers too fast, but mix it in until the mixture becomes a smoother sand. If it seems you need more moisture to get to the stick-together dough, mix in the egg, and if you still need more, add the vinegar. Vinegar adds a nice flavor, and sometimes, I switch out a tablespoon of vinegar instead of egg.

MOMO FILLING

1¼ pounds yellow potatoes, diced into ½-inch cubes

2 tablespoons olive oil

1 tablespoon cumin seeds

1 tablespoon brown mustard seeds

1 tablespoon garam masala

1 tablespoon curry powder

1 jalapeño, seeded and finely chopped

5 cloves garlic, minced

1 cup frozen peas, defrosted

6 green onions, finely chopped

Juice of ½ lemon

1½ to 2 cups bone broth

1 (32 ounce) bottle vegetable or canola or grapeseed oil

Place the potatoes in a medium pot, then cover with water. Bring to a boil and simmer for 10 minutes, just until tender, but potatoes still hold their shape. Drain well.

Heat the olive oil on medium high in a sauté pan. Add the cumin seeds and mustard seeds and heat until they start to pop, then add in the garam masala and curry powder. Add the drained potatoes and stir until well coated. Let the potatoes begin to brown, about 5 to 8 minutes. Mix in the jalapeño and garlic, cooking for another 2 minutes. Remove from the heat and stir in the peas, green onions, and lemon juice. Add the bone broth as needed to create a thin sauce. Set the mixture aside and let it cool. You want the filling to be cool so it doesn't melt the dough when you put together the dumplings.

Divide the dough into two flattened disks. Then cut those into quarters, and the quarters into thirds. Make these pieces into little balls. Using a smaller rolling pin, if you have one, roll these balls out into 4-inch diameter circles. Spoon a heaping tablespoon of potato filling into the center. To make the dumpling shape, gather the edges of the circle with pinch after pinch, folding over into the next all the way around until the edges gather together at the top like a drawstring bag. Place the raw dumplings on parchment paper on a cookie sheet. As you make them, put the cookie sheet in the fridge while you make the rest. Let them get chilled before frying so they maintain their shape when dropped in oil.

Heat up a big, deep skillet with at least 4-inch-high sides. Pour in the bottle of oil and heat to medium-high, or until a piece of dough starts to sizzle when dropped in. With a slotted spoon, place a few of the dumplings in the oil. Let them turn a golden brown before lifting out with that slotted spoon and placing on a paper towel to drain. Repeat until all dumplings are fried.

You can make these into any shape you want, of course. I just love the little dumpling shape. Make them flat semicircle hand pies, or triangles, or disks. Or add meat. The Dalai Lama would.

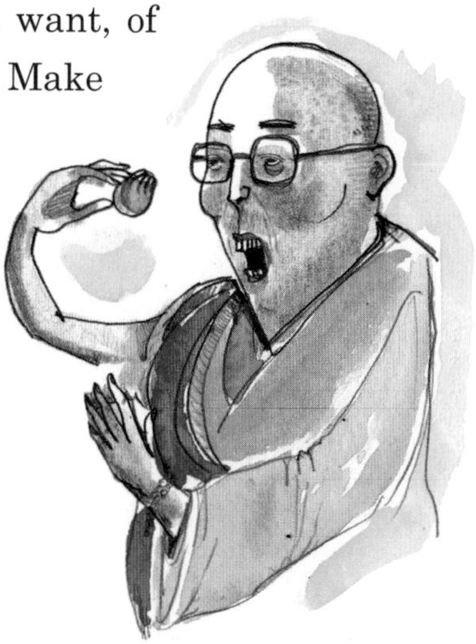

CHAPTER NINE

It's Drafty in HERe
Is This the ENd?

Early on I mentioned the anecdote about the writer E. B. White putting his manuscript in the corner postbox to mail to his agent. He then changed his mind and waited beside the postbox for the mailman to show up so he could retrieve the manuscript to take it home and revise it. These were the days when we sent hard copy manuscripts via snail mail, when there were postboxes on the street corners, and when mailmen were called *mailmen* even if they were not men. A lot has changed since those days when E. B. White was an anxious writer. What hasn't changed is knowing when we're finished.

It can be addicting—just one more draft, just one more. I know I can stop anytime, really, I can. Wondering when the ending will arrive can also be frustrating. It's not like your novel just pops its head up and says, "I'm done!"

I hear students often say they feel their book is good enough after a couple of drafts, and they'll just let the editor fix the things that aren't working.

Once upon a time, back when hard copies were snail-mailed and postboxes sat on the corners, and mailmen were women in disguise, there was an editor named Maxwell Perkins who was famous for helping authors write their best books. F. Scott Fitzgerald, Ernest Hemingway, and Tom Wolfe were some of Perkins's authors. He nurtured their gifts and helped them grow as writers. Editors still exist who want to help writers and who "love books," as Perkins was famous for saying, but time has become money in publishing. Today, editors don't have the time to work with a writer and their rough

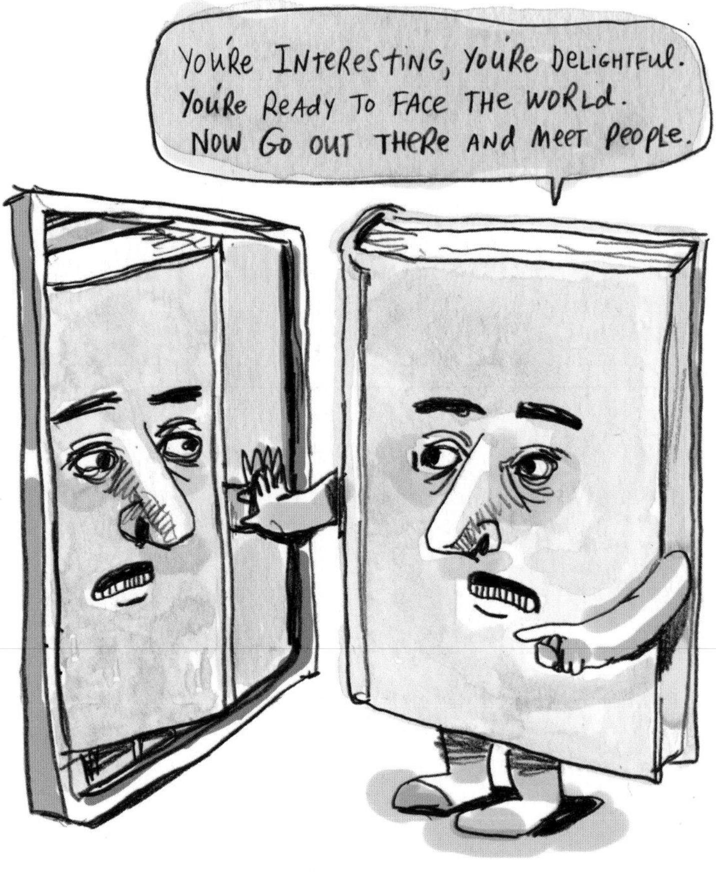
YOU'RE INTERESTING, YOU'RE DELIGHTFUL.
YOU'RE READY TO FACE THE WORLD.
NOW GO OUT THERE AND MEET PEOPLE.

gem of a book. Despite the swiftness of email, texting, and mail carriers being free to be who they are, time is even more precious for editors. The painful truth that sends many less diligent writers than yourself running, is that the process inside those big publishing houses is about the sales and not the art. Editors have to meet the numbers the larger conglomerate who owns the publishing house demands. This doesn't mean they don't respect art or the process of polishing a gem to its brilliance. It means they have a marketing department that has a say in who the editor picks for their list. It means your book has to be brilliant before it shows up in their inbox. Which means it should be pretty shiny before it hits the inbox of any agent.

So many of us, especially those of us who believe in self-affirmation, want to shout, "But I am a gem!" And your book may be the next bestseller,

Pulitzer Prize winner, or book club sensation. If you're reading this book, I believe in you! But if you've been paying attention, then you know this is where I'm going to say, *again*, perseverance is important—you need to take that faith in yourself and your book and keep revising until you don't see any more cracks in the prose. Then revise again.

How do you know when the cracks are sealed, and the story is solid? As I wrote this chapter, I was also working on the Nancy Drew novel. I felt a sense of urgency to get the novel written because I wanted it to come out when this book came out. So, I pushed through the drafts of this new novel. I motored along like a manic typist, staying focused on the page, making my page count of revisions every day—fifty! I pushed myself to do more. I could do one hundred if I really tried, if someone else would walk the dogs and make dinner. Still, the book didn't just sail out of my fingertips and into my agent's hands. Or, rather it did, and I regret that I made her read that draft. Now I'm revising the novel again.

This novel-in-progress has had several rough starts because, first of all, it's a mystery and I've never written in the mystery genre before. Mystery writing is a mystery to me! That took a few drafts—if the detective character is in the kitchen with a rolling pin, and Colonel Mustard is in the library with the lead pipe, and Professor Plum is tying knots in the rope around the candlestick, while Miss Amy is in the attic with the typewriter, how do I get the detective to tell the writer who the culprit is? I know, that makes no sense, but that's how my first few drafts went. Finally, I got the hang of how to make all the threads connect. Whew.

This is where an outline comes in handy even if you aren't an outliner. I use note cards thumbtacked to my wall. I know where the story is headed, where and how the character will change, and even how it ends, but the outline, no matter how detailed, doesn't tell you if you've just written the final draft.

What takes so long when it seems the character and plot are figured out? And, with a memoir, what could take so long with that when—hello!—shouldn't you already know what happened, and who it happened to? If only it were that easy.

Mrs. Peacock in the Secret Passage with a Pitchfork

Outlines are great for keeping track of both where you're headed and where you've been. They keep us on track with the story like a road map. But like any journey, at least one that gives you new perspectives and provides ample adventures, you will come across tangents and forks in the road. Like Robert Frost said, you should take the road less traveled by for that will make all the difference, or you may find a new path that no one knew about before. You never want your story, any part of it, to be cliché, so when you are posed with a choice to make for your character or the plot, or even the structure or story, choose a direction that will take you and the tale to someplace new. "But won't I finish faster if I follow what is already proven to work?" you ask. You will finish faster, but when you're told that has already been done before, you'll have to go back to the beginning anyway.

This isn't to say you should make up stuff and scatter your fictions willy-nilly across the page, especially not in nonfiction. But try a new idea on for size and see how it fits the story, even if it means another draft. You'll know fairly early on if it's going to work, or maybe you won't know until it's been tried on and didn't fit. Or, it may fit like the proverbial murderer's glove.

MoonPies took twelve drafts before I even sent it to an agent. I saved everything I cut from each draft and kept it in a Trash file in case I might need it later. My novel manuscript ended up being over three hundred pages long. The Trash file was over 1,200 pages long.

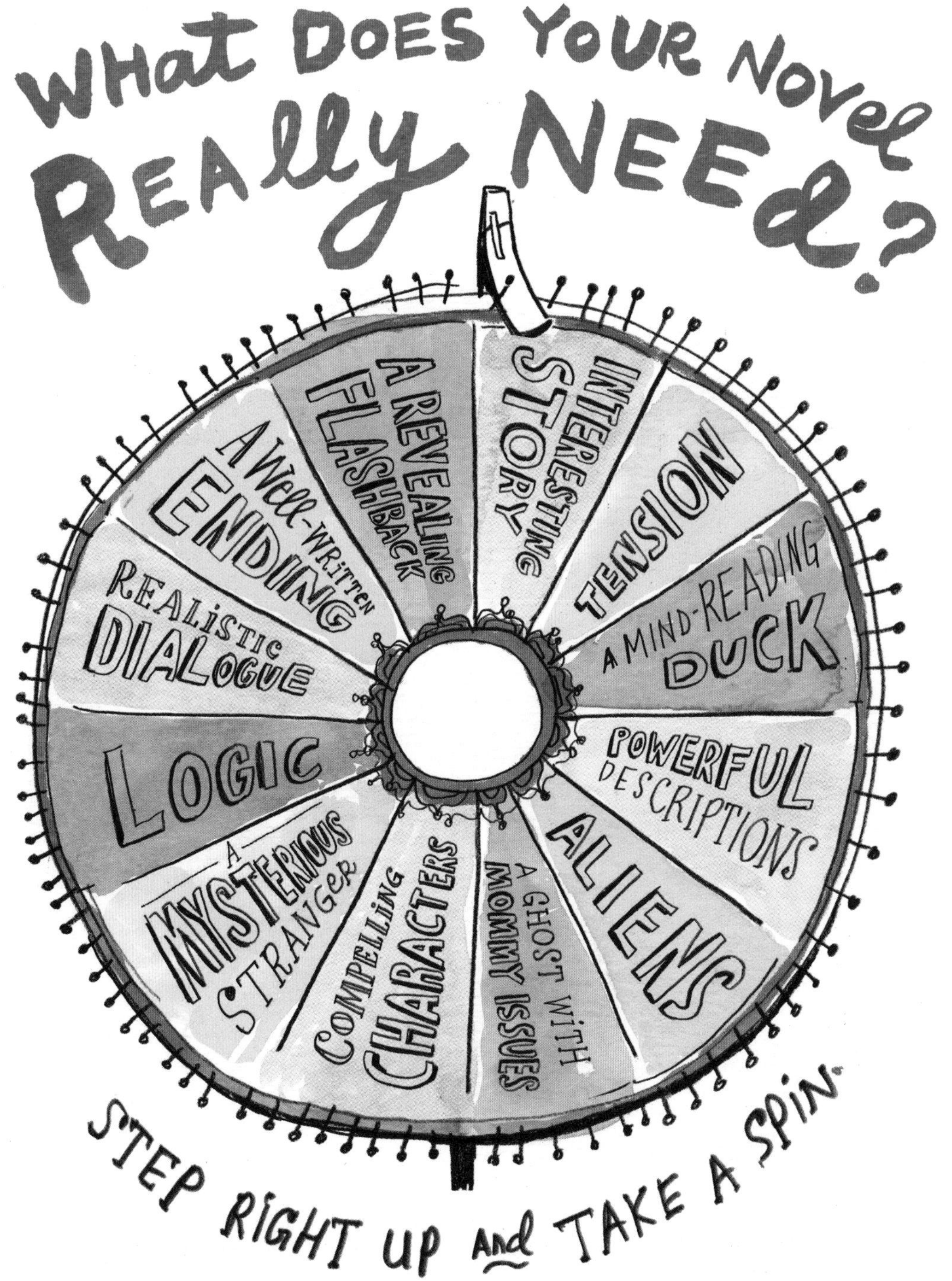
WHAT DOES YOUR NOVEL REALLY NEED?
INTERESTING STORY
TENSION
A MIND-READING DUCK
POWERFUL DESCRIPTIONS
ALIENS
A GHOST WITH MOMMY ISSUES
COMPELLING CHARACTERS
A MYSTERIOUS STRANGER
LOGIC
REALISTIC DIALOGUE
A WELL-WRITTEN ENDING
A REVEALING FLASHBACK
STEP RIGHT UP AND TAKE A SPIN.

You may be saying, "Oh, you're just indecisive and anxiety-ridden," and you'd be right. And you may be saying, "I can make up my mind faster than that," and again, you are probably right. And, you are quite likely saying, "I still don't understand why I can't just follow my outline, write the damn thing, and be done." You can. But there's one more thing to consider.

Consider the devil that's in your details. The devil in this idiom refers to the mystery that lies inside your work. Not all devils are evil. But this bugger is sneaky. In every chapter, every paragraph, every sentence, and with every word, drafts are where you finesse the details to make sure everything is cohesive, not just the story line, but sentence structure and word choice. With each revision, as you sift through the details like sand, this is when you'll find gems to polish. This is a devil who might slow you down, but he's worth keeping an eye out for.

Mr. Domino on the Staircase with a Spoon

Because I keep delivering bad news about how it really could take you a long time to finish and that this writing game really is hard, my evil side wants to add one more horror to your worries that's hiding around the corner: the domino effect.

As you get close to feeling like this draft is your last draft—"This could be it!" you say to your annoying friends who keep asking when you are

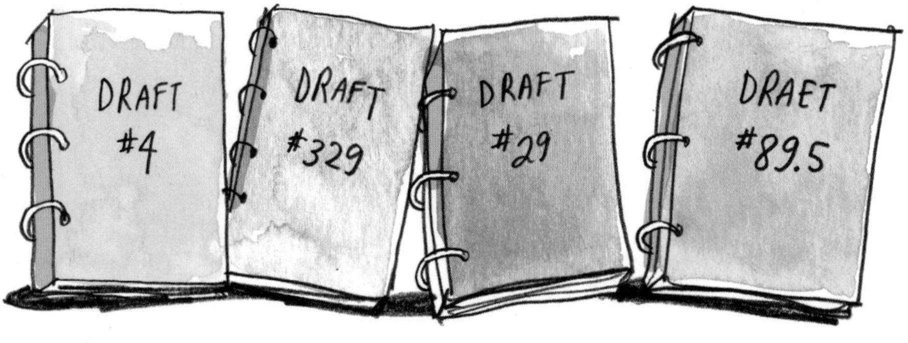
DRAFT
#4
DRAFT
#329
DRAFT
#29
DRAFT
#89.5

going to be done—you start back at the beginning of your novel to do one last read-through, when . . . you see in page after page where you made the last changes, everything that came before it needs to be changed to work with that set of changes, and then everything after that needs to be adjusted to work with the adjustments you made going forward, and next thing you know this supposed last draft is a new tangled mess of minced meat, which is usually best reserved for pie.

This, my dear readers and writers, is when you are quite possibly close. When you start to unravel the knots and reorganize the threads of the latest mess, you'll start to see the pattern in the fabric. Don't be surprised if the heart of the story leaps out at you during this process. This is when the weaving you've been doing, the placement of scenes, character development, subplots, themes, and even the plot itself, often gel, sometimes surprise you, and maybe raise your self-esteem because you realize you truly are a fantastic writer because you kept at it.

After all of this is said about drafts and more drafts, there will be one or two of you who will write to me and tell me that you wrote your first book in one draft while letting only your wife or hamster read it for spelling errors, and you are now #1 on Amazon's soon-to-be-published list. To that I say, celebrate your success, but don't be surprised if we use your name in vain while the rest of us rewrite trying to get closer to the jewel we aspired to.

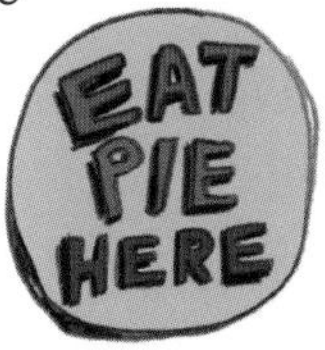
EAT
PIE
HERE

Mr. Theme in the Closet with a Mask

We learn in all this revision and rewriting that writing takes us on a path to discovery. Every story solves a mystery. Not necessarily a mystery about whodunit, but a mystery about why we write the story we are writing. What did we want to find out when we took on this story, this book? This discovery process is what keeps us writing. We don't always know what we are hoping to discover when we start. But as more of the story becomes apparent, the more clues reveal themselves in each draft. In *MoonPies*, I wanted to find out why people abandon other people, why anyone would abandon children. I didn't know this is what I was looking for when I started, but once I realized this about four or five drafts in, I couldn't quit until I figured out the answer.

It took someone in my writing group who asked me if I knew I was writing about abandonment to bring it to my attention. Once they said it, I could see where abandonment and loneliness were everywhere among my pages. In my memoir, a reader suggested the theme was "Are we hideous people?" Both of these suggestions took me on a whole new path with my next drafts, as I finessed the story lines in order to reveal the answers to me and my future readers.

What if you don't know what it's about, and no one tells you? You just keep making the book, the writing, and the story itself be the best it possibly can be, and don't give up. Themes are curious creatures that like to hide, but not so subtly as may be first suspected. They usually leave a foot in the aisle for us to trip over eventually. A great place to start looking is in the metaphors you create. More than likely, you'll begin to see subjects that repeat themselves or patterns in objects. Maybe in one form or another, masks keep showing up in all the scenes. Could the characters be hiding behind their true selves? Is there a reluctance to show their vulnerabilities? Or maybe there's a subconscious desire to be a superhero?

Editor in the Library with a Pen

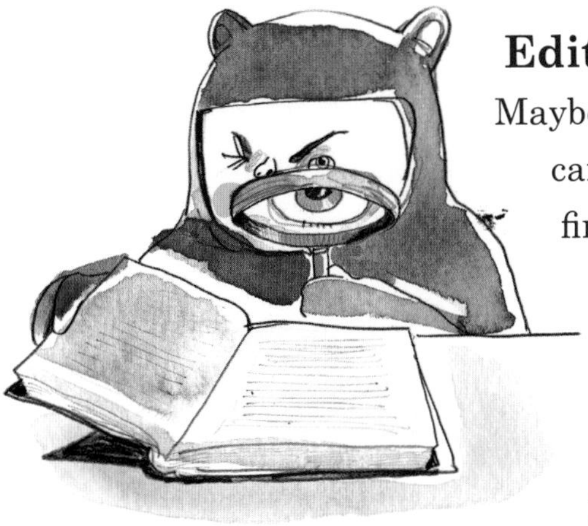

Maybe you've taken your book as far as you can go by yourself. You don't feel it's quite finished, but you don't know what more to do. You've used up your allotment of friends and family to read it for free. It can be helpful to have a professional set of eyes on your pages. The Maxwell Perkins-esque editors are outsourced now. Freelance editors, writing teachers, and book coaches have filled this void. They can be expensive but are worth every CryptoByte if you do your homework and find one that meshes with what you need and want. Online you'll find a swarm of people professing that they can take you to publication. Often, they offer to publish you themselves, and they'll claim they published some other huge hit. Looking for an editor can be like trying to meet your future mate by hanging out at a bar. You may find the love of your life that way, but you'll more likely end up with a venereal disease. Often, the best matches come from friends who match you up. If you're in a writing workshop, ask if anyone has any referrals. If the workshop is led by a teacher, ask them if they do manuscript editing, or if they know someone who does. Look up your favorite authors' websites and see if they offer mentoring or editing services. In other words, don't go home with some random person, and definitely don't have unprotected sex.

Having an editor means more editing. As your story unfolds, and you start to see what sort of resembles The End, be open to revisions big and small all along the way. Be open to making your story the best possible story it could ever be. It's your story, only you can write it, and it deserves to be told well, so make it pie-worthy!

A legion of editors is not waiting for your book. Trust me on this one. Not even a back-alley agent waits for your unedited book. The tighter the prose, the faster you will get an agent, and the faster they will sell the book to a publisher. Your book needs to be rock solid. It must have a bod of steel—it must be the Arnold Schwarzenegger of novels.

Every Novel Writing class, I have a student or two who tells me they are just going to let their publisher edit their manuscript. They assume, I presume, that all they must do is type up the story. It's a great idea, they put it down on paper, and let (with wave of hand like Marie Antoinette) the little editors deal with the nitty-gritty. But editing isn't the nitty-gritty. It's the bones, the exoskeleton, *and* the electrical impulse that brings the monster to life. Otherwise, you have a bunch of flabby flesh and some gross organs lying around trying to stand up.

Being at the page every day, maintaining a connection to the story no matter how minimal, this is the electricity, the connective tissue, that sometimes feels like "magic" or being in the "zone." This is what editing does—it turns offal into steak.

As my dear author friend Hope Edelman said to me as she read this chapter, "Tell them they can dial 1945 on their rotary phones if they want to reach their editor to help them write their books."

THIS IS THE
END OF
THE ROAD

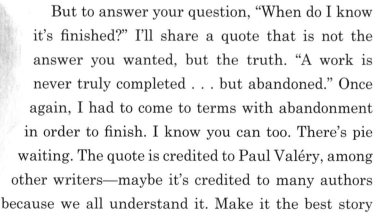

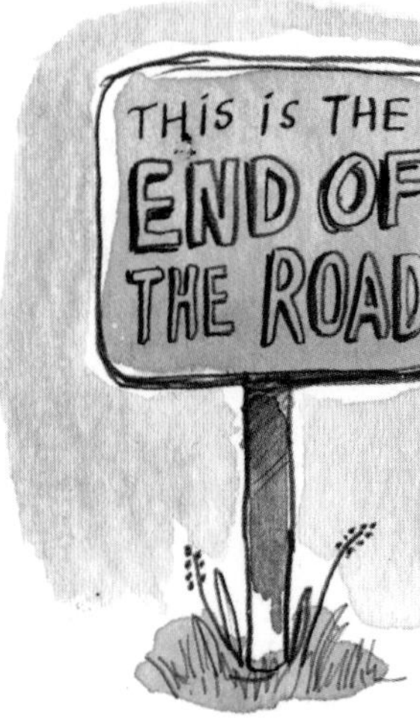

But to answer your question, "When do I know it's finished?" I'll share a quote that is not the answer you wanted, but the truth. "A work is never truly completed . . . but abandoned." Once again, I had to come to terms with abandonment in order to finish. I know you can too. There's pie waiting. The quote is credited to Paul Valéry, among other writers—maybe it's credited to many authors because we all understand it. Make it the best story you can, and if you feel the book needs another revision, it probably does. Look for professional help and consider that it is not just an investment in your project, but it's an investment in you, an investment in your dream. If you can't afford a professional, revise yourself into a good book.

Now, I must go bake a pie, so I can see something finished.

When WRITING gives you LEMONS, Make SHAKER LEMON Pie, OR not.

The first time I made Shaker lemon pie, I thought it was the easiest and most delicious one I had ever made. So I made it again, only this time it had a soggy bottom, and the lemons were too tart and so bitter it was hardly edible. So I made it again, still trying to attain that original flavor stuck on my taste buds. This time I made it a single crust, which I prebaked before adding the lemons. This got rid of the soggy bottom but the top burned. So, I made it again and turned my oven down, but the soggy bottom came back. It dawned on me that my oven might be broken.

After my husband pulled the stove out from the wall, repaired the oven, and I recovered from seeing what all had fallen behind the stove, I was ready to try that Shaker pie again. That afternoon, a friend showed up with a bag of kumquats. If you aren't familiar with the kumquat, it's surprising when popped in your mouth. You eat them whole because the skin is sweet like an orange, but the juice is tart. Like a Shaker pie that uses the whole lemon, I figured a kumquat version would be a cinch. Sometimes things fall into place in unlikely ways.

In the middle of writing *MoonPies*, I had a scene where Ruby finds a little girl tied to a front porch. I took it to my writing group and they pooh-

poohed it. I revised it and took it back to my group again. They still found it not linked to the rest of the novel. I tried revising it again. "It doesn't belong in the novel." "It has nothing to do with your story." "It just isn't working." They tried to be kind, to let me down easy. Janet said she didn't want to see it again, to move on. I came home to my writing desk and tried to just forget about it. But the scene niggled around inside my skull. *I* was trying to move on, but *it* wouldn't. I decided to allow myself one more rewrite before I said stop. When I rewrote it, I thought of how I could better connect it to the story. I made it a flashback: the little girl in the scene became Violet, Ruby's adopted daughter before she adopted her. When I took it back to the group, again, Janet cried. She cried not because I'd disobeyed, but because the scene moved her. It became the novel's pivotal scene.

That anecdote is meant to connect to my broken stove, and Violet is the kumquat that arrives and creates a whole new pie that works better than before. Or maybe I just want to tell you about listening to your gut and knowing when to let go, and maybe when to try figuring out how to link what you feel in your heart of hearts should.

SHAKER KUMQUAT PIE

I was inspired to bake Shaker lemon by the very first pastry cookbook I ever owned, *The Complete Book of Pastry: Sweet & Savory* by Bernard Clayton Jr. The lemon version was one of my earliest pies I ever made.

Make this Shaker pie with any citrus revisions you want. They all work. I'll share my kumquat version with you, mostly because I think more people should delight in saying the word *kumquat*.

WHOLE WHEAT CRUST

Using the Basic Pie crust recipe on page 11, substitute ½ cup of whole wheat flour for ½ cup of the all-purpose flour. Chill in the fridge.

FILLING

6 ounces kumquats, halved, de-seeded, and sliced thin

½ teaspoon salt

½ cup brown sugar

½ cup granulated sugar

1 tablespoon chopped fresh or crystallized ginger, optional

4 eggs

1 tablespoon turbinado or demerara sugar, to sprinkle

I always think of how simple this pie is, but then I forget this part, so I'm going to remind you up front—this recipe takes overnight to make because the citrus needs to sit overnight with the sugar, so plan ahead. The cutting and deseeding of the 6 ounces of kumquats reminds me of pitting cherries—

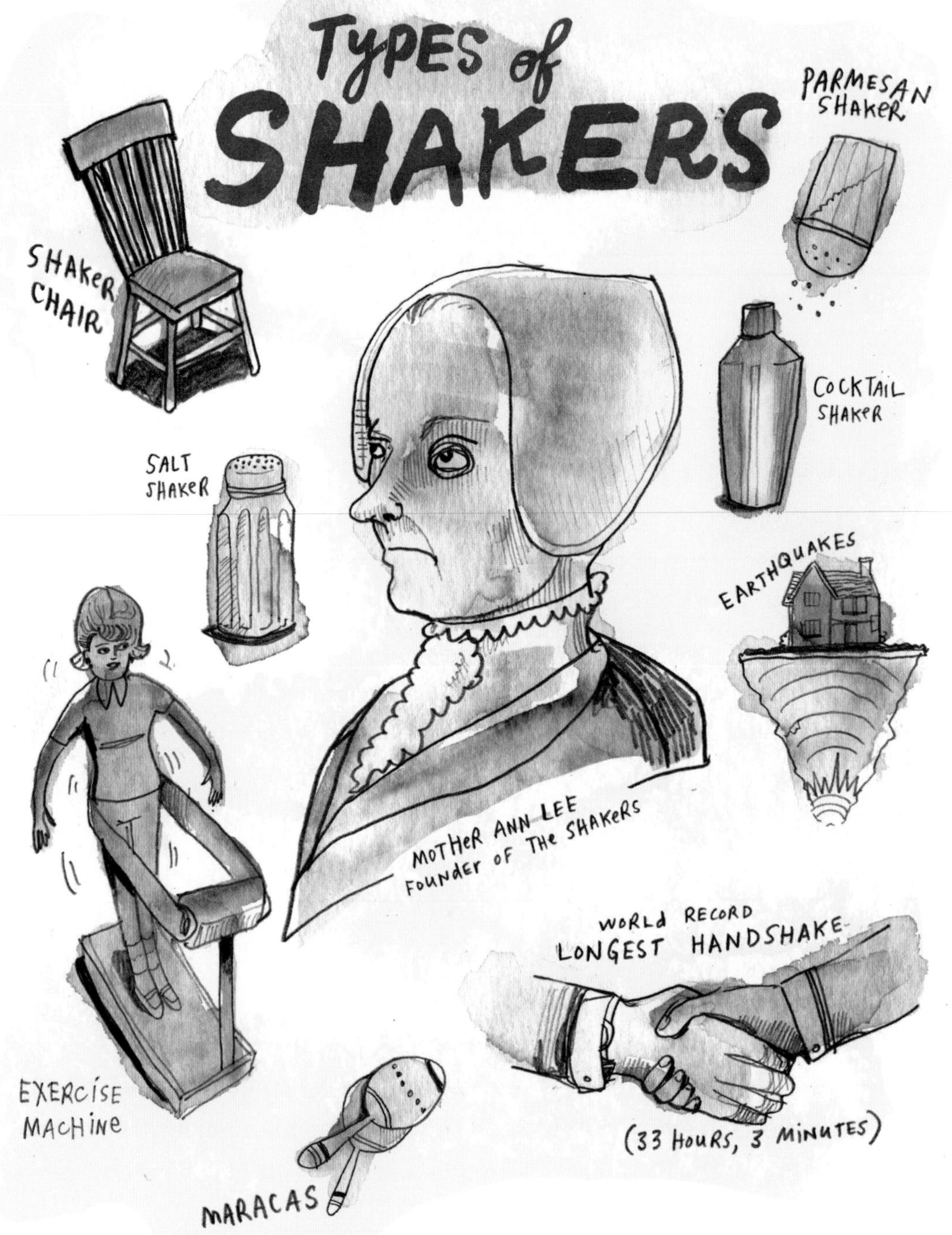
TYPES of SHAKERS
PARMESAN SHAKER
SHAKER CHAIR
COCKTAIL SHAKER
SALT SHAKER
EARTHQUAKES
MOTHER ANN LEE
Founder of The SHAKERS
WORLD RECORD
LONGEST HANDSHAKE
(33 HOURS, 3 MINUTES)
EXERCISE MACHINE
MARACAS

a meditative process. Cut them in half, then remove the seeds. Flesh side down, slice thinly. Again, watch out for those seeds.

In a large bowl, add the kumquats, salt, brown and granulated sugars, then stir. This is where I add a tablespoon or so of some fresh or crystallized ginger, especially if it's a lemon version, but this is optional. Let the mixture sit overnight, stirring here and there.

The next day, preheat your oven to 425°F.

Beat eggs.

Stir the kumquat mixture together with the egg mixture.

Roll out your bottom pastry, then press into an 8- or 9-inch pie pan.

Pour the kumquat and egg mixture into the pie pan. I often make a lattice top crust so I can see the yellow or orange peeking through. Brush with milk and sprinkle the top with a tablespoon of turbinado or demerara sugar.

Bake for 30 minutes, then turn the front to face the back and cover with foil. Reduce the oven temperature to 350°F and bake until a knife inserted in one of the vents of the crust comes out clean, about 25 minutes.

If only it was that easy to know when your book is done—just insert a knife in your gut and see if it comes out clean. Let pie rest for 30 minutes or more, as should you.

SOMETIMES YOU JUST CAN'T MAKE AN IDEA WORK.

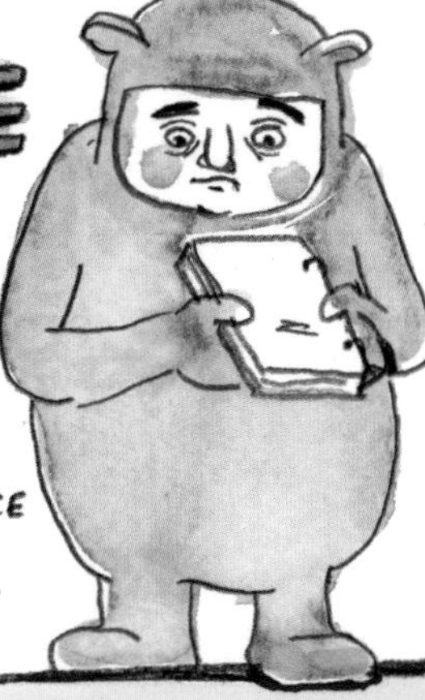

YOU TRY DIFFERENT WAYS TO RESCUE IT, BUT SOON IT BECOMES OBVIOUS THAT NOTHING WILL SAVE YOUR BOOK AND YOU HAVE NO CHOICE BUT TO GIVE UP AND WALK AWAY.

YOU'VE ALL BEEN GREAT CHARACTERS. BUT WE NEED TO MOVE ON. SO, I GUESS THIS IS IT.
BUT WE'VE BEEN THROUGH SO MUCH TOGETHER.
YOU SAID WE WERE BEST FRIENDS
YOU THOUGHT ABOUT ME CONSTANTLY
I FEEL REALLY TERRIBLE ABOUT THIS, BUT IT'S NOT YOU, IT'S ME.
DUH. OF COURSE IT'S YOU

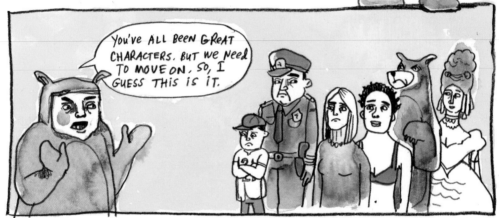

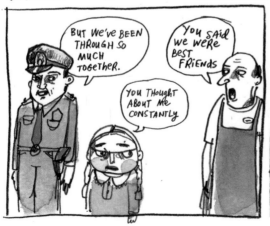

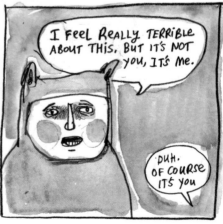

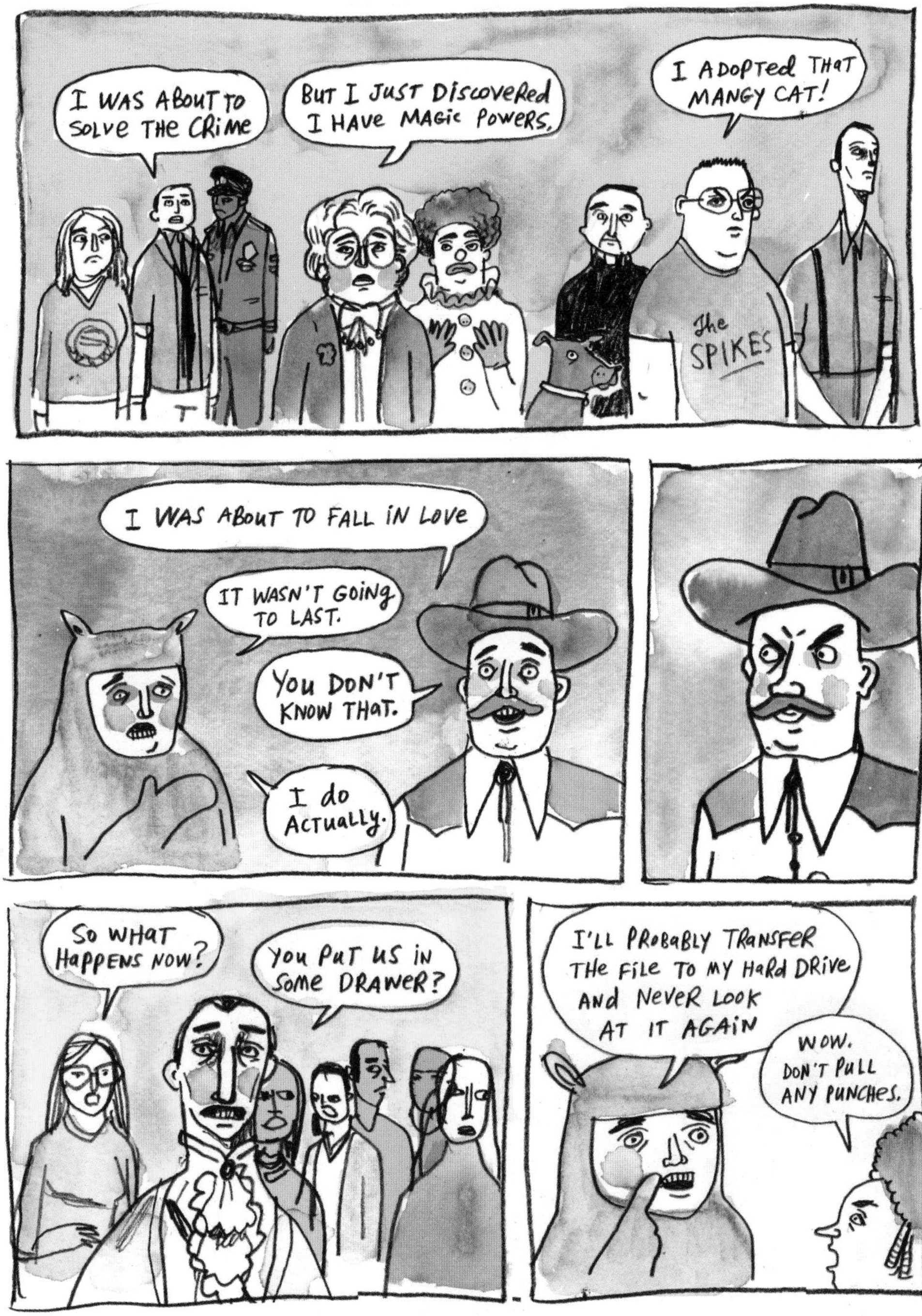
I WAS ABOUT TO SOLVE THE CRIME
BUT I JUST DISCOVERED I HAVE MAGIC POWERS.
I ADOPTED THAT MANGY CAT!
The SPIKES
I WAS ABOUT TO FALL IN LOVE
IT WASN'T GOING TO LAST.
YOU DON'T KNOW THAT.
I do ACTUALLY.
SO WHAT HAPPENS NOW?
YOU PUT US IN SOME DRAWER?
I'LL PROBABLY TRANSFER THE FILE TO MY HARD DRIVE AND NEVER LOOK AT IT AGAIN
WOW. DON'T PULL ANY PUNCHES.

The best thing to do now is to make a pie for all those characters who are never going to see the light of day. Maybe you can mourn the entire story while you're at it.

IT'S SO SWEET, you'll FORGET TO CRY

WHAT YOU NEED IS A FUNERAL PIE

Deciding to stop working on your book can happen without warning, any day of the year. A Funeral Pie uses ingredients usually found around the house: dried fruit, raisins, maybe a handful of nuts. Throw it together when you need to ease the grief from saying goodbye to a loved one. Or that good-for-nothing book you've been working on for months.

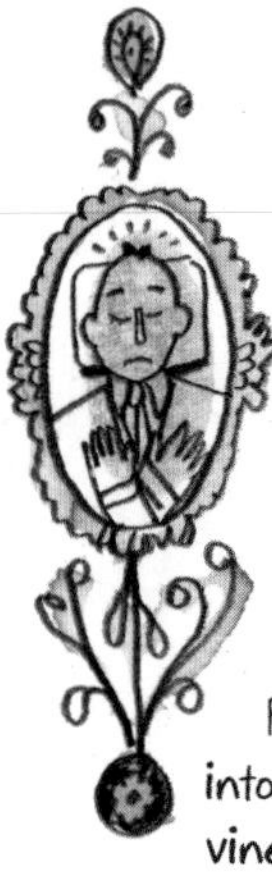

CRUST

3 cups all purpose flour
1 teaspoon salt
1 cup (2 sticks) cold butter
1 egg
1 tablespoon apple cider vinegar
Some cold water

Put flour and salt in a bowl. Grate cold butter into mixture and rub until crumb-like. Add egg and vinegar. Add enough water to hold together, then gather into a ball, put in refrigerator until chilled.

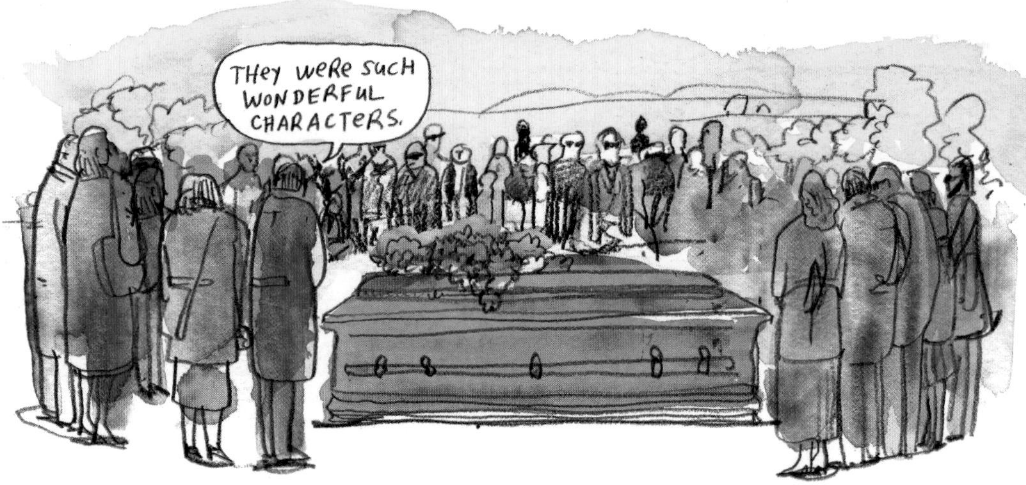
THEY WERE SUCH WONDERFUL CHARACTERS.

THE FILLING

For the filling, you'll need 3 cups of dried fruit. Any kind will do: golden raisins, dried apricots, dried cherries, dried apples or pears, whatever makes up the three cups OR you can do 2 cups of fruit and substitute in a cup of chopped nuts (walnuts and almonds are both good choices). Try golden raisins and apples. Or maybe dried cherries, blueberries and cranberries. Or dried apricots and oranges. There's lots of possibilities.

Now for the soaking liquid. You'll need 2 cups and this will turn all that dried fruit juicy and soft. Some recipes call for water, which seems like a waste. Instead, you can try any kind of juice like orange, cranberry, or apple cider. Or why not use some booze and live a little? Grand Marnier, rum, or bourbon would taste delicious. Who doesn't want to be drunk at a funeral?

MIXED NUTS
Cherries
GOLDEN RAISINS
DRIED APRICOTS
ALMONDS
DRIED ORANGES
CRANBERRIES

Let that simmer for 7 minutes. Then add ½ cup of sugar (white, light brown, etc.) and 2 teaspoons of spices. You can use cinnamon or a bit of allspice, pumpkin pie spice, ginger, orange rind, vanilla extract, whatever. Add three tablespoons of cornstarch and a pinch of salt.

When it starts to thicken, take it off the heat and stir in 1 tablespoon of cider vinegar and 3 tablespoons of butter. Then let it cool completely. Set the oven for 400°F. Roll out dough and put in a tin pie plate (it doesn't have to be tin, but the bottom browns better). Put the cooled filling into the bottom crust then cover the whole thing with a top crust and crimp the edges. Brush it with egg if you have some. Bake for 25-30 minutes. Start grieving! That book is in a better place already.

LIQUEUR

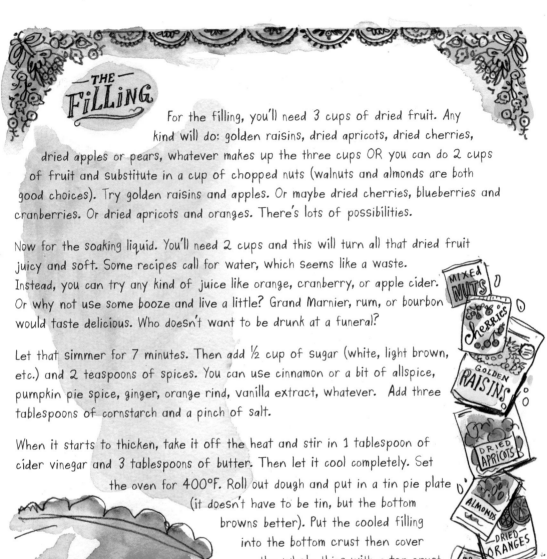

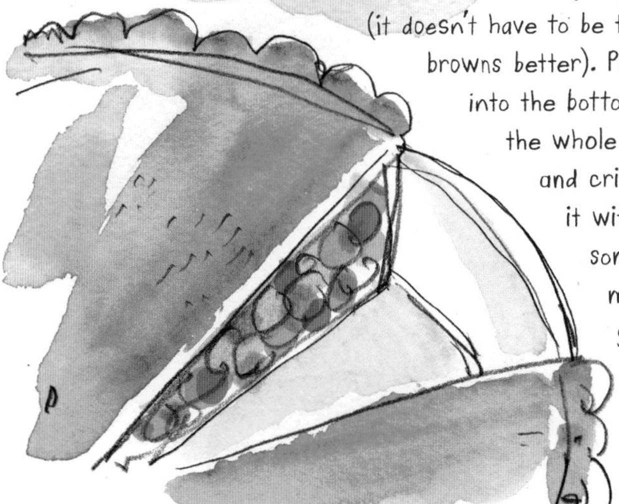

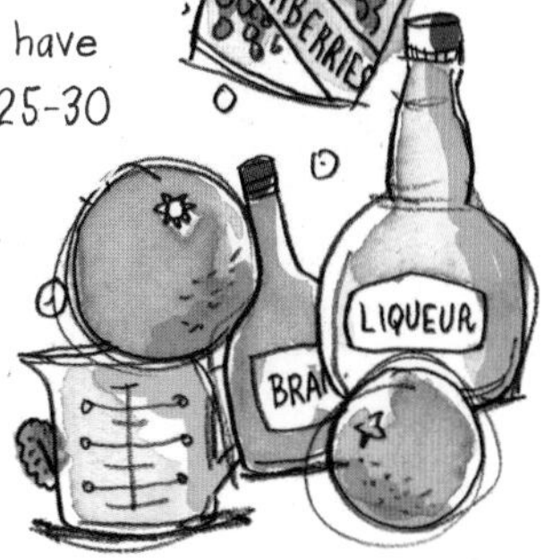

COMMON DISTRACTIONS

That will cruelly distract you from your novel

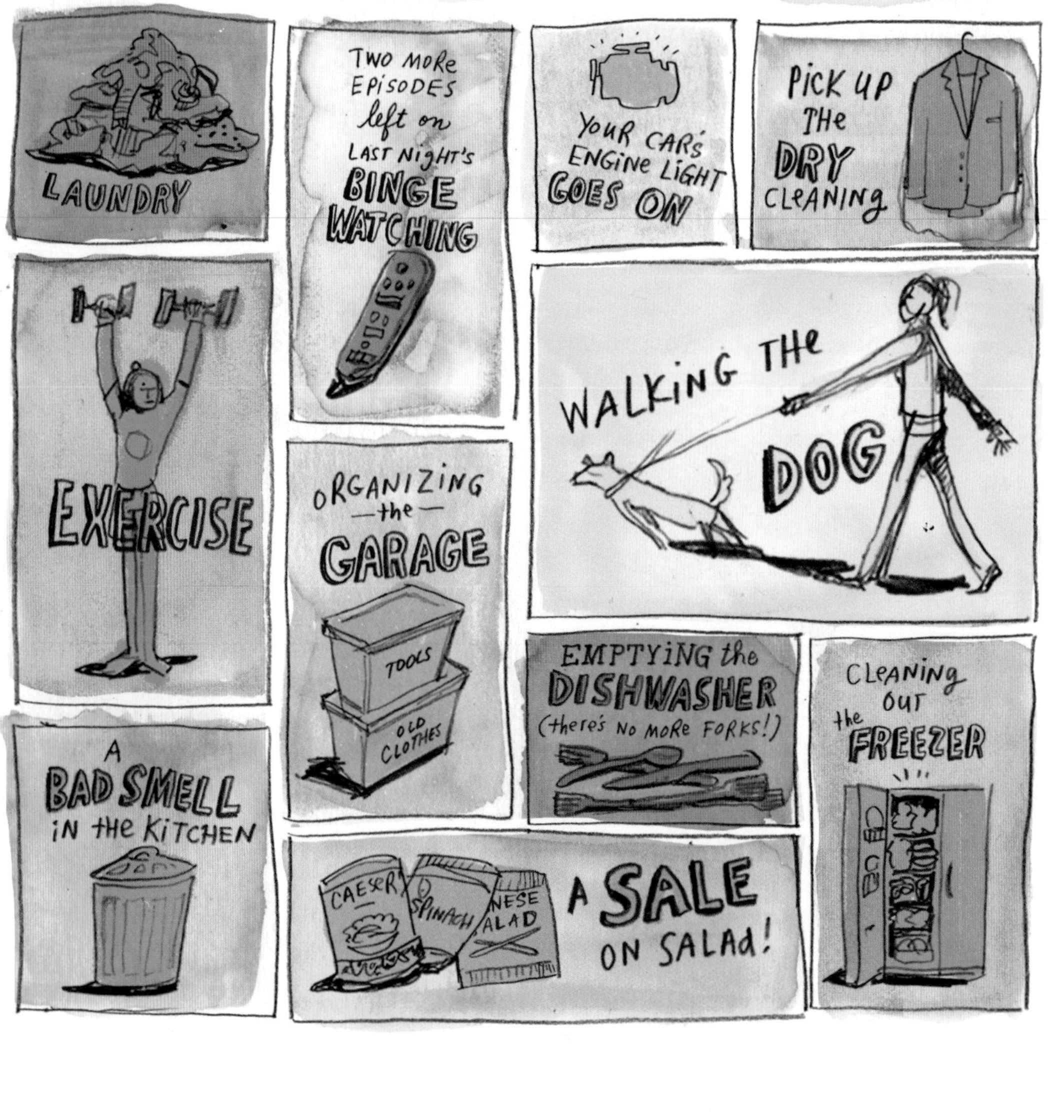

LAUNDRY
TWO MORE EPISODES left on LAST NIGHT'S BINGE WATCHING
YOUR CAR'S ENGINE LIGHT GOES ON
PICK UP THE DRY CLEANING
EXERCISE
WALKING THE DOG
ORGANIZING the GARAGE
TOOLS
OLD CLOTHES
EMPTYING the DISHWASHER (there's no more forks!)
CLEANING OUT the FREEZER
A BAD SMELL IN THE KITCHEN
CAESER
SPINACH
A SALE ON SALAD!

CHAPTER TEN

DATING and REJECTION AREN'T JUST FOR LOVERS ANYMORE

I had finished the last draft of my first novel, or so I thought, and was ready and all set to send my baby out into the world. I signed up for a local writers' conference where agents and editors read your work. These places are a hotbed of schmoozing and bumping elbows. Conferences are a baker's dozen and often are affiliated with a multitude of genres—romance, mystery, horror, etc.—but also are focused on both literary fiction and nonfiction. Often, they offer what I call Speed Dating for Writers.

Speed Dating for Writers is an addendum to the regular programming. You pay a fee to have up to three or four agents or editors review your work. It's like speed dating for a mate because you sign up in advance, then when the time comes, you go in the special room in the conference center, usually a big room with small tables spread out, and you get five (5!) minutes with the representative you paid for. In all of five minutes, you present your elevator pitch (practice this!) to the agent or editor and they fall in love or diss your book. The agent or editor may read a short sample you have brought along, or maybe just judge whether or not they would be interested in your work (and you) by listening and asking a few short questions. Then, ding, the bell rings and it's on to the next agent or editor.

I signed up for three of these, all set to find my perfect agent.

I borrowed a miniature bowling bag purse from my fashionista friend, since my main character Ruby owns a bowling alley, and I aspired to look like a creative person with a flash of personality. I located my first agent, slid into the seat across from her, exchanged the requisite greetings, then spat out the elevator pitch I had memorized and practiced in front of the mirror for umpteen hours: "When Ruby Kincaid, the owner of a six-lane bowling alley, spots her runaway daughter on a ButterMaid commercial, she sets off for Hollywood with her rattlesnake-rattler-earring-wearing sister, the mother-in-law, and two grandkids in tow to find Violet and get her to own up to why she would abandon two kids. Along the way, they encounter Hells Angels, are contestants on the *Price Is Right* game show, and find out unconditional love is not always reciprocated." (Stop and catch breath.)

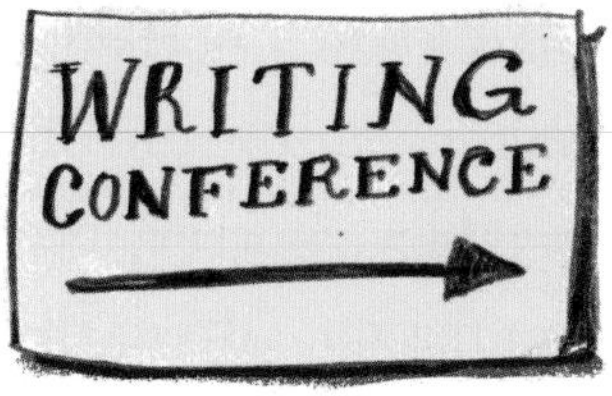
WRITING
CONFERENCE

On my first speed date, the agent offered me an exclusive. I had to ask what that meant. The agent replied, "Send me your full manuscript, give me three weeks to read, and while I have it, I request that you don't send it out to anyone else. It's mine exclusively to choose." She added, "This book sounds exactly like my kind of book."

This, I thought, *was worth every extra penny I paid. Should I even bother going on the other two speed dates?* I'm like that with men too—they say they like me and I'm theirs.

I did go to the next speed date, I mean, it was paid for and all. This next agent was also very positive about my story and asked me to send her a copy of the manuscript. 2–0! But I was already dating someone—I had that exclusive with the first agent. I liked this second agent too. I explained my dilemma. "Congratulations, that's wonderful," she said, "but if that agent decides it isn't right for her after all, will you send it to me?" "Oh sure," I said, thinking, *I'm going to marry the first agent, so I'll just say yes to be nice.*

Third speed date is a charm. Not. The third appointment was with a well-known editor at a big New York publishing house. I slid into the booth, smiling, and feeling confidence bounce off my smile. My book was practically already published. I complimented the editor on her earrings—a little schmoozy, but I was feeling generous.

I recited my blurb about Ruby and the gang heading to Hollywood.

She looked at me while a long silence hung between us.

"I'm not sure why you signed up with me when your book is nothing I would ever consider."

Is this when I should tell her about my exclusive? She doesn't seem to get that I'm pretty much already a *New York Times* bestseller.

"From your bio, and the research I did, I thought my book was one you'd be interested in." My voice trailed off at the end as my confidence began to smell soured.

"You've wasted my time, and yours, I'm afraid."

I silently took back the compliment I gave her on her earrings. I didn't really like them in the first place. I was just being friendly, unlike her.

We still had about four and a half minutes left of our speed date.

"Should we talk about something else?" I tried to joke. My nervous go-to.

"I'm heading to the bathroom," she said, and slid out of the booth.

That pretty much sums up how "subjective opinions" work in the publishing business.

But never mind, I would go home with my exclusive in my back pocket and knew down the road that editor would be wishing she'd been a teensy bit nicer to me.

Only that's not at all what happened when I got home.

My husband was out of town that weekend of the conference.

When we spoke on the phone, I regaled him with details. With great enthusiasm, he purported support for my writing career. I blabbered

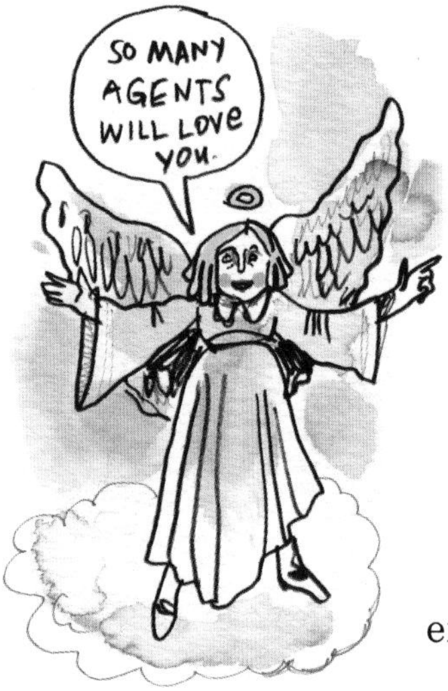
SO MANY AGENTS WILL LOVE YOU.

on and on about the exclusive and the rest of the conference filled with panel discussions and presentations, and the authors I saw speak, and—

"Why does it sound like you're sitting next to a dryer with tennis shoes tumbling in it?" I asked mid-sentence.

"The woman I'm staying with is doing laundry."

"Woman you're staying with?"

"Yeah, my client put me up with one of the employees to save money."

"Why don't you sit somewhere else, so you aren't next to the tennis shoe-palooza?"

It took me a few days after he had returned to fully grasp that this was no money-saving activity, but an extracurricular activity that included hanky-panky without tennis shoes.

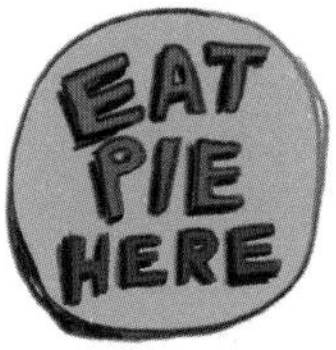
EAT PIE HERE

I kicked him out of the house.

But the exclusive! I was going to be fine without him, because I was about to get my book published any minute now.

Then the rejection came, I mean aside from my husband. While I was rearranging my life to fit the news that I was soon-to-be-divorced, the first speed-date agent sent an email within the three weeks she had promised that read, "While I am enamored with your characters, the plot just doesn't work for me. Someone else may feel very differently about this. I wish you all the luck in placing this book."

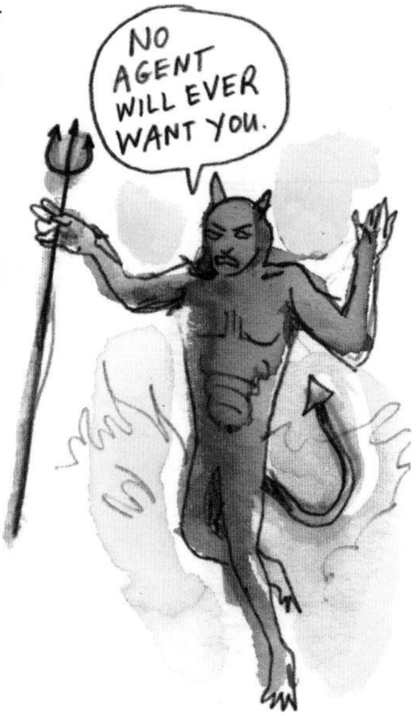
NO AGENT WILL EVER WANT YOU.

"No, no, no," I wanted to write back, "you are supposed to publish this book and make my deadbeat husband see that I don't need him because

I am a successful author." But I didn't. I wrote back, "If I revised the plot, would you be interested in looking at the book again?" I was determined more than ever to make this work. She had loved me once, couldn't she love me again?

The agent agreed to look at the revision, so I revised like the maniac I was, in between running around trying to find a divorce attorney. I received a new rejection email that read, and I would have found it funny except nothing was funny at that time, "While I am enamored with your plot, your characters just don't work for me . . ." The opposite of the first letter.

This was not how I wanted it to go. But things in life don't usually go the way I want them to. What would we have to write about if they did?

Wait! I thought. I still had the second speed date agent who said she wanted to see my manuscript if the exclusive didn't work out. A rejection came almost before I even got my letter in the mail to her. Then divorce became full-time, what with the attorney research, preparing documents, and the lengthy telephone conversations with every friend and neighbor I could tell about my disastrous marriage.

I put a sign over my desk with my favorite quote, most often attributed to Winston Churchill, "When you're going through hell, keep going."

That's what I tried to do—keep going. While revising my plot for the agent who practically promised me marriage, I realized the book still had loose threads. I began revising again. My life looked like it had been shaken loose, then dumped out on the driveway where someone ran over it a few times with their F-350 pickup truck.

Then, I left for the summer of writers retreats and workshops you've already read about.

My summer sojourn turned out to be helpful in a myriad of ways. While I needed lessons from unbiased strangers to open up my writing, I also needed distance to gain clarity on what direction I wanted my life to go.

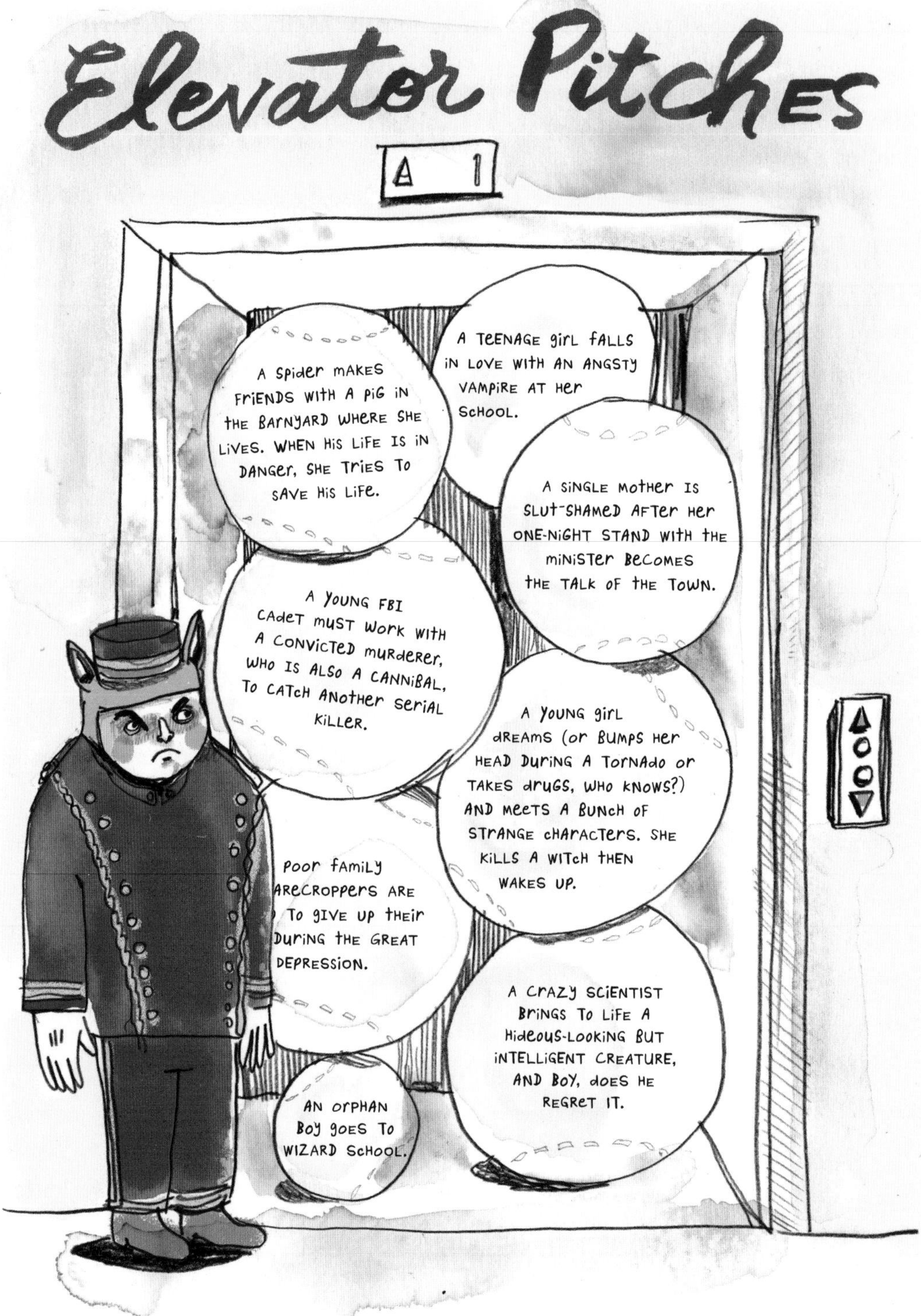
Elevator Pitches
1
A spider makes friends with a pig in the barnyard where she lives. When his life is in danger, she tries to save his life.
A teenage girl falls in love with an angsty vampire at her school.
A single mother is slut-shamed after her one-night stand with the minister becomes the talk of the town.
A young FBI cadet must work with a convicted murderer, who is also a cannibal, to catch another serial killer.
A young girl dreams (or bumps her head during a tornado or takes drugs, who knows?) and meets a bunch of strange characters. She kills a witch then wakes up.
Poor family
arecroppers are
to give up their
during the great
depression.
A crazy scientist brings to life a hideous-looking but intelligent creature, and boy, does he regret it.
An orphan boy goes to wizard school.

The teacher who had said, "Write, then publish" gave me the incentive not to give up on *MoonPies*. *MoonPies* needed smoothing and straightening. When I returned home, I had calmed down enough to begin doing the research on which agents out there would love my book. That's when I organized my plan of attack on a whole new set of agents.

When life gets in the way, as it inevitably will in small and big ways, it's okay to take a break. It doesn't have to be a monthslong trip somewhere. The cool thing about a novel is that, unlike a relationship with a human, the novel will wait loyally for you to return. You may feel distant from it at first, but by returning to it every day, reigniting your rituals or process, the story and your intentions come back to you as though you had never left, right brain muscle memory.

Just remember to keep going, no matter the heaven or hell you are going through. Did I mention falling in love can be a distraction too?

Salmon & PortoBello
in a sour cream crust

I was close to creating Mrs. Lovett's pies during that crazy time in my life, but I refrained. When my husband was no longer in the house we shared, I looked in the freezer and found it stocked full of salmon he'd been bringing home from his trips to Alaska where he sat next to noisy washing machines. What to do with a freezer full of salmon? First thing I did was invite all my friends over for a barbecue. I needed comfort food more than grilled salmon, though. My sister told me about a salmon and mushroom pie she'd eaten, and I wanted one. I hadn't yet ventured outside the chicken pot pie realm, but this new life of mine would begin with a new favorite pie. I concocted my own version below after years of finding what made me happiest. I worked my way through that freezer of fish, and I worked my way through to the final draft, and I found I could not only write a novel, but I could write a recipe too.

Once you're proficient at making pie dough, and you probably already are, you can add just about anything as long as you keep the fat and liquid balanced. In the same way, you want to make sure your prose is balanced—if there's too much drama, it's helpful to add some humor.

SOUR CREAM CRUST

Using the Basic Pie Crust recipe (page 11), I make a sour cream crust for this pie, which means I substitute about ½ cup of sour cream in place of water—add it in tablespoonfuls so the dough doesn't get too wet. I also add a couple of tablespoons of horseradish if I'm feeling particularly spicy. Make a double-crust pie dough of your choice and let it rest in the fridge while you make the pie filling.

FILLING

    1 pound salmon, poached

    5¾ cups chicken broth or vegetable stock, divided

    4 tablespoons butter, divided

    1 pound baby portobellos, sliced

    2 to 4 garlic cloves, minced

    4 tablespoons all-purpose flour

    ¼ cup half-and-half or milk

    1 teaspoon salt, plus additional to taste

    3 teaspoons dried tarragon leaves

    1 tablespoon sherry

    ½ pound hot-smoked salmon

My freezer was stocked full of Pacific fresh-caught salmon, and also the pantry had some packages of hot-smoked salmon. When I combined them, I found the flavor was bolder than only the delicate poached salmon. But try out your own version using a pound and a half of whatever kind of salmon.

Poaching is simple. Fill a straight-sided deep pan with 4 cups of the broth, or enough to cover the salmon. I tried Trader Joe's Miso Ginger Broth for the poaching once and haven't done it any other way since. Bring the broth to a boil, then add the raw salmon. Turn the heat down to a simmer. Cover the pan and let simmer for 5 minutes. You don't want to overcook the salmon, especially since it will cook more inside the pie.

While the salmon poaches, start the rest of the filling.

Preheat the oven to 425°F. Melt 1 tablespoon of butter in a heavy, nonstick deep skillet over medium heat. Sauté the sliced portobellos in butter until the mushrooms lose their water, then add the garlic and continue to sauté until the garlic is fragrant, about 2 minutes. Shift to a separate dish and reserve.

Using the same pan the mushrooms were in, add the remaining butter. Stir over medium heat until melted. Add in the flour one tablespoon at a time and cook slowly, stirring, to make a roux.

Let the flour flavor cook out, about 2 minutes. Slowly stir in the remaining broth and the half-and-half or milk. Turn the heat down to medium-low. Add seasonings to your desired taste: salt (remember the smoked salmon will be salty, so be wary of adding too much or any more at all), tarragon, and sherry. Add additional broth as necessary to reach the desired

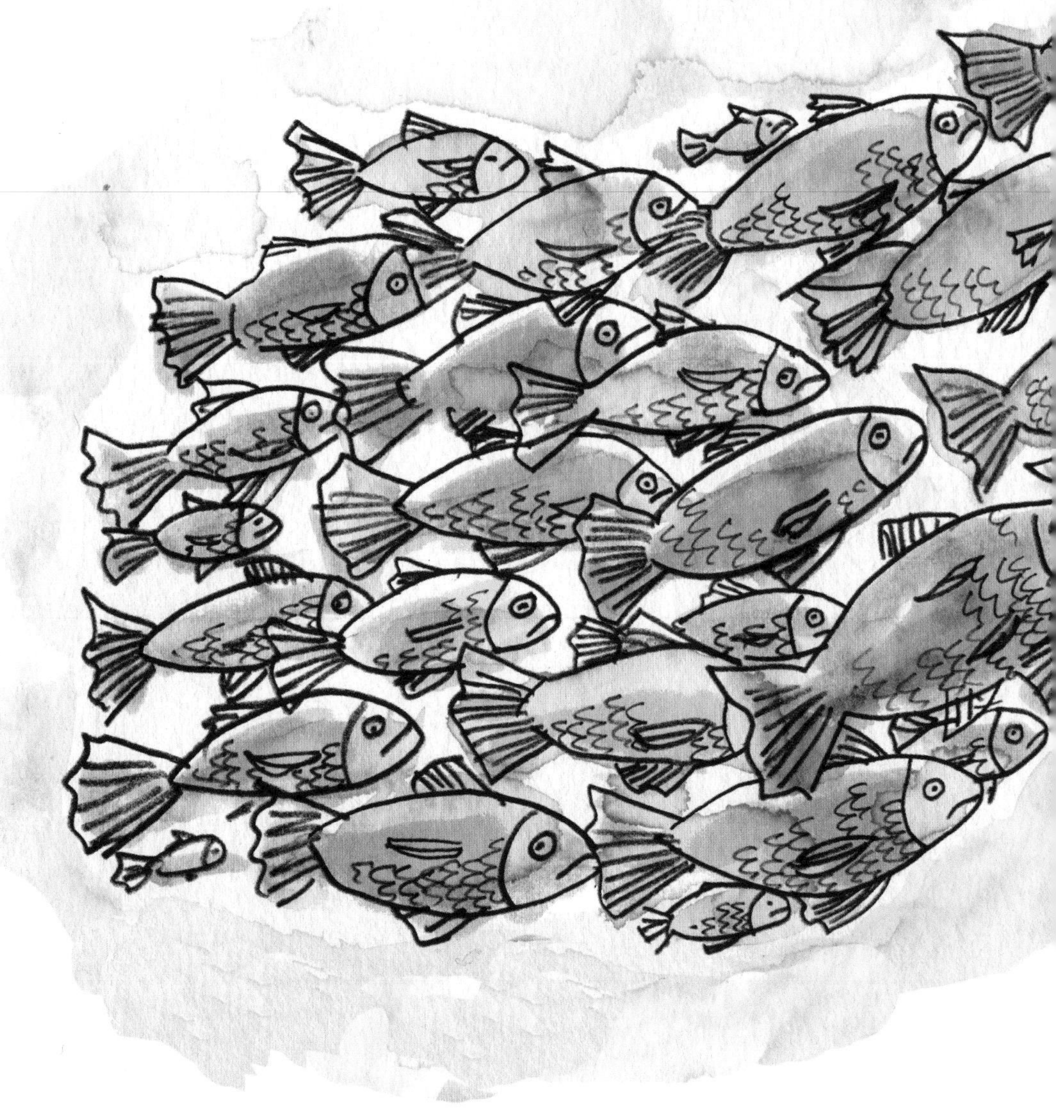

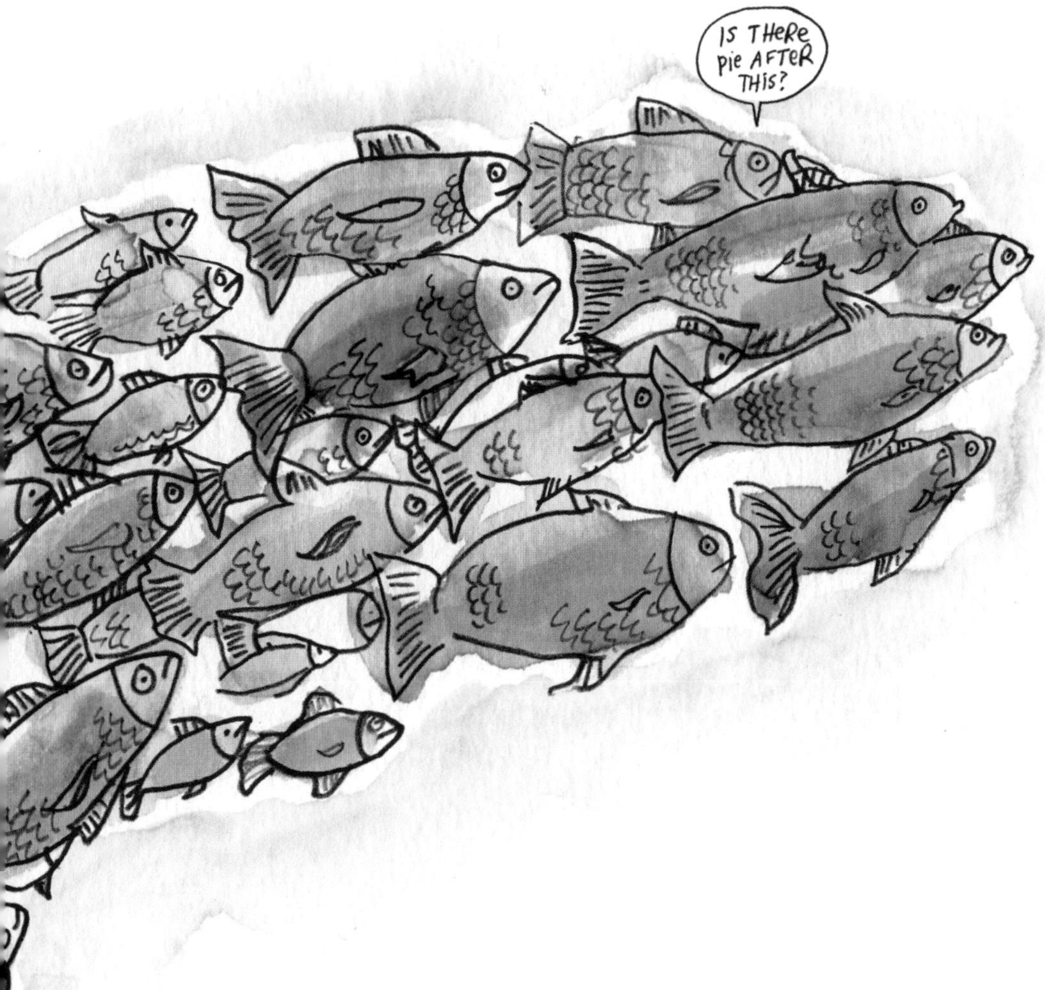
IS THERE PIE AFTER THIS?

consistency of sauce for the pie. I like a medium thickness that isn't too runny when I cut into the pie, but not so thick that it stands up on its own like pudding. Adding the sherry helps to thin the consistency too, but too much sherry can make the flavors bitter. But taste as you go!

Once the sauce reaches the consistency you like, turn the heat to low. Stir in the mushrooms. Break the smoked and poached salmon into 1-inch pieces and stir into the sauce. Mix well. Taste for desired seasoning. This is your last chance to season.

Roll out the bottom crust to the desired size of the pan. This recipe makes one 10-inch pan or three 5-inch individual pans or five 3-inch pans with double crusts. It's pretty rich, so consider the smaller pies to serve yourself, or the one big pie to serve your friends.

Roll out and place the top crust on the pie. Slice steam vents in the top crust. Crimp the edges decoratively or mash with a fork. Bake for 35 to 40 minutes, or until the crust is golden brown, the sauce is bubbling out of the steam vents, or a knife jabbed in the center comes out steaming hot.

Invite friends over to amuse them with the latest tales of your agent search.

CHAPTER ELEVEN

OH AGENt, WHeRE ARt THou?

Remember back at the beginning of this book when I said some of my students want to know how to get an agent without even having written a book? This is the chapter you should turn right to, if you are one of those people. You'll still need to write the book first, but this is where I tell you about why, how, when, and where, plus how to write the dreaded query letter.

Why?

Your first question may be: Why do I even need an agent? Why can't I just send my masterpiece directly to the editors? The reason I'm such a big agent advocate is because I've had three agents, and each have helped me in ways I could not have helped myself. But it was my first agent's adroitness, which untangled a few unexpected knots in my career, that convinced me that I wouldn't have survived publishing if I hadn't had an agent advocate.

Now, you may be saying, "But an agent is so hard to find, can't I just mail my manuscript to all the editors who would like it? Seems easier to just bypass all the people in between." While there are some editors at publishing houses who will accept manuscripts over their own transom, most will not. When I tell you my story, maybe you'll find it may be worthwhile to have an agent looking out for you in the wide, wild world of publishing.

First of all, my agent got me a lucrative two-book deal on my first-ever book written. When I got off the phone from learning about that deal, I was certain they had me, Amy Wallen, confused with someone else named Amy Wallace, since that's the name everyone confuses for mine. *They will realize their mistake and call me back at any moment*, I kept saying to myself for about the first, oh, year. When it sunk in that Penguin really did like my book, and maybe even me, I focused on that second book of the two-book deal.

The Two-Book Deal Curse, I started hearing from friends. This second book turned out to be harder for me to write. The contract requested a book with the same characters as the first. We had negotiated this because I didn't want to write a sequel, but my editor wanted a sequel. But sequel or just the same group of characters, it wasn't going well. Working with the same characters over and over obviously works well for writers who keep a series going. But for me, it was like having my relatives come to visit and they had overstayed their welcome. Ruby constantly tidying around the house without being asked, Loralva was sleeping in and drinking all my beer, and none of us were getting along. My writing group helped me brainstorm a plot, but even that didn't seem to help me move forward. In the middle of all of this struggle, I received an email that my editor had accepted a new position at another big New York publisher.

When I looked up the list of books represented by the new editor who was assigned my book, I was impressed but wasn't sure how her list meshed with my book. I spoke to her on the phone a few times, and we chatted about what my first draft needed. I had never met her nor even seen a photo of her, but I kept picturing someone who was so out of shape that she could barely get around her office. She'd make a suggestion, then she'd let out a heavy sigh. My impression was she pushed herself around on her office chair,

NEW YORK! LOS ANGeles! GARY, INDiANa!
TYPES of AGENTS
you'RE LiKely To MeeT

THE GO-GETTER

She's young and has little experience but by hell or high water, she's gonna make you a bestseller.

THE TOUGHIE

Do not disappoint her. She says that this business will spit you out if you're not careful.

THE MOTHERER

Available for therapy appointments about your marriage, mother, weight, or manuscript.

THE CELEBRITY AGENT

If you're Danielle Steele, great. But otherwise, whoever you are, get out.

SUPER BUSY

Doesn't have time to return your calls. Or emails. Might be on vacation. Can she get back to you in a couple of years?

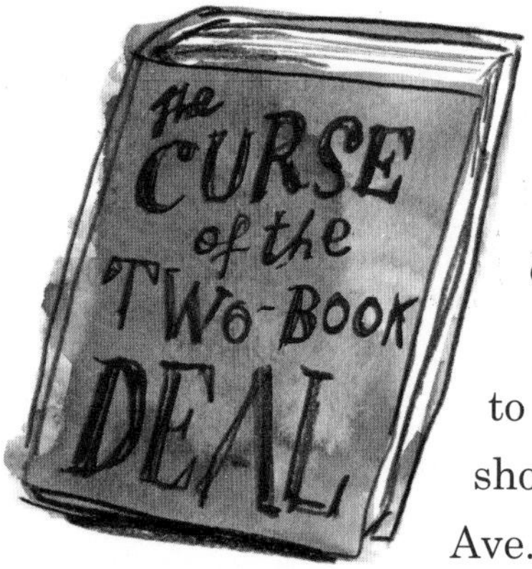
the CURSE of the TWO-BOOK DEAL

the wheels struggling to carry her girth as she tried to find a file or flip a page. I pictured her as rather portly, to be honest, because she sounded exhausted just picking up the phone receiver.

The next time I went to New York City, I offered to stop by to meet her in person, and she agreed we should have coffee. I got to the building on Hudson Ave. The security guard told me to which floor to take the elevator. I got off and walked down the hall, then stood in her office doorway. I took one look at her svelte build and instantly realized she wasn't portly at all; she just had no enthusiasm for my book. To be honest, neither did I.

In the meantime, my agent was negotiating a tricky situation with my previous editor who was now over at Hyperion. We arranged a meeting in a crowded restaurant near Grand Central Station—a place we would neither be noticed nor overheard. Our clandestine gathering was to talk about a contingency deal. The editor had read an article in the *New York Times* about a group of characters who were ripe for a novel. I read the article and knew immediately I was familiar with and loved these characters. I read the article and said, "I know these characters. I don't *know* know them, but I know them." I was willing to oust the squatters in my second book and invite these new characters to move in.

My agent negotiated a deal that made it possible to leave one publisher and move to another without having to pay back any of the monies paid to date.

Me, myself, and I began a fast and furious friendship with the new characters. A group of has-beens and wannabes from Hollywood, California, living the bohemian lifestyle in a retirement village in Burbank became my new best friends. We laughed, we played, we cried. We swam in their apartment complex swimming pool.

And, then we cried some more when I got another email from the editor at Hyperion, the editor who had been at Penguin. "I must leave you at the altar for a second time." She returned to Penguin to have her own eponymous imprint. While I was happy for her, I watched the publishing revolving door spin on its axis.

I was assigned another new editor. This one was not portly, and she didn't sigh politely into the phone either. She told me straight up that the new friends I had were not who she wanted to invite to her party nor her booklist.

My agent came through for me again. She negotiated out of Hyperion, and I paid back none of my second advance.

Without an agent, I wouldn't have known the first thing about negotiating the ins and outs of the agreements. I want to write more books, not learn contract law. I encourage anyone to have an agent. Looking back, I should never have agreed to write that second of the two-book deal. I wasn't passionate about it. I agreed to it because I wanted the deal, and I wanted to make the editor happy. I was naive thinking I could just type out another book when I had not even a plot or experience or desire to write that kind of book. Paying close attention to what kind of writer we are is key to finding a great agent, but also in connecting to our editors, and knowing what kind of books we are meant to write.

Without an agent, I would have been stuck at Penguin writing a book I could care less about with a gorgeous and intelligent editor who eventually would have sent me packing. Without an agent, I wouldn't have met the bohemian Hollywood wannabes and has-beens who still make me laugh and cry. Without an agent, I wouldn't have had any of these deals, no matter how they turned out.

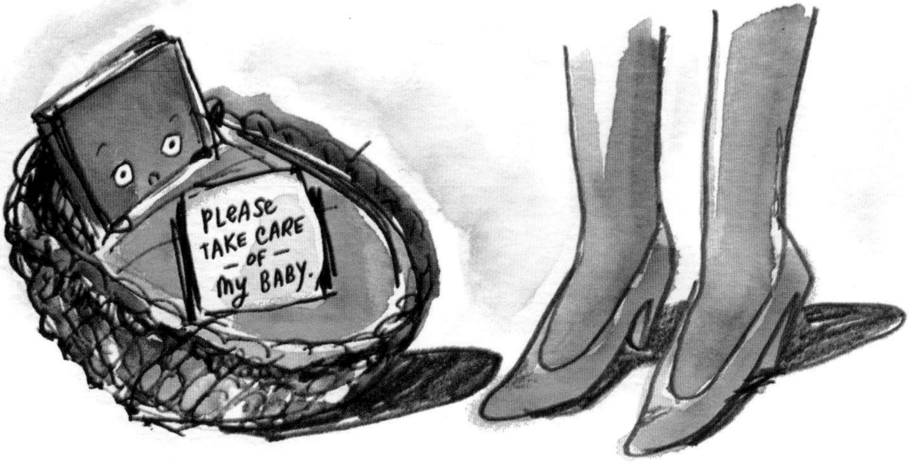
PLEASE
TAKE CARE
— OF —
MY BABY.

After all the publishing hullabaloo, it was up to me to start a new book, and write I did. That's when I wrote my memoir, a book I needed to write before I could go back to fiction for a while.

Agents work hard. They don't just read books all day—they have your back when it comes to contract negotiations. The publishing house is a business and wants to make a profit. An agent wants you to make the most money you can, so that they, in turn, earn their standard 15 percent on domestic sales (foreign rights and film deals, those will be mentioned in another book after my dream where this one is made into an animated flick). Fifteen percent of more is more for them, so while they, too, are a business, they all want you to succeed. Agents are on your side.

How do I know that agents don't just eat lunch with editors, and the rest of the day lie around their offices reading, eating bonbons, and drinking vodka? I don't, but I do know that years ago, when I first started writing, I lived across the street from the offices of one of the top recognized agents. She represented some big-name authors, and I mean big. Household-names big. While I fantasized she might one day see me at the nearby Postal Plus and invite me to submit my manuscript to her based solely on the fact that I could work the self-serve copier with aplomb, I never once ran into her.

But I did see her staff come to the store to pick up her mail. One day, when I overheard a young woman say she was there to pick up Big-Name Agent's mail, I then watched as the staff person was given a handcart stacked five feet high with boxes. As she wheeled the cart out the doors, I asked the Postal Plus employee, "Wow, does she get that much mail every day?"

"No," she replied, "She gets at least three stacks that tall every day.

"Three? Three stacks of boxes? Every day?"

The Postal Plus employee nodded, then returned to filling the Scotch tape dispenser.

That was the moment I knew it would take a lot for an agent to notice my manuscript coming in the door. I would have to edit and revise until it sang.

How?

To start, you'll need to dust the cobwebs off your Left Brain and start thinking without your emotions. Emotions are Right Brain's most important tool. Right Brain helped you go deep inside your story, helped your characters have at least three dimensions, and even helped you see inside conflicts and how to solve them in your scenes. Right Brain deserves a whole pie and a nap while you work on getting published with Left Brain.

Although there may be some altercations across the amygdala about this, you still don't need the answers to those algebra problems that seemed useless in eighth grade, but you may need to recall the research skills from social studies and analytical skills used in writing book reports in English class. While you don't need an MBA, people skills never hurt—they may be rusty after spending so much time in your attic writing. Maybe that's just me.

Next, you'll need to think about whose book yours may resemble. Maybe you've already done this. You've already pictured whose book yours will be sitting next to on the table at the front of the bookstore. You've imagined the author interviewing you onstage when your books are compared in the *New York Times* book section (my fantasies require that newspapers still have book sections). Maybe you already know which movie star will be playing which character in the movie. All of these imaginings are the best kind. It's quite possible they can come true, and even if it takes a long time, it keeps your passion invigorated. Chances are, other more wonderful things will happen that you never imagined, which makes the book journey more enticing, because you don't know all the parts to the carnival ride until you pay the ticket vendor and enter the gates of the fairgrounds. That's what you're doing—getting an agent is paying the ticket price to get on the rides.

I described my memoir as a cross between Alexandra Fuller's *Don't Let's Go to the Dogs Tonight* and Michael Ondaatje's *Running in the Family*, with some Indiana Jones thrown in. Like Fuller's memoir, mine is an African childhood, and like Ondaatje's childhood memories, mine are blurred and

fantastical, but that's where the similarities end. Indiana Jones comes along because my story starts with my family digging up a grave. We were ghouls, as the title suggests—though more the goofy Munsters than the sexy Addams family.

Query letters are not your first step to finding an agent. Your first step is to really know what your book is about and how you can describe it well so you can research which agents would be interested in your story. Then you research agents. Finding an agent, take heed, is like finding a mate. It can be daunting, but this is where rejection becomes a badge of honor.

When?

Throughout the writing of your book, it's a good idea to do some schmoozing— I mean, networking. Attending writing workshops, conferences, and getting to know other writers. Getting to know other writers helps with the camaraderie and also in sharing resources about agents and publishers. I was pretty sure I was finished with *MoonPies* when I took the advice of an agent I had heard speak on a conference panel, and I subscribed to *Publishers Marketplace*. Joining *Publishers Marketplace* is like stepping inside of a world of information on how the leg bone connects to the hip bone, and the agent bone connects to the editor bone, and the author tibia connects to the agent kneecap that connects to the editor clavicle. Once you're inside, there is so much to learn about agents and editors that is not visible from the outside. *Publishers Marketplace* works as a cross-reference to most agents, the editors they work with, and the books they represent. The best part is being privy to the deals that are made on the books. This is why you'll want to know what books are like yours—you can see who agents that book, then submit your manuscript to them, stating, "If you like that book, you'll surely like mine."

I also made a lot of good writing friends in the years it took me to write that first novel. A few had been published and offered to refer me to their agent. *This,* I thought, *was going to be my "in"—someone who knew someone who would want me.* When I was dating, I always preferred meeting a friend of a friend.

Before finding an agent, a longtime writing friend and I had an ongoing conversation about the best way to find the right agent. She believed the thorough research of an agent would find you the best connection, but I thought that it mattered more who could help you squeeze in the door. In the end, I found my agent by mentioning in my query a book the agent represented and its similarities to my manuscript. A little while later, my writing friend found her agent from a referral I passed on to her. This proved that both methods work, but one never knows which one will, so try them all.

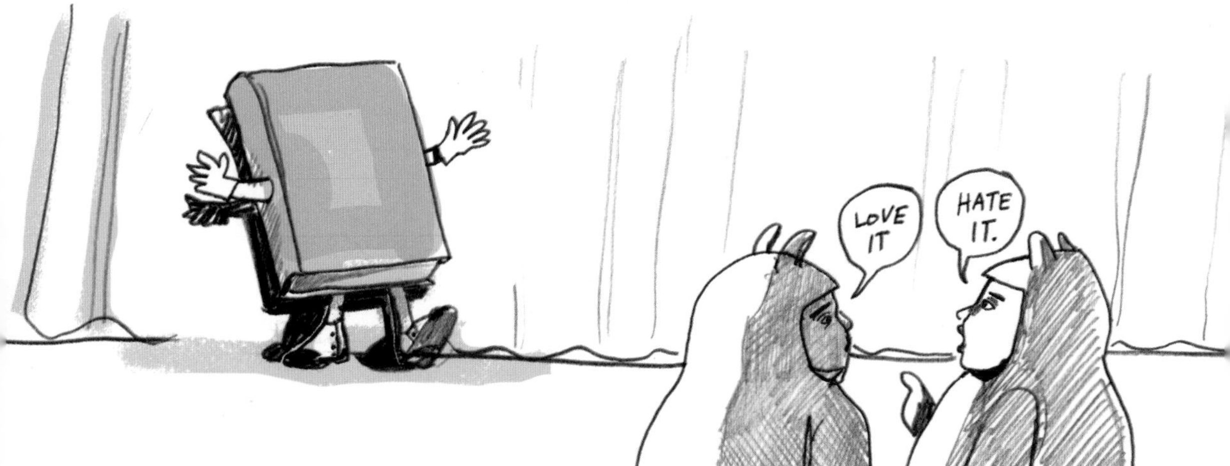
LOVE IT
HATE IT.

Where?

Should it be a New York agent only? Agents can be agents from anywhere, especially nowadays with the World Wide Web of connectivity. The Big-Name Agent next door to the Postal Plus is an agent on the West Coast. My current agent has her office in Los Angeles. I've had two other agents who were in NYC. If you're a good match and listen to your gut, which will tell you if you are a match, then it doesn't matter where the agent lives or works. Okay, maybe Micronesia in an office with bad Wi-Fi is not the best option, but again, listen to your intuition. Maybe you've written about deep-sea diving and that Micronesian agent is perfect.

The Query Letter

An enticing query is what lies between the slash of the letter opener and getting your manuscript read. The letter is a simple equation: reason + description + gushing = a compact three-paragraph query.

Paragraph 1 should contain a short reason why you are connecting to this particular agent. This is where that research comes in handy. Look in the acknowledgments of a book you admire to see if the author thanked their agent. If they did, perhaps you should query that agent. If they didn't thank their agent, maybe that's a reason not to query them, or do a Google search. But let the agent know you know what kind of work they represent and how it relates to yours.

1) Hello
2) DESCRIBE BOOK
3) SELF—PROMOTE
4) CALL ME!

The QUERY LETTER

Paragraph 2 should describe your book. This is where your creative side should shine—let the agent see a snippet of your ingenious prose. Provide a few-sentence synopsis. "A few sentences" may sound like pushing your entire novel through the eye of a needle, but I use a simple A + B = C formula that works well for a character-driven novel. *A* is who your character is (for example, Ruby Kincaid, the owner of a six-lane bowling alley in Devine, Texas), *B* is what situation your character is in (. . . spots her runaway daughter on a ButterMaid commercial), *C* is what happens (. . . so Ruby sets off for Hollywood to find her daughter and make her own up to her responsibilities, such as the two kids she left behind). This is where you may also say your book is the lovechild of Shirley Jackson's *We Have Always Lived in the Castle* and Franz Kafka's *The Trial*, or in my case, a cross between Mark Childress's *Crazy in Alabama* and Eudora Welty on speed.

Paragraph 3 is where you should gush about yourself, your publishing feats, no matter how small or big (everyone has something to brag about, so don't be shy—if you won the local newspaper's hundred-word essay contest, that's good writing), and what makes you the best author for this book, especially if it's a nonfiction book, and why this agent will want you as their client.

Follow all the submission guidelines the agent has on their website to a T. This means the query process is never just sending out the same email as a form letter to as many agents as possible. Research and create a list of as many agents as you feel would be a good fit. You will have fewer agents you are querying this way, but you'll be more likely to catch a whale of an agent than if you're just flinging your net out there willy-nilly having to throw back the fish every time. Besides, who wouldn't rather read a savvy query than a boring form letter?

Remember, not everyone will like you, but make everyone want to. Start sending out those queries, and don't let the rejections get in your way as you get busy writing more.

Looking for an agent can be both disheartening and exciting. It can be frustrating at times, as just as you think you have found the right agent when you read their website, you then find out they don't accept new clients. Or, from the books they represent, you glean their sense of humor meshes with yours—and you picture telling funny stories over a bottle of wine after your first book is published, but then you find out they don't accept novels, only nonfiction. The trek to finding the right match for you and your book can be a constant letdown. That's even before the rejection. I know I sound like your mother, but I promise, there's someone out there for you.

I SCReam Pie

Sometimes in the process of looking for an agent, you just want to scream. A long, primal scream. Or maybe you want to scream at someone. The latter is not advised. Instead, I suggest Dark Chocolate Ice Cream Pie.

I had seven leftover egg yolks in my fridge after trying to invent another pie, which I'll tell you about later. I didn't want the egg yolks to go to waste, so I googled recipes with egg yolks. I figured I would end up making some sort of custard, maybe even a savory dish, something heart attack-worthy. When the recipe for "Chocolate Ice Cream" popped up on Epicurious.com, I almost breezed past it since I had no intention of making ice cream, plus I don't own an ice cream maker and most recipes want you to use one. Then I had an idea. Ice cream pie! I changed the level of dark chocolate to even higher than they suggested, but choose your own. This ice cream is so easy you don't need an ice cream maker. Just a spoon to eat it with. It might not even make it into the crust, and maybe not even into the freezer once you've made the pie. But just in case, make a graham cracker crust and have it chilling in the fridge while you make the ice cream.

GRAHAM CRACKER CRUST

10 graham crackers

⅓ cup brown sugar

1 teaspoon salt

6 tablespoons butter, melted

Preheat the oven to 350°F. Place the graham crackers in the bowl of a food processor and pulse until you have crumbs. Add the brown sugar, salt, and butter and pulse until the consistency resembles wet sand. Pour crumbs into the bottom of an 8-inch pie plate and, with your fingers, spread them out evenly across the bottom and up the sides of the pan. Chill in the fridge for 10 minutes, then bake for 7 minutes. Set aside.

FILLING

    7 ounces chocolate, broken

    2 cups whole milk

    ⅓ cup dark cocoa powder

    6 egg yolks

    13 tablespoons granulated sugar, divided

    2 tablespoons water

    ¼ cup heavy whipping cream

I have a chocolate that I'm partial to that is so dark, so rich, that I almost *have* to drink red wine with it. It's 85 percent cacao, which is a little more than most bittersweet chocolates you'll find. Feel free to use a less concentrated version—65 to 75 percent, or go all milk chocolate if you're not up for hardcore.

Melt your chocolate of choice in a double boiler, or a small metal bowl placed over a saucepan of simmering water. Stir until smooth. Set aside while it cools slightly.

Whisk the milk and the darkest cocoa powder you can find in a medium saucepan over medium heat until it begins to boil. Set this aside too. I love Droste cocoa with its high fat content (high fat and pie go together like agent and author), but every chocolate maker has a dark version, just like every character has their dark side.

With an electric mixer, beat the egg yolks and 7 tablespoons of the sugar in a medium bowl until it thickens and is well blended, about 3 minutes. Whisking constantly, gradually add the hot milk mixture to the egg yolk mixture. Return the combination to the saucepan. Add the melted chocolate and whisk to blend. Stir over low heat until a candy thermometer reads 175°F, about 5 minutes. It will be slightly thicker, and your finger will want to scoop out a taste. Let it. Stir until the chocolate custard is cool. Taste as you need to.

In a small saucepan, mix the remaining 6 tablespoons of sugar and the water and bring to a boil over medium-high heat, stirring until the sugar is dissolved. Keep swirling the pan until it turns a light caramel color, about 5 minutes. Gradually whisk in the heavy whipping cream. Whisk the caramel into the chocolate custard.

Pour this into your graham cracker crust. Freeze the pie overnight.

CHAPTER TWELVE

The Joy of RejecTion

Waiting, Waiting, Waiting

You created a whole book and now you are ready to send it out into the world. Congratulations. Be sure to celebrate and enjoy every satisfying moment of this time when you can feel you accomplished your goal. So far.

On the page, you put your heart, your soul, your funniest humor, best details, everything you ever learned in an MFA program, all the really brilliant suggestions from your writing group, that pivotal plot point that came to you while driving, the heartbreaking scene that came to you in the shower where you cried along with your characters, and all those scenes that flowed out from your dreams—waking and sleeping. Your book is gushing with greatness, and you know it's going to be snatched up and New York is going to be fighting over the chance to publish it.

Hang on, all of this is true—your book is the best it can be, and you've written query letters to the list of agents who are perfect for your book, but now you're waiting. Waiting for the phone to ring, an email to appear in your inbox, maybe even a text message (who knows how they'll contact you because this agent who is going to fall in love with your book will want to reach out to you before anyone else does).

The first response you may get will be an email that pops into your mailbox right after you hit send. *Already!* you think. *They want me already!* More than likely, it will be an auto-responder saying, "We've received your submission. We will be in touch if your manuscript is of

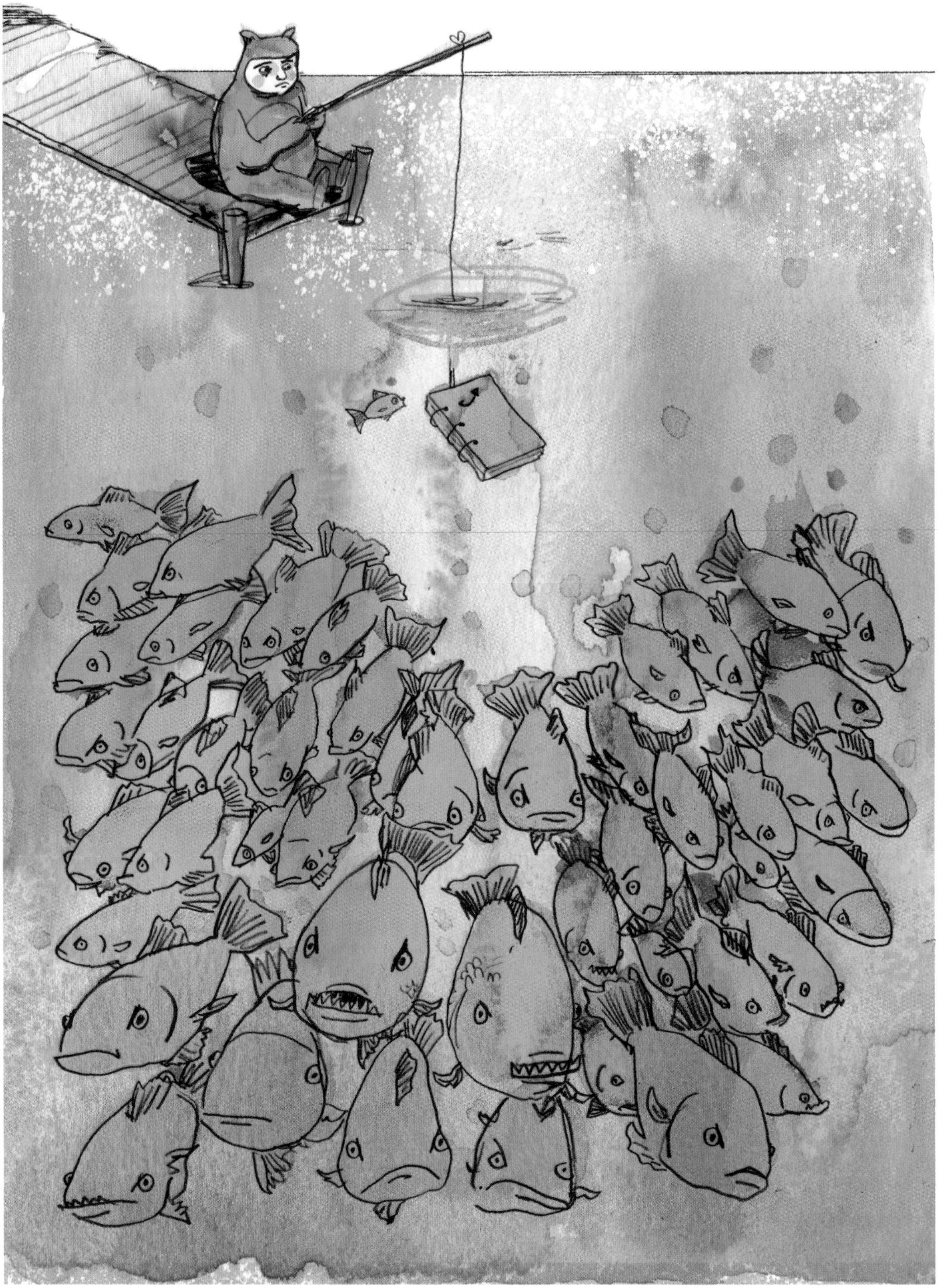

interest to us. If you don't hear from us in six to eight weeks, it did not fit our list." Six to eight weeks! But you were planning to stop off at Party City and get streamers and cake (or pie) decorations on your way home from work today.

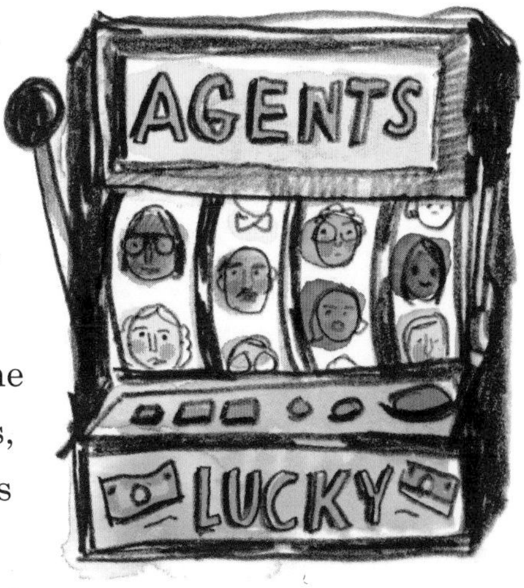
AGENTS
LUCKY

Agents are humans, more or less like the rest of us, and work at different paces. Thus, this part of the journey can go in all sorts of ways.

First of all, I'm going to divulge a secret that will probably get me in trouble with some agents. Some agents request that you don't multiply submit, meaning only submit to them and no one else, until you hear back from them. Now, in my mind, the reason not to heed this is based on one simple equation—take that six-to-eight-week turnaround mentioned earlier, multiply it by the number of top-tier agents you want to submit to, divide by the number of years it took to write the book, then add in a pound of heartache for each rejection, and you won't get an agent for somewhere close to ten years. Instead, how about I give you full permission to submit to as many agents at one time as you'd like. If you get more than one agent wanting to represent you at one time, then you've hit the jackpot, and all your friends will be jealous.

What will more than likely happen is you will hear from some agents who will ask you to send fifty pages, some who will ask for one hundred pages, and others who will ask for the whole manuscript, and still others who will never respond to your query. These latter agents are still nice people, they are just busy and maybe they are just the kind of person who doesn't like to reject people, so they do it silently. You may not hear again from the ones that have asked for a portion or all of the manuscript either.

Maybe their mothers never taught them how to write bread-and-butter notes, or maybe they are too busy reading the next manuscript on the pile next to their desk. Whatever the reason, your best bet is to just keep in mind that there are more than enough agents to go around the world a few times, and you will find the right one in due time.

Do They Just Want Me for My Book?

The first few times someone requested fifty or more pages of my manuscript, I immediately started calculating how long it would take them to read those pages, which publishing houses would probably want the book, and how I should dress for my *Oprah* appearance—casual chic, sophisticated librarian, or frumpy author (guess which is the real me?). One agent asked for fifty pages, then a couple of weeks later asked for the entire manuscript. Then, nothing.

To keep myself motivated, I set a goal of always having at least three queries out in the world at one time (feel free to do more). If I received a rejection letter, I immediately found an agent on my list, or researched another one to submit to, always keeping three out there in the unknown.

It was Agent #15 who called to make me an offer. She and her coagent called and told me they loved the premise of my novel and were laughing all along the way. They asked me a few questions that I am certain I was unable to answer as I was in shock that I was on the phone with a New York agent. I'm in my skivvies, don't have my glasses, and am standing in my attic office trying to find the list of

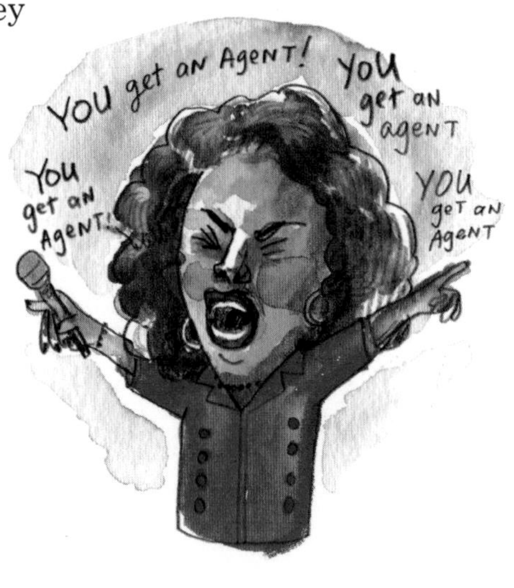
YOU get aN AgeNT!
YoU get aN ageNT
YoU get aN AgeNT!
YOU geT aN AgeNT

questions I'd read and saved, but never really thought I'd need. I eventually found the list dog-eared in a book on finding an agent, but couldn't read it without my glasses. By the time I had found the list, the agents were ready to get off the phone. "Just called to get to know a little about how you see your book in the world," they said. With promises they would finish reading it and that they would get back to me by the end of the week, we hung up. I went back to bed because it was o'dark thirty since they had called not realizing Pacific time is very different than East Coast time, and I stared at the ceiling for an hour. When I finally convinced myself that I would probably never hear from them again, I got up and went about my day.

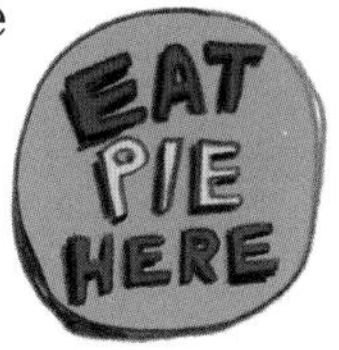
EAT
PIE
HERE

On Friday, they called again, as promised. They offered me representation. As I write this memory, I get a thrill up my spine.

My story is just one story, though. So many other writers have stories that take longer, or shorter, or involve more rewrites. Personally, I have four finding-an-agent stories, and each one is different. My author friends have more stories still.

When I finished writing my memoir, my novel agent and I had already parted ways. To be honest, I got a little scared of writing after the incidents with the publisher revolving door, and the publisher now owned the bohemian retirement home story. So, I had run off to get my MFA and learn about essay writing. I ended up writing an unintentional memoir. My first agent didn't represent memoir, so I was back in the non-agented boat. I queried a dozen or so more and was in conversation with one in particular who seemed perfect. I guess you could say we were on our first date, because she was reading my pages and sending me emails telling me how much she loved the story. She represented Chigozie Obioma, the Nigerian writer who had just won a jillion awards for *The Fisherman*, a book I had been in awe of, and one of the reasons I had queried this particular agent. While she and

FAMOUS PRESSES   START-UP PRESSES   FANCY PRESSES   SCRAPPY PRESSES   UNIVERSITY PRESSES

I were communicating, my professor from graduate school referred me to her editor at University of Nebraska Press. I was impressed and familiar with several of the memoir titles they had published under their American Lives series with Tobias Wolff as editor. The smaller independent presses don't always necessitate an agent and often have some incredible titles on their list to aspire to be among. I let Obioma's agent know I had met someone else at the university press who I was also interested in.

This is a goal you want to hope to attain, and it's why you want to keep more than one live submission out there at all times—when one agent (or in my case, editor) shows interest, you can let the other agents you've submitted to—all of them who have not outright sent you a letter saying "no, thanks"—that you have someone who is interested in your book. All the agents you've previously submitted to will read or at least review your manuscript to see if they want it. No one likes for someone else to snatch up a bestseller that was sitting in their basket too.

You may be asking: "Why don't we just occasionally email the agents we have sent work to and say, 'Hey, someone wants me'?" Because that would be dishonest, and trust me when I say that in this business things catch up with you, because they do. Leave the game-playing to the dating world.

I went with the university press not *just* because the agent decided the manuscript wasn't one she could place, but because I felt UNP was the perfect home for my memoir. Sometimes this process feels like what I imagine it's like finding the right private school for your kids. You apply to all the ones that sound good, then you interview them, and they interview you. Sometimes they aren't who you thought they were, and sometimes your kid isn't accepted where it seemed the best. But in the end, you find a good school where they can get a strong education, and ultimately, it's up to the kid on how well they do out in the real world.

Small, reputable presses are different than the fancy-schmancy New York presses. For one, with Penguin, I was offered a six-figure, two-book deal. With the university press, I negotiated up from zero to a three-figure, one-book deal. But it isn't about the money, remember? What it's about is being taken seriously. A reputable and respectable press will get you into libraries and make you eligible for awards—these are the things to look for in a press. Maybe I didn't get hotels and champagne this second time around, but the university press provided plenty of publicity, and my editor bought me breakfast when she came to town for a conference.

After the Breakup, Get Back out There

After my memoir, I got busy on this book. It's such a quirky book that I really didn't have a clue how to market it. I was still friends with my agent for *MoonPies*, so I sent the proposal to her—the first five chapters with some illustrations. "It's great," she said, "but it's not anything I know what to do with."

That's what makes an agent a good agent, and this is the truth about rejection: They aren't rejecting your manuscript based solely on the off chance it sucks. They often reject your manuscript because it's not something they know how to pitch to an editor. The manuscripts have to sing for them. Some agents like rock and roll, and some like rockabilly. Some like ambient

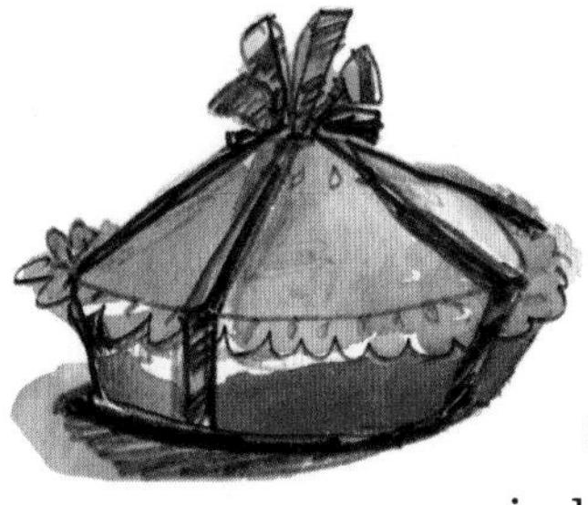

music, and some like K-Pop. But just because they like rock and roll, and your book is a Beatles lookalike, doesn't mean they don't prefer the Rolling Stones. See, it gets all nitty-gritty and really is about an individual choice. That subjectivity thing again.

I could say here that you shouldn't take rejection too personally, but then I'd be assuming you aren't a typical writer. Rejection bites. It can feel like a rainstorm at times. Maybe try to picture yourself in a cool yellow slicker letting the raindrops slide off. Or maybe run around and jump in the mud puddles of rejection and burn off that frustration.

For instance, this book—since it was different than a traditional book, how was I to find an agent who would consider it? I didn't know how to describe it—part memoir, part how-to, part crazy-pie-lady book.

When I don't want to waste anyone's time, or rather when I am about to waste their time but want them to do something for me anyway, I bake them a pie. So the owner of my neighborhood bookstore, The Book Catapult, is a good friend. I baked him an apple pie with a crumb topping and asked him to look at my proposal and see if it was viable. "Does it have a heartbeat?" I asked. Seth told me he could see it on his front shelf by the cash register and, yes, it would sell. He'd choose it for his store.

I felt we had a chance, so Emil and I picked out all sorts of agents from the various resources who liked books with illustrations, how-tos, and had a sense of humor. To us, it was the sense of humor that mattered the most.

Guess what? My tippy-top agent who represented my all-time favorite illustrated books never called. She still hasn't. I think the proposal must have gotten lost in the email postal system. But when I look back at why I wanted her—because she was famous, and her books were mega-sellers—I realize that she was probably retired and living on an island somewhere not bothering to check her email except one day a year. I was small potatoes—hopefully, those little red ones served with butter and dill.

Another agent who I would consider my first realistic choice signed us up. She was perfect for the book in every way. She sent it out to twenty top editors, and they all sent rejection letters that were essentially this: "Love the concept, not sure how to pitch it."

I slumped around for a few months until our contract with that agent ran out. Then I started thinking about where else I could go. A friend who had published a chapter in her literary supplement at the news media outlet where she's senior editor suggested I send it to an agent we both know and love. So, I did. Betsy took it on immediately.

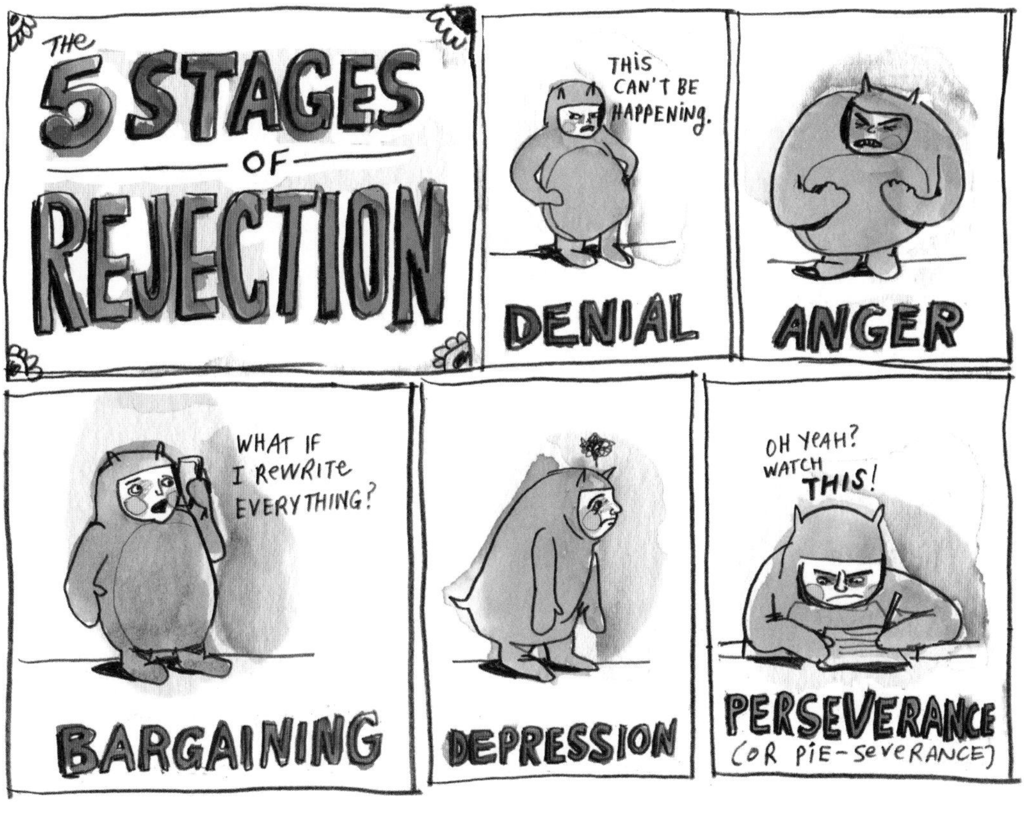
THE 5 STAGES OF REJECTION
THIS CAN'T BE HAPPENING.
DENIAL
ANGER
WHAT IF I REWRITE EVERYTHING?
BARGAINING
DEPRESSION
OH YEAH? WATCH THIS!
PERSEVERANCE
(OR PIE-SEVERANCE)

Isn't that what happened with the other agent? It is, but Betsy had ideas for other types of editors who had plenty of experience with books like this one. We ended up with four editors vying for the book.

Unless you've got a quirky how-to memoir-y kind of book with illustrations, the example is probably different than what you are working on, so it may seem this story doesn't apply, unless you take into consideration that I didn't give up. Okay, I did mope for a while, but that annoys even me, so I quit after the sobbing made my pie dough too salty. "Get back out there," my amygdala yelled at me. Just because one agent didn't find the editor she thought would fit the book, doesn't mean it's over. A new agent took a new approach. This opened up different doors. Sometimes it takes a persistent author who pokes her nose in every cracked door she can find.

When to Say, "I Love You."

Many days you'll be getting rejections, or staring at an empty inbox, feeling like all your effort to write a gorgeous, sexy book that sings like Lady Gaga and dances like Beyoncé is all for naught. Then, one day, you might get an agent who says they like your book, but they feel it needs something else. They may offer suggestions and ways to revise it. This can sometimes be a tough decision, one that involves that gut that has probably been tied up in knots waiting for responses.

They may suggest you make changes with the caveat they will look at the manuscript again, or they may ask you to make the changes and still reject you. It's not guaranteed they will sign you as a client if you make the changes. So, think hard—are these changes that you agree are necessary? Do you see them as changes that will make it a better book? Maybe others have suggested something similar, so it seems to be a trend? Before you make major changes, consider all your options—will it make it not just a better book but a better book that you would feel proud to write? Will the agent ask you to marry them afterward? If the agent wants to sign you but would like to work with you on revising the book, that makes it a little easier to decide—they like you the way you are, but they want you to dress a little better. Again, determine if you feel the new style they've chosen for your wardrobe suits you. Will the new clothes make you professional or take away your originality? Do they want to take your deep love story and turn it into a playful romp? Maybe playful sounds more fun, or maybe you think, love should not be fun.

When an agent calls—and they will—make sure they are right for you, just like they will make sure you are right for them. It's so tempting to say yes to the first, or even the second, agent who calls. Getting that call is such a big part of our whole dream that when it happens it's easy to miss when it's a wrong number. Consider how the relationship will work best for you and your book. Ask them what they love about your book, ask where they envision submitting the work, ask them how they work with clients long-term. Ask anything you want to know because you will be working together

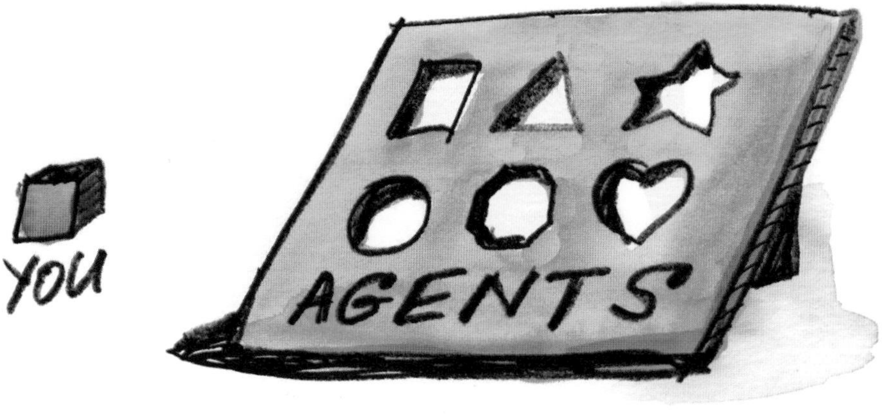
YOU
AGENTS

for a while, hopefully. It helps if you have your glasses and clothes on when they call. Dog-ear this page.

I still recall the very first agent who ever emailed me. An author friend had referred me to his friend who was starting out as an agent. I screamed when I opened the email—just someone wanting to read my pages made me ecstatic. After he sent the manuscript back, rejected, he also pointed out that I had misspelled *damn it* on the first page. Bad first date.

When I was offered representation by my first agent, I sent her an email with a rather humorous and snarky message, and probably not as professional as I may have been otherwise. I wanted to know if she had a sense of humor. When she wrote back and made me laugh with her response, I knew we were a good fit. That, and she had a reputation for being the best kind of agent for my kind of book.

Every traditionally published author has an agent story. Just ask.

Black & Blue BERRY PIE

Navigating the muddy Amazonian waters of the agent world is fraught with the piranhas of rejection, the crocodiles of self-doubt, and the green anacondas of disappointment. The constant spurning of your work can feel like you've been beaten black and blue. Keep paddling, and don't give up just because your arms are sore. Around the next bend of the long, wide river may be the port with the agent of your dreams. Then, when you are published, you'll have your own agent story to tell.

This is a traditional and simple pie. You can make it any time of year with fresh or frozen berries. Mix the berries up. Add some raspberries if you're feeling a little bloodier than usual. Add peaches if the future seems fuzzy.

FILLING

4 cups berries

⅔ cup brown sugar

1 teaspoon ground cinnamon

¼ teaspoon salt

1 teaspoon freshly squeezed lemon juice

4 tablespoons tapioca flour

1 tablespoon orange zest or orange liqueur

Make your double-crust pie dough and chill in the fridge.

In a big bowl, add all of the filling ingredients and mix until the fruit is well coated.

Roll out one-half of the dough and place it in an 8-inch pie pan.

Pour the filling into the pie pan.

Roll out the remaining dough. If you just want to hurry up and eat pie, place it on top and cut some slits for ventilation. If you're feeling fancy, make a lattice top so the berries seep out, leaving beautiful purple stains.

Preheat the oven to 425°F. Rest the pie in the fridge while you wait.

Bake for 30 minutes. Add an egg wash (egg white mixed with a splash of water) by brushing on before returning the pie to the oven. Turn the pie so the back faces front to even out the crust, and turn the oven down to 375°F and bake for another 30 minutes.

Remove the pie from the oven and sit on your hands for an hour while it sets up. This is probably a good time to run to the store and buy the best kind of vanilla ice cream to serve on top. You deserve it.

CHAPTER THIRTEEN

My AGenT's going To CAll

Agents Hanging with Editors

You got an agent! Soon you'll be published and living a life of leisure.

Don't be silly, this is the creative world—prepare for more rejection. Without rejection, how would we build character, and wallpaper our bathrooms?

This doesn't mean go crawl under your desk and weep. Getting an agent, especially one who feels like the right fit, means your writing has been accepted by those who have gatekeeping authority. They have the ability to help you connect with the editors who will publish your work. In addition, you can now say to people, "I'd love to meet you for lunch, but I'm expecting a call from my agent."

And right you are to be waiting for that call. But, like waiting for the call from any agent before you had one, you might want to go ahead and go about your day. Maybe go to lunch with your friend and say instead, "I'd love to go to lunch with you. I'm expecting a call from my agent, so if they call, I will have to take it while we eat. Do you mind?" A fabulous and true friend will say, "Of course, I want to be there when you find out who is taking your book." A good friend will say, "Sure, that's fine," and probably smile at your optimism. A lousy friend will say, "Yeah, right. Like that's going to happen." Here's a response for your lousy friend, "Since I don't have a book deal *yet*, I'll let you pick up the tab."

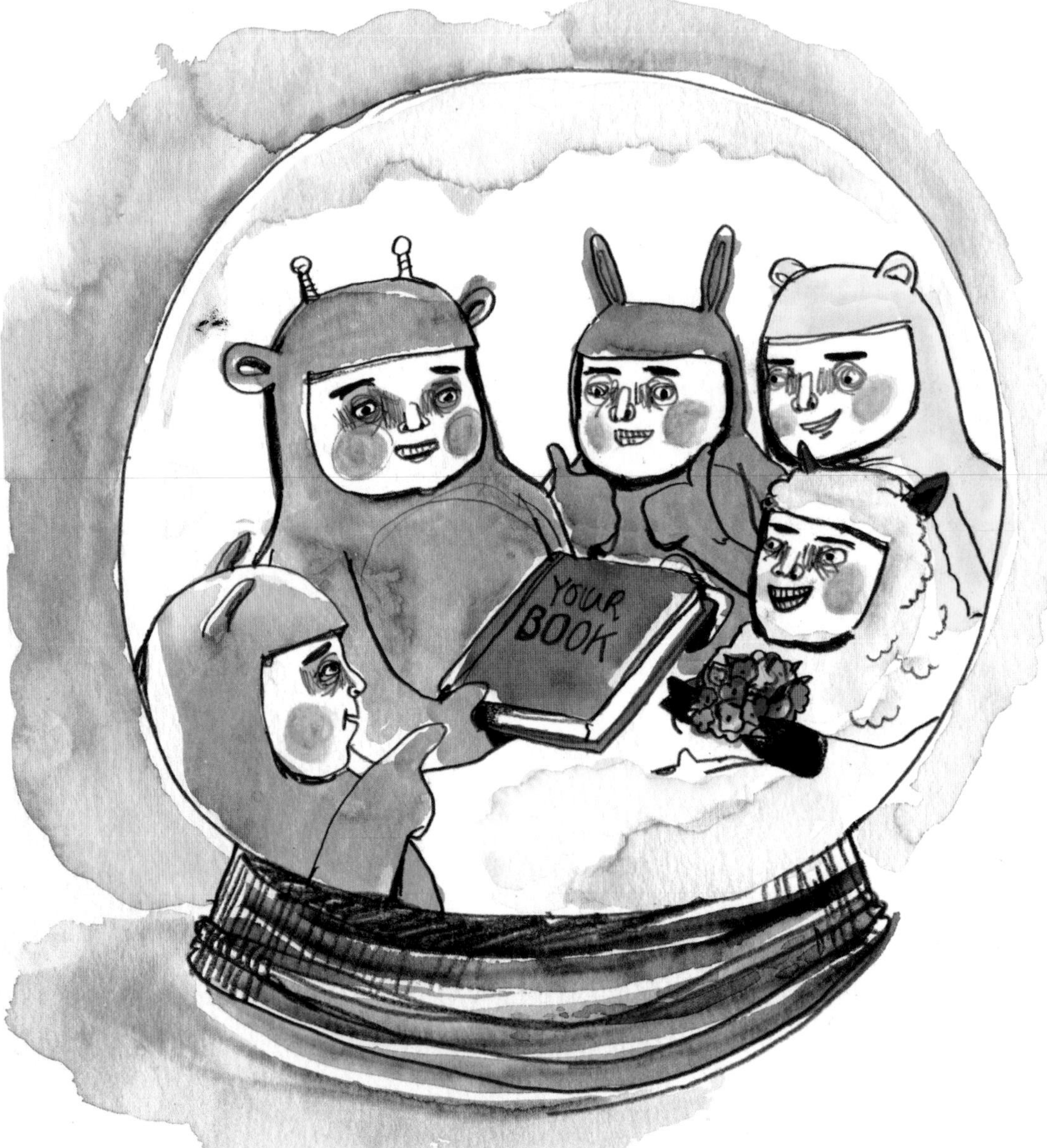
YOUR BOOK

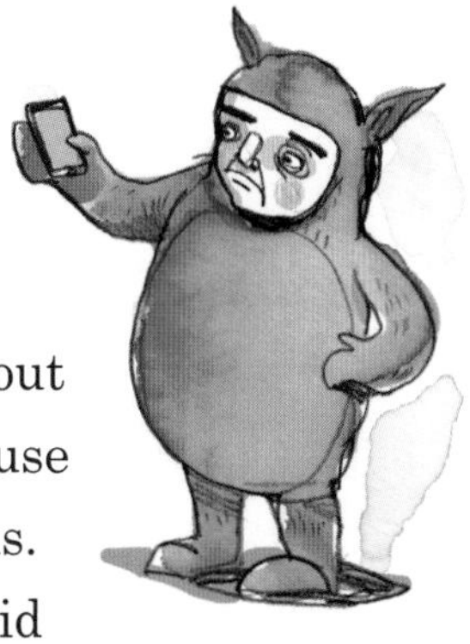

While you are at lunch with your group of friends, your agent will be at lunch with editors. Or on the phone with editors. Or emailing editors. Wherever they are or however they are doing it, they will be gabbing about your book, about how it's a book the editor will love because they love similar books, have even published similar books. They will tell the editor how brilliant your book is, how said editor has bought other books like this one, but yours is clearly the tippy-top. Your agent will be telling the editor about other books at the same time, because remember, the publishing world is about finding that next new hot author. But the matchmaking has begun. Your agent is trying to find the perfect editor to fall in love with your story. Your agent loves you and your book and wants the right editor to fall in love too. The agent's job is to find the *three* in *threesome*. They are pitching all your book's good qualities—its cheerful disposition, its adventuresome frolicking plot, its upbeat humor, its good looks, and a personality to wow the world. They probably share about your blog if it has a zillion followers, or your Instagram photos series of front doors if you get tens of thousands of clicks, but don't fret if you don't even have an Instagram account, although you might want to know what Instagram is.

Hanging Out on Social Media

Social media has us all in a tizzy that we need to be the most popular person. I'd rather be reading a book, but I find myself checking to see how many likes my Facebook posts get. But just like that age-old popularity contest in high school, it's important to be your authentic self. Your agent fell in love with your book because it has promise and resonated with her because it made her laugh or cry, or laugh and cry at the same time. Having a million and twenty-three followers on Instagram can certainly help get you noticed by an agent or an editor, but if you have just twenty-three followers and each and every one of them wait with great anticipation for your next post of your pet snake's aquarium antics, then that makes all the difference. The numbers are not the only story, anyway. The cheerleader who smiled at everyone in the halls, invited you to sit at her lunch table, and genuinely cared about you as a classmate, her photo series of rock formations is the one we all want to watch on social media. The cheerleader who spent more time worrying that her skirt wasn't short enough and never noticed your locker was next to hers, her selfies with her and her pet panda may get more likes, but most folks know pandas don't make great pets. Like anything, followers can be bought for a price, and you can have all the surface popularity you want. Those purchased followers can be detected by an editor. They know when you are genuine, so remember to be yourself. That's exactly what my mom used to tell me when I asked why I wasn't popular—just be yourself. *That*, I thought, *was the whole problem.*

Editors Hanging with Your Book

Like any good matchmaker, an agent will focus on the positives.

The agent pitches your book, something sparkles in an editor's eye. The more the editor hears, the more they love the book, the more they want it for their very own list. On the way back to the office, or as they are turning off their Zoom account, the editor is already dreaming of flying you out to New York, hiring a limo to pick you up at JFK, and wooing you with champagne and pie. Okay, that part I know doesn't happen. It's what we writers hope editors are doing. The editor does get pretty darn excited, asks the agent to email a copy of the book to them tout de sweet as pie. Your agent (and don't you just love being able to add the possessive pronoun to that noun?) sends over a copy, and the waiting begins. Again.

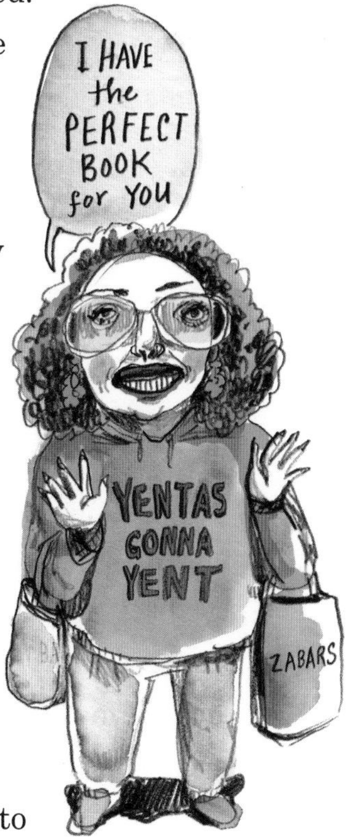
I HAVE the PERFECT BOOK for YOU
YENTAS GONNA YENT
ZABARS

A lunch or meeting may not have even happened. That's another author fantasy of how all this works. More than likely, your agent is so busy reading manuscripts both for potential new authors and current clients, working with the authors' contracts and billings, and negotiating deals with editors, that lunches probably don't occur that often. Instead, just like you were emailing and sending a cover letter with a stunning pitch to agents, the agent does something similar, sending a note and maybe a copy of your manuscript to editors who the agent has an educated hunch will be a good fit. There's a chance your agent has never even met the editor they send your book to. But your agent has probably sent your manuscript out to a list of editors that she feels confident will want to at least crack it open. Some may be longer shots than others, but they aren't just blind throws. Your agent wants to sell this book, remember, because that's how she makes a living. Aren't we writers glad we don't make a living by trying to pitch our books to people? Oh, wait.

Anyway, let's stick with the fantasy version, because whether it was via blind letter or eight-Moscow-mule lunch, when an editor falls in love, the next steps to publishing are similar. Sometimes.

The editor rushes back to their office in the high-rise New York City building. They take the stairs three at a time up to the twenty-seventh floor. They hardly notice their staff, which is vying for their attention to tell them about the movie deal for another of their blockbuster books. The editor waves them off and says, "This new book that I just heard about is bigger than even Hollywood." The underling staff all scatter as the editor dives into the book to read it from cover to cover before someone else snatches it up.

Reality check: it's doubtful there's an underling staff, or even a twenty-seventh floor. The publisher could be in NYC or Kansas City. Taking the stairs three at a time, unless it's the front stoop, is also unlikely. There's probably an editorial assistant who works diligently trying to bring the best of the best books into the world. Depending on the size of the press and the rung of the hierarchy where the editor sits, this assistant editor probably read your manuscript first from your agent's email. I like to think that editors do get excited when they read something that surpasses all the other pages in their full-to-bursting inbox, but they reserve shouting to the world until they've gone through the next steps. Reality: the editorial assistant loved your book, then passed it along as a possible book the editor should consider taking to the acquisitions meeting.

The Acquisitions Meeting. This is where Decisions are made. This is the weekly meeting where your nose will itch because your book will be talked about from all angles. Mostly the sales angle. I've never been to one of these meetings, but I do know these meetings include the editor, the sales and marketing teams, the editor-in-chief, and/or THE PUBLISHER. This is who has the final say. The publisher presides over the meeting and listens to what the editor says about your fabulous book and how the editor just loves it. The publisher also listens to the sales and marketing team. This is when the sales pitches start and the discussion includes what's already on sale, what the trends are, what author has a TikTok following, and who has just dropped off the *NYT* bestseller list. They talk about what's working and what's not. They decide how to change the world with books. This is when, no matter how much good juju your agent passed along with your manuscript, and no matter how much the editor is head over heels in love with this book, the industry comes together in one meeting to predict your future. This is the day your group of friends should be taking you out to an eight-Moscow-mule lunch.

Editors Hanging with Publishers

Your agent has probably notified you of the interest by the editor. She may have even told you who she sent your book out to. My agents have asked if I want to know who they've sent my book to, or do I want to be kept in the dark? Some authors just want to know when a book deal is imminent. I like to know every painful detail. One agent updated a monthly spreadsheet with columns such as "Who," "Date Sent," "Date Responded," and "Comments." I read and reread the rejection comments. It's like reading a spreadsheet of every person you've ever been on a date with and the columns are "Who," "Date," "Called Again," and "Why They Never Called Again." For example, "Amy's writing is funny, but I have no idea where I would place a book like this." Or, "Love this idea, but it's really not my thing." But the most painful ones are the blanks in the spreadsheet where the editor never even called

PUBLISHER
DESIGN
DISTRIBUTION
MARKETING
EDITING

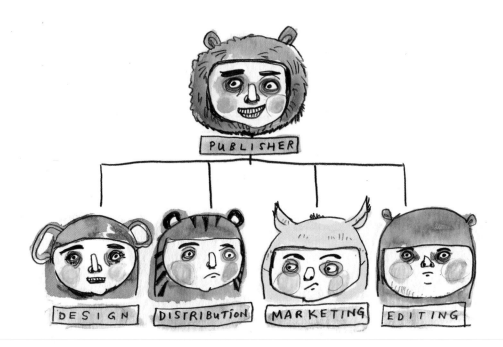

at all. All of these are versions of, "It's me, not you," except maybe the last one, where in my neuroses I decipher the lack of response to mean, "Who told her she could write?"

All the responses are helpful in some way. Often, the editors will have similar responses, like for a novel, "The last third seems to drag," "I was enthralled for most of the book, then lost interest in the character," and "The story has potential, but I felt she needs to work on her plot." These could all mean that it isn't them, but also that there is a flaw in your book. Sometimes it's fixable, sometimes the editor will ask about fixing it, sometimes the agent will suggest you fix it, or "sometimes" it's just subjective opinion. Sometimes—there are so many sometimes in this arena because so much is possible, and so much comes close and seems possible, but not possible yet. But despite all the sometimes, don't give up hope.

While there are many possible rejections, there are as many positive acceptances. As many varieties as there are of pies, there are possible outcomes from this stage of publishing. The editorial board may say,

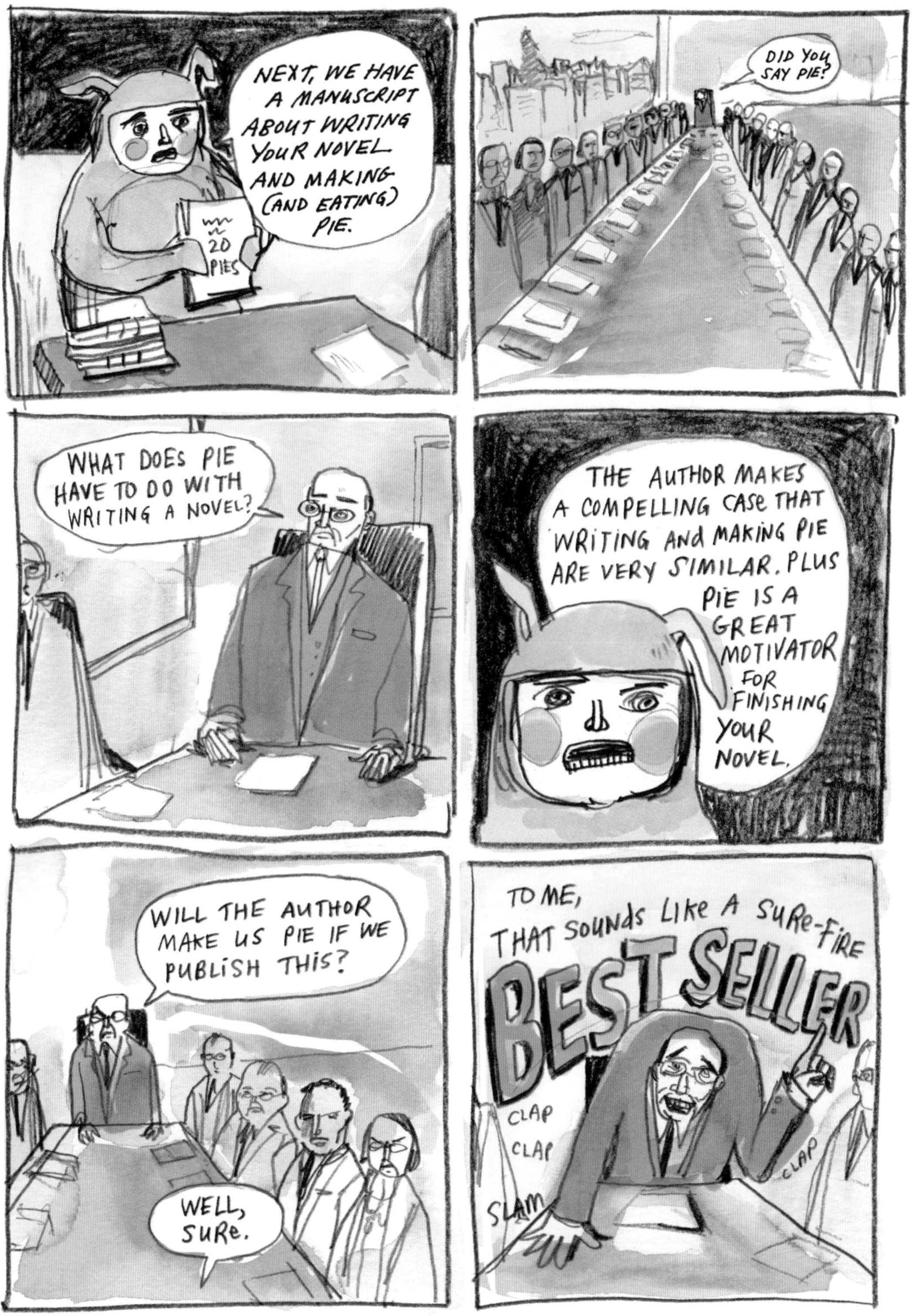
NEXT, WE HAVE A MANUSCRIPT ABOUT WRITING YOUR NOVEL AND MAKING (AND EATING) PIE.
20 PIES
DID YOU SAY PIE?
WHAT DOES PIE HAVE TO DO WITH WRITING A NOVEL?
THE AUTHOR MAKES A COMPELLING CASE THAT WRITING AND MAKING PIE ARE VERY SIMILAR. PLUS PIE IS A GREAT MOTIVATOR FOR FINISHING YOUR NOVEL.
WILL THE AUTHOR MAKE US PIE IF WE PUBLISH THIS?
WELL, SURE.
TO ME, THAT SOUNDS LIKE A SURE-FIRE
BEST SELLER
CLAP
CLAP
CLAP
SLAM

"There's nothing out there like this, let's do it!" Or, they may say, "There's nothing out there like this, not sure we should take a chance on an unknown." Or they may say, "We've seen this type of book sell like apple pie at a county fair, let's add this to our list." Or, the sales team might say, "Hmm, well, a book on how to write has been done before, but the pie thing, well, hmmm." And the editor says, "Who doesn't love pie?" because he's hoping he'll get a pie out of this. Then the publisher says, "These illustrations, now that's impressive. This proposal—it's well done." Then the marketing team asks if the pie baker has a TikTok following or a pie shop or maybe she could send a sample of her pie first.

I've said it before and I can't say it enough—make sure your book is the tightest and best of the best you can write before you get to this stage. You want the publisher to say, "This is the best book proposal I have ever seen." That's your goal. Now, go make a pie, eat every bite, and get to work on fine-tuning.

It's not just the agent you have to make fall in love with you, this is a whole editorial team you have to get to crush on you and your book. It's more than just your new boyfriend taking you to meet his family, it's your new boyfriend taking you to meet your future mom-in-law, the judgmental sisters, the nitpicky aunt, a slew of cousins, and the godfather. They have to want to share pie recipes with you and put you in the will.

In our society of self-care and motivation, we try not to force perfectionism on each other. I fear a well-edited book sounds like a daunting task. When we are busy trying to spark joy with our sock drawers and big-box furniture stores that put the Swedish word for comfort and happiness on throw rugs, we need to remember to put the pie in writing. The reality is that if you have a very strong book with a solid story where the prose flows smoothly, then finding the right agent, then editor, then pleasing the editorial team is a whole lot easier. You only have control over the book, not the rest.

But with perseverance, your socks will be joyfully color-coordinated; your living room wall art will remind you to live, laugh, and love; and with pie-like comfort, you will have a real chance at achieving your dream of publishing a book.

This is the final stretch to the end goal, but it can be arduous with everything out of your hands and constant wringing of those hands. While you wait for the editorial meeting and the resulting call from your agent, use your hands to start on your next book. Next book? Yes, because what if they want to make you a two-book deal?!

All this work, all this waiting, you need some hygge and a hearty Warrior Steak and Cheddar Pie. You'll need it because there's more to come, and being a warrior will be important. Or a worrier. That's part of being a writer too.

WaRRioR SteaK and CHEddaR PIE

As hearty as this pie is, it's easy. Or as easy as you want to make it—you're in control. If you are a make-it-from-the-ground-up kind of cook, and some days I am and others not, you can make this pie by marinating the meat yourself and making a puff pastry from scratch. Or, you can get a nice rosemary and balsamic marinated sirloin at Trader Joe's and a frozen puff pastry at your local grocery store, and you'll have easy pie that evening. Edit as your gut desires.

MAKES SIX 5-INCH PIES

Remove 1 package of puff pastry from the freezer and let it thaw for 1 hour. The first time I made homemade puff pastry, it turned out delicious and easy. It just takes more steps and more time to prepare in advance. I encourage you to try it, but enjoy the ease of frozen too as you deserve someone else to do the work for you on occasion.

FILLING

2 tablespoon olive oil, divided

¾ pound marinated sirloin, chopped small

1 tablespoon butter

3 cloves garlic, minced

1 red onion, thinly sliced

6 ounces sliced mushrooms

3 tablespoons Worcestershire sauce

salt

pepper

4 tablespoons all-purpose flour

½ cup half-and-half

1½ cups beef or vegetable broth

1 tablespoon sherry

3 cups grated sharp cheddar cheese

1 egg

1 tablespoon water

Preheat the oven to 425°F.

While the pastry is thawing, begin the filling. In a medium-size pan, heat 1 tablespoon of olive oil over medium heat, then sauté the sirloin. Once the beef is cooked through, transfer to a bowl and put in the fridge to let it cool. In the same pan, add the remaining olive oil, butter, and minced garlic. Heat until the garlic is fragrant, about 2 minutes. Add the red onion and cook until translucent. Add the mushrooms (shiitake or creminis or your faves) with the garlic and onions, and add more oil if needed. Once the mushrooms have lost their water, add 2 to 3 tablespoons of Worcestershire. Season with salt and pepper to taste. Once the mushroom and onion mixture is browned, transfer to the same bowl as the sirloin in the fridge to cool.

You want the filling to be cool before putting in the pastry so the pastry doesn't melt. Don't clean out the pan. Add 4 tablespoons of flour to the pan, 1 tablespoon at a time, stirring as you add. The flour needs to cook as you stir to release the flour flavor. Then, gradually stir in the half-and-half, then the broth to make a roux. Add more or less broth as needed to reach your desired thickness. Stir in the sherry.

Take the beef mixture from the fridge and stir into the roux. Remove from the heat and set aside to cool.

Roll 1 puff pastry sheet to ⅛ inch thick. Cut into 6 even squares, about 6 inches each. Place the 6-inch squares in 5-inch pie pans with the corners hanging over the edges. Place these in the fridge to stay cool while you cut the rest of the pastry.

Roll out the second pastry sheet and cut into six 5-inch squares. Remove the bottom pastries from the fridge. Sprinkle ¼ cup of cheese in the bottom of each pan. Fill the pans to the brim with the beef mixture. Sprinkle another ¼ cup of cheese over the top of the filling. Brush the edges of the bottom pastry with an egg whisked with 1 tablespoon of water. Place a 5-inch square pastry over each pie, corners offset from the bottom pastry corners so you have 8 corners draped over the side of each pie pan. Brush the egg and water mixture over all the pastry tops. Cut a few steam vents in the top.

Bake for 30 minutes.

Eat these little pies like you have a giant book deal coming your way. Or, in case you have to wait a few days to get the news, they reheat really well too.

CHAPTER FOURTEEN

The BOOK Deal

You've received the call from your agent telling you how the acquisitions meeting went, or what the next steps may be. Unless you're out to lunch with the lousy friend and want to gloat, you might not want to be sitting in a noisy restaurant for this call.

Here are a few episodes of the *Writer's Life* romantic comedy spin-off to give you an idea of what may or may not happen.

Episode 1: "Saddest Day in a Writer's Life"

The editorial staff doesn't feel your book has what it takes to make it out in the world. Perhaps the publisher squashed the idea. Your agent will explain that there are plenty of other publishing houses out there who will be interested in your work, and in fact, she already has a couple in mind. All you can think about is how that's what your mother said about men, but then it turned out that no one else asked you out for the next three years. Or, you might be thinking, I got this close! Why bother writing? It's all so stupid anyway, I should just run off a dozen copies of my manuscript and hand them out to friends. You may want to throw pie in that publisher's face. But why waste a good pie?

Listen to your agent. They will know the next steps. Maybe they will have received input that will help you decide on more revisions, or maybe it's clear that that particular publishing house just wasn't a good fit, or maybe . . .

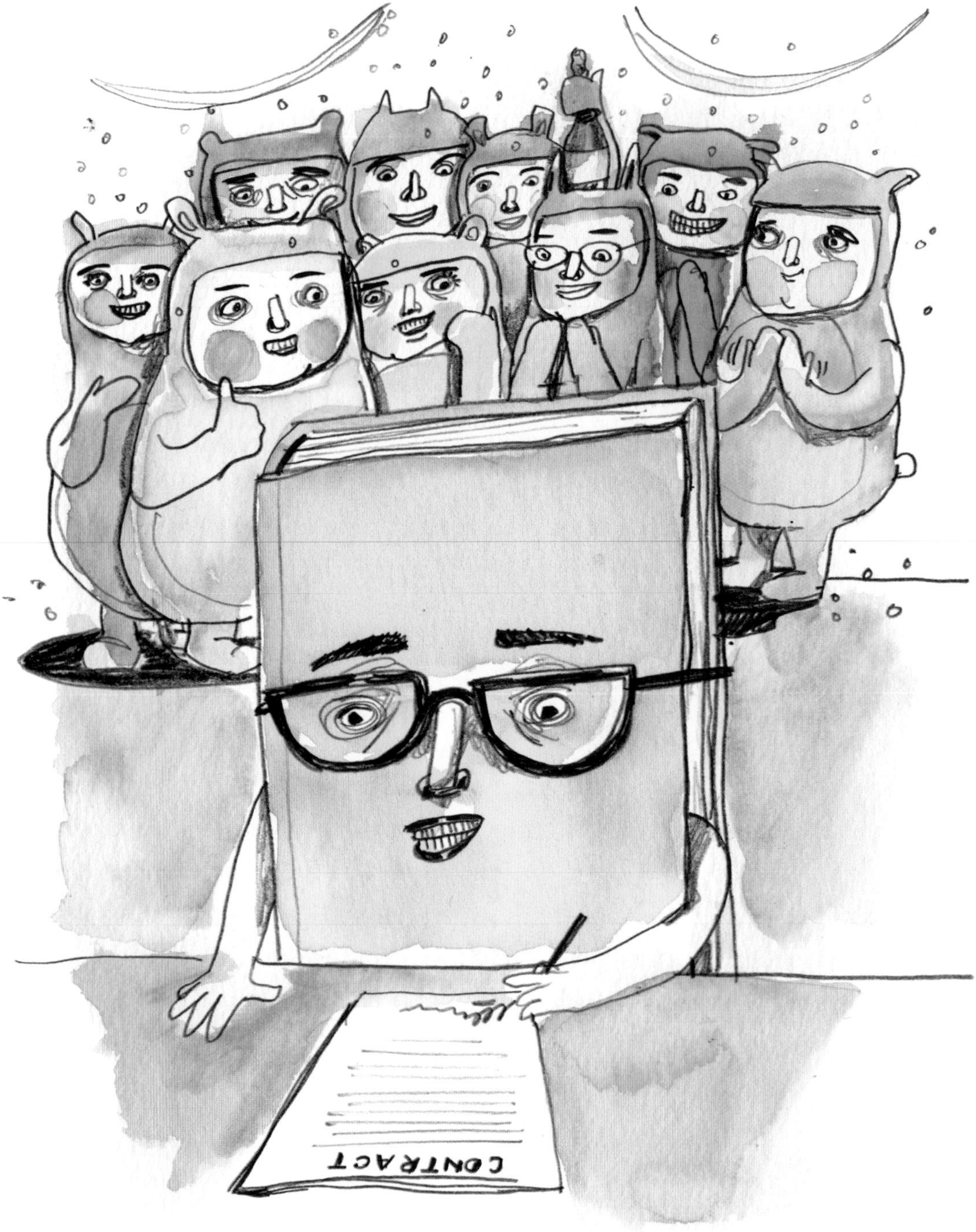
CONTRACT

Episode 2: "Someone Else Was There All Along"

Flash back to when you find out from your agent that an editor is interested—Agent reaches out to other editors on the spreadsheet and another one was interested too. When Editor #1 comes back to say their marketing team didn't see your book as part of their list, Editor #2 has their acquisitions meeting the next day, and they will be in touch. This is when it's okay to sit at home and stuff your face with pie while staring at your phone.

Episode 3: "The Whole World Wants You"

Revise the flashback of when one editor was interested and make it four editors were interested. Now you have to wait around for all of their meetings, and you have to pretend you have patience for this. You can spend the day baking pies and fantasizing about how you will call Lousy Friend and gloat. Beware of gloating, though, because as soon as you say anything prematurely, like, "I owe you lunch since you bought the last time, and I'd love to take you to the fancy restaurant with chandeliers and tablecloths, but I'm going to be busy working with my editor on my soon-to-be-published novel," you could jinx the whole situation. Gloating is always best as a fantasy, anyway.

Soon you will start hearing back from your agent about the results of the acquisitions meetings.

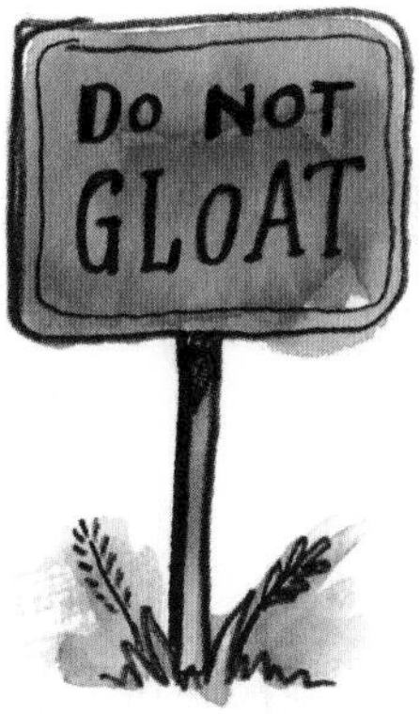
DO NOT
GLOAT

I know you are wanting to ask, "When does the money stuff happen? When do I get offered that ten-figure, five-book deal? What time does the limo arrive? What should I wear for my author photo?" Hang on to your selfies.

Doing Vegas in a Business Suit

Remember back when the editors first started saying they were interested? That's not when it happens. Surely, by now, you know this isn't about the money, right? Back when the editors get interested, and they find out, as you did, that others want your book, more interest ratchets up. They know this book is something. Now is when they start considering The Deal. It's business. Every writer hates this part because it sure didn't seem like business when we were toiling away for months and years only to be rejected time and time again. The only time I felt I was a businesswoman was when I'd go to conferences, but even then, I felt like I was wearing a name tag that said, "Hello, my name is . . . Sisyphus."

When I got my first book deal, which was a wow deal to me, I calculated how many years of hours of toiling it took to write the book and came up with the whopping hourly rate of sixty-three cents. Not quite minimum wage. But it's not about the money. It's about this—The End. The Achievement. The goal that your tenacity got you to. That big pie in the sky that is yours.

The editors have budgets, which we hope they'll decide to just throw at our book because we know the world is waiting for this bestseller. Remember those marketing and salespeople who were in the meeting? And that publisher and editor-in-chief? They all have input and there's a part of the discussion about not only which flavor of pie they expect to be sent their way for publishing a how-to-write book with recipes, but they also have a secret way of predicting how well the book will do and what they can spend on your advance so that they don't lose money, but instead make money. It may sound like Vegas and the roulette wheel is your book, but they actually have statistics and data and what all their combined experience says the market wants and needs. And they have a gut feeling they are putting their money on a good bet. Maybe it is just Vegas.

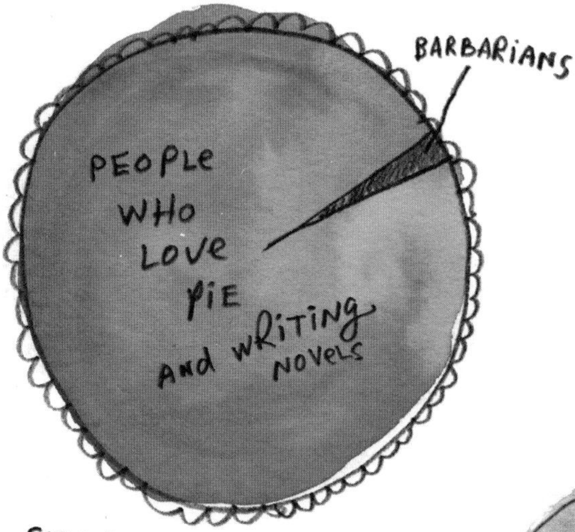
BARBARIANS
PEOPLE WHO LOVE PIE AND WRITING NOVELS

GET IT?...IT'S A PIE CHART that's ALSO A PIE.

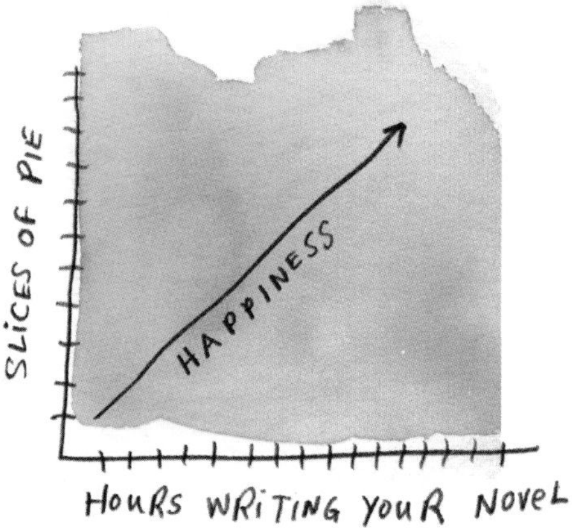
SLICES OF PIE
HAPPINESS
HOURS WRITING YOUR NOVEL

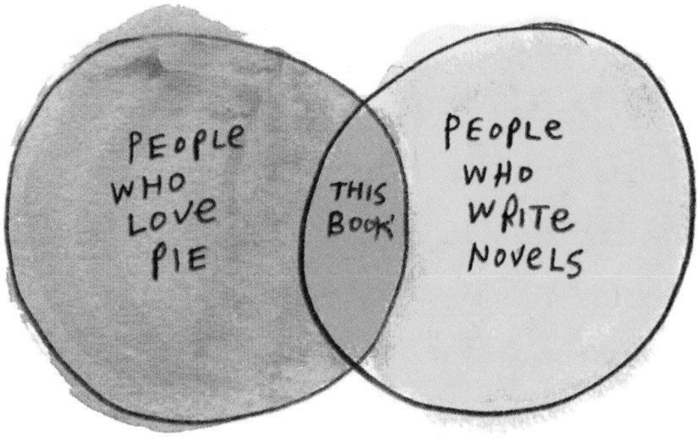
PEOPLE WHO LOVE PIE
THIS BOOK
PEOPLE WHO WRITE NOVELS

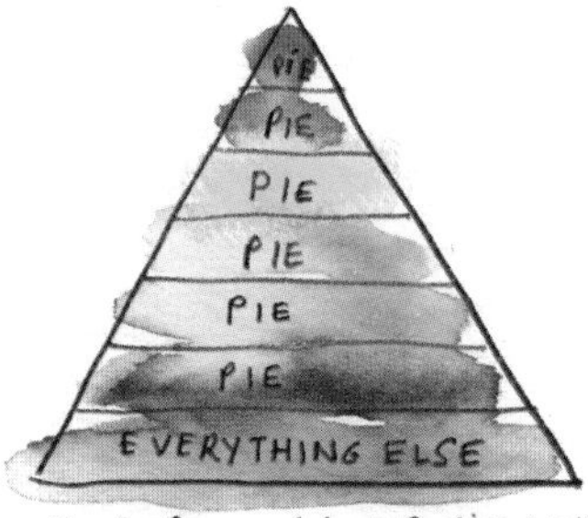
PIE
PIE
PIE
PIE
PIE
PIE
EVERYTHING ELSE

Food PYRAMID FOR PIE LOVERS

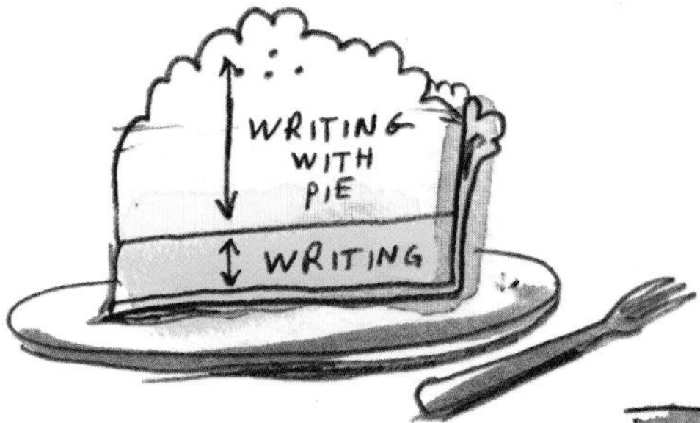
WRITING WITH PIE
WRITING

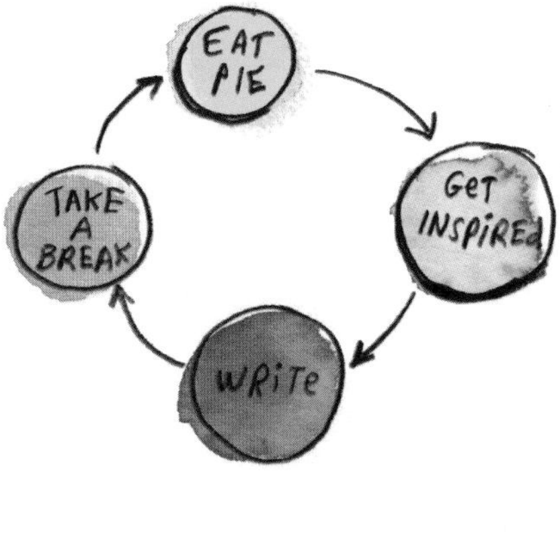
EAT PIE
GET INSPIRED
WRITE
TAKE A BREAK

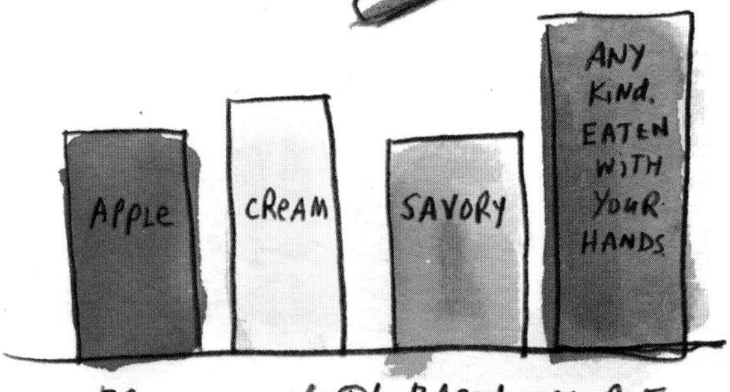
APPLE
CREAM
SAVORY
ANY KIND, EATEN WITH YOUR HANDS

PRODUCTIVITY BASED ON PIE

The meetings and decisions take place over a matter of days. A week or two at the longest, also known as the longest week of your life. Your agent will keep you updated on news, if any, that she has along the way. Some agents will ask if you want to have a phone meeting with each editor. This is a good idea, so that you can also know that you feel good about the match. You'll be working with them on the final edits of your book after all, and you might want to make sure they at least know what your book is about.

When two editors were vying for *MoonPies*, I was, well, over the moon. They both heard about each other and decided to take the weekend to determine how much they wanted to offer me for the novel. They had to outguess the other one, determine what their budget could handle, and determine what the market would handle in the long run. That weekend was a holiday weekend. I made my boyfriend, now my husband, take me hiking to burn off the excess energy I had in my system. I knew I wouldn't be able to sleep until I heard back on Tuesday. Even though it was fifteen years ago, I still remember that first deal because I had to wait over the three-day Memorial Day weekend. Who doesn't forget the day you were scrambling over boulders wondering if all your hopes and dreams and fantasies and secret wishes were really coming true?

When Tuesday morning came, I was sitting by my phone. As would any sane author. My agent gave me the details of the two deals that were offered. Included in the details were her experiences with both editors, what she knew and didn't know. One editor she had worked with for many years and always had great successes, but they were smaller and couldn't offer as much as the other editor. Would I go for the money and prestige of the bigger publisher? Yes, I did. But that wasn't the only reason. I also considered both publishers' lists. Did I see *MoonPies* among those books? Which list felt like home?

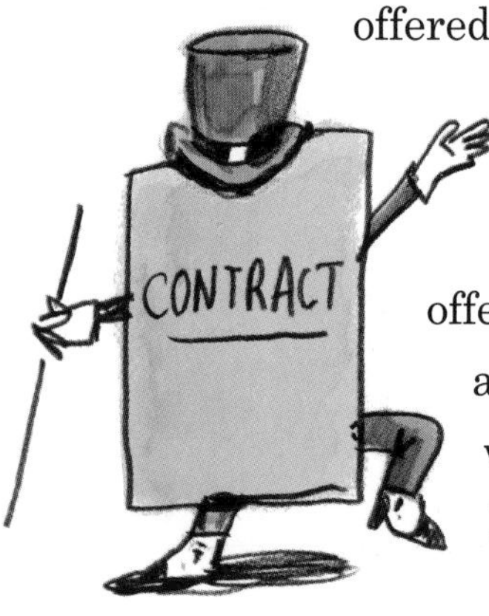
CONTRACT

For this book, I spoke to all the editors who were interested. There were four. That made me feel that Emil and I had a book that was worthy. Consider how much better this felt after the other list of editors from the previous agent had all rejected it. If I hadn't knocked on one more agent's door, I wouldn't have been able to have the opportunity to meet all these editors. But just another reminder that it is always about finding the right fit. You can't fit a round pie in a square pan—well you can, but then it feels more like a casserole.

The editors want you to know why they like your book, how they see it on the shelf, what appealed to them among all the submissions they get. I did not take the highest bidder this time. Not because I didn't like that editor, I liked them all, but because I could see this book among the list of books my editor had published. From everything my editor said, I could tell he got the book 1,000 percent. Not one thing in our conversation sounded even the quietest of alarms that this might not be a good match. You want that kind of confidence when you decide, because from here until the book is sitting on a shelf at a bookstore, it's a partnership. Plus, I liked my editor's sense of humor. That's how I pick my agents too. And how I picked my husband. Come to think of it, my dogs are also pretty funny.

Put on Your Big Girl Business Pants

Now is when it all becomes business. Next up, contract. For the most part, contracts are boilerplate, unless your book is unique in some way, like you envision the book as having scratch and sniff for the recipe pages. This, again, is where your agent is your best friend. Whether or not your book will come out as a hardcover or paperback first is negotiated. If the book was written on proposal, the number of pages is negotiated. The deadlines and payment schedule are determined. And how many copies you'll receive to give to your mom and dad and all those really wonderful supportive friends. That lousy friend—they can buy it at full price.

This is when it really starts to feel like it's happening, that you will be a published author.

On the Tuesday after that fateful Memorial Day weekend, right after I chose which publishing house to accept, I got in my car to go to my job. My mind spun with elation and giddiness that *I WAS GOING TO BE PUBLISHED.* As I pulled onto the freeway with cars zipping around me, I found myself clutching the steering wheel tightly. The old rumor of when Edgar Allan Poe got his first big royalty check so he headed to the tavern to celebrate spun in my head. The story I was told went something like this: After many pints, Poe stumbled out the doors of the bar, tripped on the curb, hitting his head. He died in the gutter, never getting to live as a paid author. I drove the whole way to work in the slow lane way below the speed limit, watching and worrying about every car that came near me. *This would be how I died*, I thought: *My dream is coming true, and I'll die in a pileup on Interstate 5.*

I made it. The book came out. And I lived to celebrate it. And more.

Now it's your turn. Just keep at it. Sign that contract, drive safe, and buckle up for the ride ahead!

This moment calls for a fancy-schmancy celebratory pie!

A book deal might not make you rich, but this recipe is so rich your lips will smack of the decadent taste of success.

HEARTS and CROWNS
Artichoke Pie

This was the first pie I made for my Savory Salon series. I started Savory Salons when I was craving a way to include my pie baking with all the author friends I'd gained over the years. To celebrate an author when they had a new book out, I would invite them as guest of honor to my living room. Reservations for an afternoon with delectable discourse were limited to ten, mostly because my living room couldn't hold more. Each author brought something different to the table, and because the guest list was small, it became an intimate conversation over pie and wine. By the end of dinner, the author and guests all had new friends.

This pie, when popped from the springform pan, looks elegant with its crown of golden-baked phyllo bursting from the top.

10 sheets phyllo dough

½ cup olive oil, divided

1 large shallot, chopped fine

4 eggs

2 cups ricotta

1 cup freshly grated Gruyère

½ cup freshly grated parmesan

¼ cup freshly chopped parsley

Zest of 1 lemon

½ tsp salt

1 (15 ounce) can artichoke hearts, quartered

Defrost the phyllo in the fridge overnight.

Preheat the oven to 375°F.

Heat 1 tablespoon of olive oil over medium heat. Sauté the shallot until soft. Set aside.

In a bowl, combine the eggs, ricotta, Gruyère, Parmesan, 2 tablespoons of parsley, lemon zest, and salt until well blended. Add the shallot to the mixture.

Brush a 9-inch springform pan with 1 tablespoon olive oil. Using phyllo is easy, but you must work quickly so it doesn't dry out. Set up your work area so the process runs smoothly. Place the remaining olive oil in a small bowl. Unwrap the phyllo from the packaging and lay it out flat on your work surface next to your greased springform pan.

Cover the phyllo with a damp dish towel to keep the pastry moist. Peel off a sheet of phyllo at a time. Replace the dish towel as you work with each sheet. Brush the top sheet of phyllo with olive oil and lay it in the pan and against the sides. The edges of the sheet will hang over the pan. Do the same with the next sheet, placing it perpendicular to the first sheet. Repeat with each sheet, and place it at an angle to the previous sheets until the pan is lined all the way around with phyllo dough hanging over the edges.

Pour half of the filling into the pan. Spread a layer of artichoke hearts, cut into quarters, over the top, and pour the remaining filling over the artichokes for the third layer.

Gently, as the phyllo has probably started to dry out, pull the sheets that overlapped the edge and fold them on the top to cover the filling. The edges will crinkle, but pull the edges up into a bouquet. Don't worry about any breakage—think of it as mantling on your crown.

Bake for 45 to 50 minutes, until the phyllo is golden brown. Stick a knife in the center to see if it's done. Let it cool. Remove the sides of the springform pan, slide pie onto a serving platter, and admire your crown. It can be served warm or room temperature.

I've added a shredded roasted chicken breast to this recipe before, and it turned out nicely for a dinner pie.

Eat, drink, and be merry, for tomorrow your book will be out in the world.

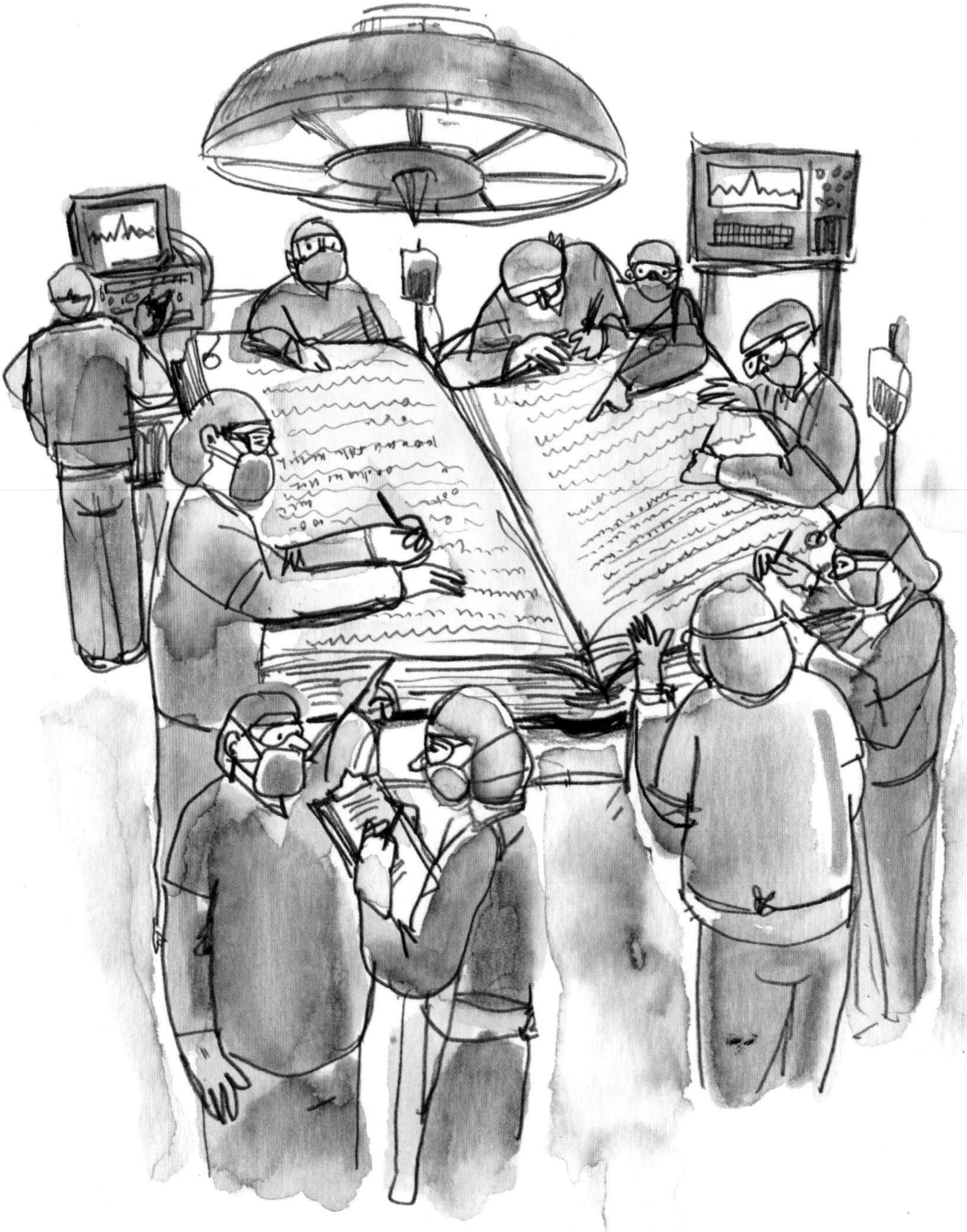

CHAPTER FIFTEEN

Now the Work Begins

Under the Editing Knife

Wait, what?

I know you were thinking that you got this far, now you just wait for the checks to come in. You did all that heavy-duty editing before, back in chapters 7, 9, 11, 12, and 14, is it really possible to do anymore? Oh, it's always possible to do more editing. Just ask any published author.

With my first novel, the editor or her assistant put big brackets on pretty much every page and wrote, "tighten." I wasn't sure at first what that meant, but over the years, I've learned to eliminate many prepositional phrases and all those unnecessary words like *very, rather, really, quite, in fact, so, just, of course, surely, that said, actually, pretty.* I'd really rather not have to be just so very picky, but of course you surely understand. That said, it's actually quite pretty easy to eliminate those words if you just use search and delete.

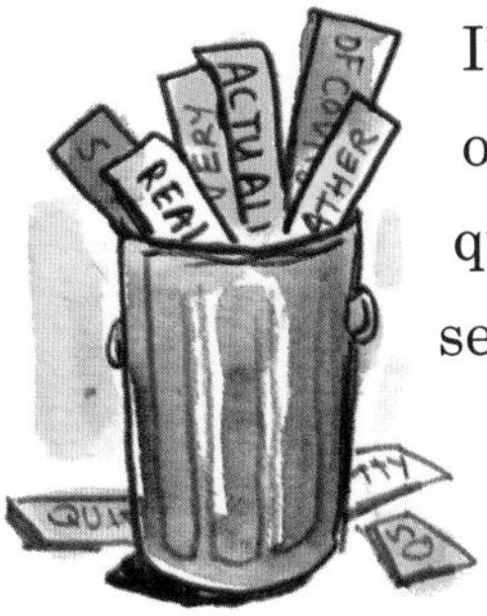
REAL
VERY
ACTUALL
OF COU
RATHER

All that tightening wasn't as hard as the biggest editorial note of all: replace the ending with one that will leave the reader with more hope. I had already rewritten the ending of *MoonPies* fourteen times. I was certain I had come up with every possible ending there was. How would I ever come up with something new? Through mulling over the story, grousing with my friends that I would never find an ending and would have to return my book advance, then getting suggestions and ideas from folks who had read the story umpteen times, I finally found a more satisfying ending. That was when the actual MoonPie was given a small but pivotal role. I took the one fetish from the beginning of the story, threaded it throughout, and made it the final clue on their journey to find the runaway. With the help of friends, metaphor, and more revision, I was able to find more hope and understanding for the characters.

Editors edit with different weapons. Some slash and burn with flamethrowers, others use crème brûlée torches to crystalize the sugar. Or, as my editor says, he uses a neon cocktail sword rather than a machete. Of course, you don't really know what to expect until you are in the midst of it, but keep in mind, the editor's goal is to make it the best book out there.

Once your edits are done, then come the copyedits. A copyeditor is much different than an editor editor. A copyeditor digs down into the nitty-gritty. They examine every word to see if it's the right one. This is when your Oxford commas are dissected. This is when you get margin notes such as, "The nutria rat is not a native Texas mammal," when you've written something about how the main character's mother-in-law chomping at potato chips was more annoying than a Texas nutria rat chewing on the cable wires. The copyeditor makes sure that if you say Ruby is wearing a checkered shirt in one scene that she can't be wearing a polka dot shirt on the next page unless she spilled guacamole on the checkered one and made a quick change. The copyeditor knows what your character had for breakfast, and quite possibly what you had too. You can't pull anything over on a copyeditor.

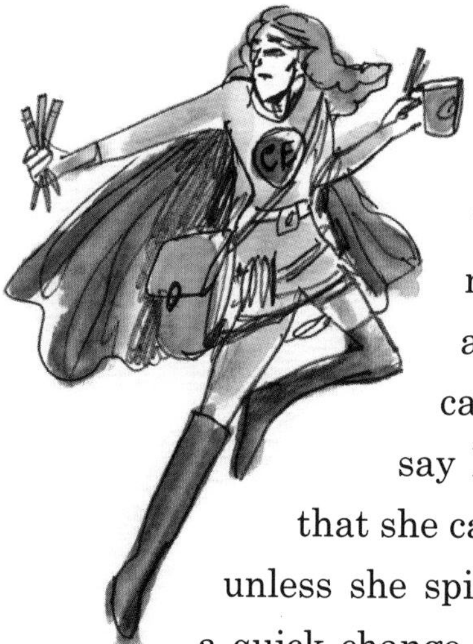
CE

After a close look at your manuscript, you will be asked to go over the copyeditor's notes and accept all that apply. If you want to argue the Texas citizenship of the nutria rat, this is your only chance.

The next stage is galleys. The copyedited version of your manuscript will be sent to you and will look almost like pages in a printed book. The pages will be formatted like a book, the final typeface with left and right justification, the little dingbat at the beginning of your chapters, if you have that, and your page numbers will be organized as they will be in the final book. You'll be asked to read this version for one more search round for typos, word choice, and comma placement.

After all of this back-and-forth, reading and rereading, editing, and copyediting, how could there possibly be any errors? But no human, nor book is perfect. In *MoonPies*, I have a *Price Is Right* scene. Everyone at Penguin and I checked it over and over, yet the calculation for the monetary cash prize for the Showcase winner is incorrect. You'll have to read the book to catch it, but this is a perfect example of how things still get past all the *proofing*. A perfect example of why there is so much review.

Don't worry, if anything does get overlooked, your readers will write to you and point out all the typos and errors.

But Wait, There's More

It's not possible to have any more revision or rewriting or editing. Not. Possible.

You're right, no more. But you still need to write your acknowledgments and your dedication. You aren't required to do this, but it's a nice little bread-and-butter note to all your friends and family and frenemies for all they went through to get you to this point.

Everyone you know, even if they didn't even so much as ask you how it was going while you were writing, will go straight to the acknowledgments to see if their name is listed. That doesn't mean you need to list everyone, but you might want to mention your writing group (yes, even that annoying woman who kept saying your publishing deal was a fluke), and the teacher who made you feel you had at least an inkling of a writer's talent, and the parachutist who described the feeling of falling, which you used for that pivotal scene, and the pharmacist who filled your monthly Xanax prescription (okay, maybe not her).

I panicked when I realized I hadn't kept a list of whom I wished to thank. All the people over the years who helped, supported, gave advice, let me cry, whine, drink their wine. I hadn't fully believed I would ever be published, so I never kept a tally. I had only a couple of weeks to try to remember everyone to whom I wanted to show my appreciation. I was certain I would forget someone vital. If I did, they never told me, and I would like to thank them for that.

Save your dogs and spouse for the dedication. Write something obscure so readers think you've got a secret message for them. They'll ask you about it at every book signing.

Now you are done writing and editing. You may be asked to weigh in on the inside jacket copy. Or you may be part of the conversation if the title of the book needs to be changed. *MoonPies & Movie Stars* was originally *Dead Armadillos & MoonPies*. I still like that title, but the publishers said it wasn't good to have dead in a title unless a dead body was involved, besides roadkill.

You'll be asked to reach out to any published friends to give you a blurb for the back of your book. Yes, this is as awkward as it seems. One of my favorite responses was from a blurber for my memoir. He was pretty famous, and I felt goofy asking him to blurb my book because he is a big deal and I'm a small fry. He'd been a teacher of mine years before, and I wasn't even

SO MUCH SUPPORT! GO AHEAD and
SO MUCH GRATITUDE! THANK EVERYBODY!

A FEW OBNOXIOUS ACKNOWLEDGMENTS

To my own brain:
Thanks buddy, you're the best!

To Homer: I'm super grateful
to you for getting this whole
literature thing. You're my
brother from another mother!

For all the snacks that
were there for me
during the writing of my
book. I couldn't have
done it without you.

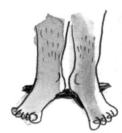

Dear feet: you were
there for every
bathroom break and
grocery run. You guys
kick ass!

To my Animal Guide:
Where would I be without
you? You're way more than
just a dog to me.

To the construction crew across the
street: You made a lot of noise, but
reminded me there was a big world out
there. Thanks for being great eye candy!

COLD and UNFORTUNATE BLURBS

I CAN'T WAIT TO TEAR INTO THESE PAGES AND USE THEM FOR SCRAP PAPER!

THe BesT Book I NeveR opeNed!

THiS Book HAS "GARAGE SALe" WRiTTeN ALL oveR iT!

THe BEST PAPER-WEIGHT I eveR ReAd

sure he'd remember the story I worked on in his class. He responded to my request, "Send the book. If I like it, I'll blurb it." He blurbed it, so I guess I passed muster. I had another teacher, also a famous writer, who I had hosted at my house, who said they'd blurb my book, so I sent it. I never heard from them, and when I ran into them again at a writers' festival years later, they acted as though they'd never met me. I'm not sure if it's easier to just say no or avoid someone forever. This business proves repeatedly that it's subjective, and it's made up of introverts. But my favorite-of-all response to a request for a blurb was from a teacher who said, "I will blurb your book, but you must promise to always pay it forward when you are asked to blurb books for others." I will never forget that advice and I try to honor it. Not to mention his blurb for my book was spot on.

Your book's cover ideas will be run past you. First, you'll be asked for input on what you imagine the cover to look like. Both my hardcover novel and memoir covers were even more wonderful than what my imagination dredged up. I felt included and pleased with the outcomes. *MoonPies'* paperback cover was revised to look more like a picnic tablecloth, or a spin-off of the old TV show *Petticoat Junction*. They ran it past me first, and I told them it didn't feel right at all. Thanks, they said, and still used their revision. I'm not certain how much say the author really has, but apparently, I was outvoted.

It's About You

Now is when you take a day off, make an appointment with a professional photographer, and get your book jacket photo taken. Or have your husband take one of you with your cats. Or use the photo from that barbecue where you have a large smile that makes you look like you're up to something. It doesn't have to be a professional photo, but it needs have all the right high-resolution JPEGs and such for the publisher to use. But another bit of advice that I'll pass on is that it can be fun to be queen for a day.

My friend Frank was an acting talent scout. He knew a professional photographer I could use, and he insisted I should have a stylist so I could have my makeup and hair done too. Movie star photo op. The stylist asked me to bring several outfits to change into, so I did. She looked through what I brought, tossed them all to the side, and pulled a few things from her own closet for me to wear instead. Then she began rolling my hair in rollers.

"I don't want to look fake in my photo," I said. "I usually wear my hair straight."

She continued to brush and roll my long hair onto big round rollers. "I'm just doing this for body," she explained. She took a hot blow-dryer to the curlers.

"My hair takes curl really well," I tried to explain. "You don't need to leave the rollers in long."

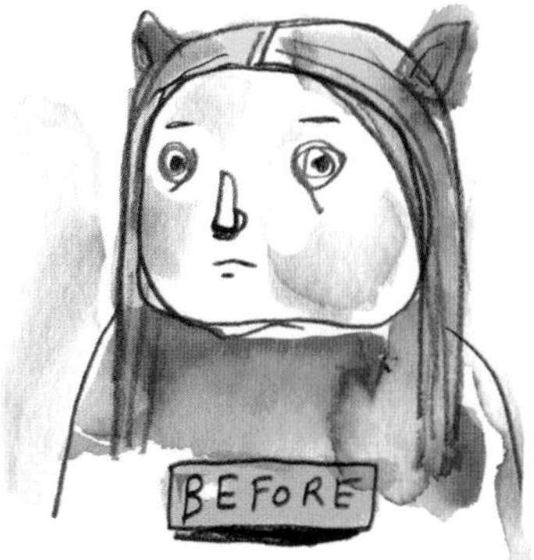
BEFORE

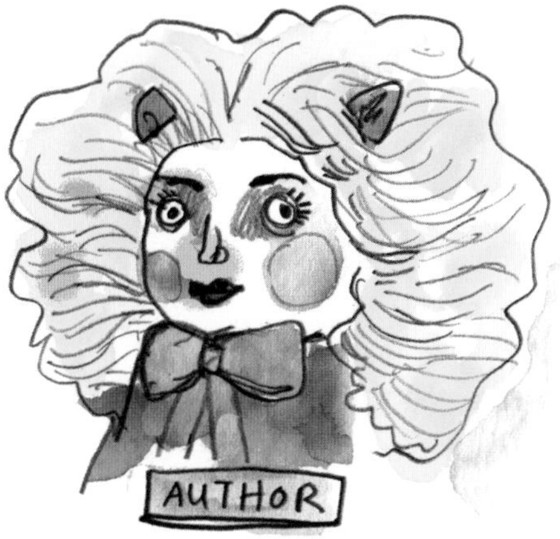
AUTHOR

"It's not that much," she kept trying to reassure me, as she sprayed hairspray around my head.

A Santa Ana wind was blowing on that day. A Santa Ana is a hot, dry wind from the desert. With no humidity, large curlers, and hairspray, every last bit of curl held on tight. My hair ballooned out all around my head as the stylist tried to comb the heck out of the Volkswagen Beetle I was now wearing.

When you attend book clubs as guest of honor, you will be asked all sorts of questions, but one of the regular questions I got was, "Why does it look like you have so much more hair in your author photo than in real life?"

But let's save all the embarrassing stuff for the book tour. Relax and enjoy this respite. Your book will be coming out into the world very soon.

Coconut-Lime Margarita Pie

With all the neon cocktail swords flailing around here, it seems a cocktail pie is in order. Besides, we all deserve a drink after all this work. This pie would make a great dessert with the spicy Carnitas and Hatch Chile Pie in the next chapter. Dessert first, as I like to say.

This is the recipe that is replacing the recipe I mentioned in Chapter 11 that I tried to make happen but just couldn't get it to come together the way I imagined it. The pie-not-seen-here is made with meringue baked crisp like a pavlova and topped with frozen margarita sorbet. My gut tells me it's a pie best created by someone who loves those flavor combinations better than I do. It's a lesson in letting go, although I'm not sure I've let go yet. In the meantime, enjoy this little-bit-tipsy recipe.

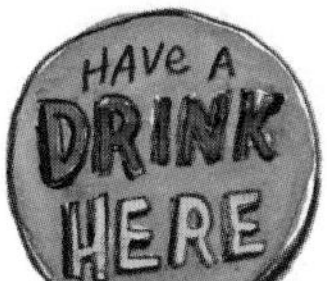
HAVE A
DRINK
HERE

- 1 (14 ounce) can sweetened condensed milk
- 1 (13.5 ounce) can unsweetened coconut milk
- 1 cup freshly squeezed lime juice (5 to 6 medium limes)
- Zest of 3 limes
- 7 egg yolks
- ½ cup tequila
- 2 tablespoons triple sec

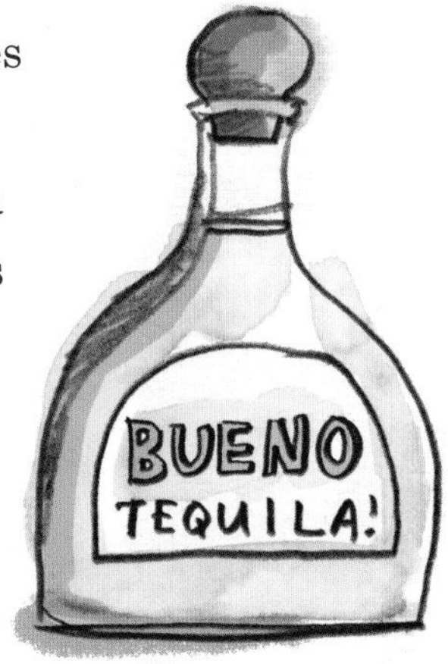
BUENO
TEQUILA!

Preheat the oven to 350°F.

Prepare a graham cracker crust as on page 154.

In a medium bowl, place the sweetened condensed milk, coconut milk, lime juice, zest, egg yolks, tequila, and triple sec and mix until well combined. Pour into the graham cracker crust.

Bake for 50 to 55 minutes. The center should still be jiggly. Let cool to room temperature for 1 to 2 hours. If you like your margaritas frozen, place in the freezer for 3 to 4 hours. If you like your margaritas on the rocks, place in the fridge for 3 to 4 hours. Cheers!

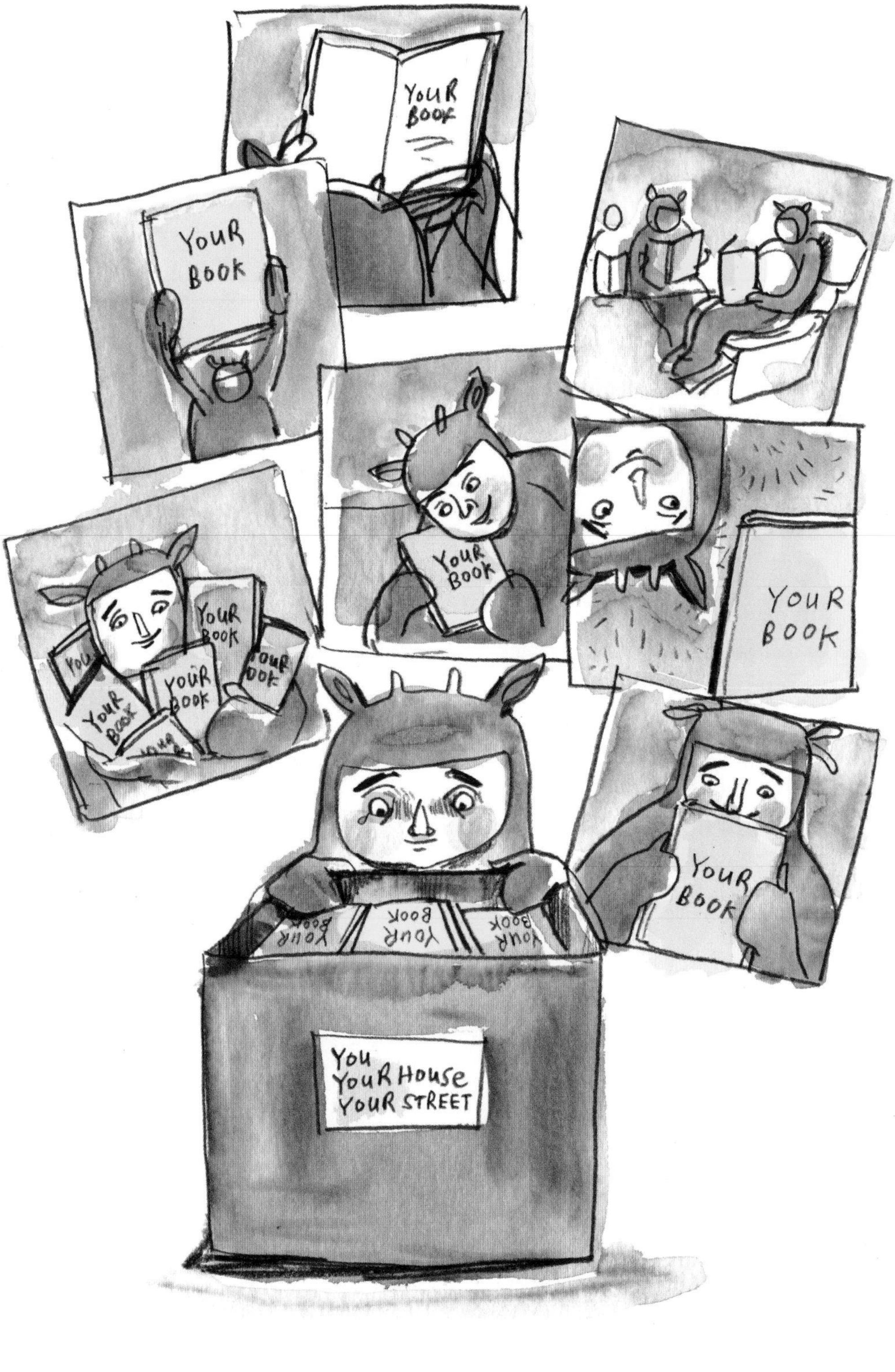
YOUR BOOK
YOUR BOOK
YOUR BOOK
YOUR BOOK
YOUR BOOK
YOUR BOOK
YOUR BOOK
YOUR BOOK
YOU
YOUR HOUSE
YOUR STREET

CHAPTER SIXTEEN

From a Box of Books —to— Book Tour

The Box

One day, when it feels like maybe the book deal was a fiction because you haven't heard from anyone asking you to read or rewrite a section in a while, and you're beginning to wonder if maybe the publisher forgot about your book, or the contract slipped between seat cushions in the board room, a box arrives on your doorstep—a box full of bouncing baby books. YOUR BOOK!

No other moment is the same as that one when you open the box, even though you know the contents, and you see YOUR BOOK. You'll pick up one book, fondle it, turn it over and over, open the pages, thumb-flip them past your nose as you inhale deeply the scent of YOUR BOOK. You might even hug it. I did.

Take selfies with you and your book. Post it on social media so everyone knows that from here on out they will be hearing about every activity you and your book embark upon.

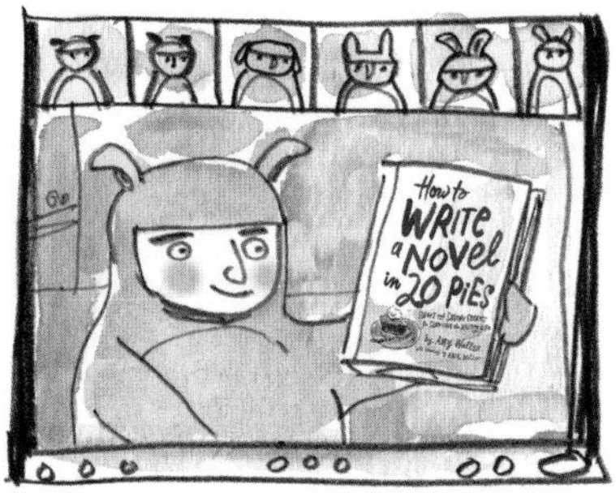
How to
WRITE
a NOVEL
in 20 PIES

Book Tour

Book tours have changed over the years, but bookstores, book clubs, and book festivals still need and want authors to come to their events. Nowadays, there are so many Zoom events that you can be all over the world without having to get on a plane. Many small writers' organizations love to have a writer come to speak, and now they can invite anyone. I can't mention enough how all the publicity, whether online or in person, is about connection. Say yes to the venues that have the vibe you want to convey, and if you're me, you'll say yes to all invitations because I never want to miss any party.

Your publicist should provide information on what outlets will interview you, what bloggers will review your book, what radio stations have a spot for you. They can give you tips on social media and how to reach or build an audience. You can also contact places and people you know. I often have authors ask me to host a Savory Salon for them. If the book and the author inspire a good conversation in my imaginings, I agree to host them. I love having people reach out to me. Even if I can't always give them my living room, I try to refer them to someone or someplace else.

Book Stores

Local bookstores always welcome a local author. Before now, you should have been kissing up to your favorite bookstore owner. I give mine pies. I highly suggest it. Pies have many uses. Your publisher can reach out to local bookstore owners to arrange a book reading or event.

An interesting fact that took me a while to get my head around is how someone achieves bestseller status. It's not because you are outselling every book out there. That's a small part of it, but not the whole pie chart. Instead, it's about how many books are sold in a certain amount of time. Let's say Joe Blockbuster sells twenty books a day for seven days. That's a lot of books. My calculator (and copyeditor) tells me that is 140 books. Jane Goodreads sold only 120 books during that same week, but she is #1 on the bestseller list. How is that possible when Joe sold more? Jane sold her 120 books in one hour at her local bookstore who reported it to the bestseller-list authorities. She sold more books in a shorter amount of time than Joe. Twisted, right? The lesson in this equation is to make sure all your friends come out to your first reading at the local bookstore. If not to make you a bestseller, at least to make sure you receive a bestseller-esque send-off for your tour.

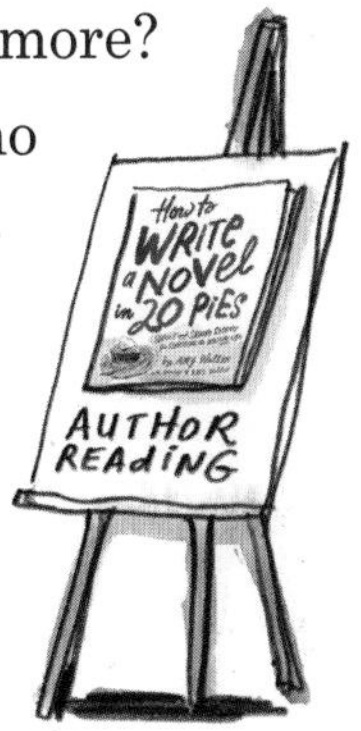
How to
WRITE
a NOVEL
in 20 PIES
AUTHOR
READING

Those nightmare stories of no one showing up for your reading, those are true. They happen to everyone, even the mightiest of authors. The first time it happened to me, I got to know the bookstore owner well because she sat and chatted with me all afternoon. The most memorable events I've had are the ones where maybe only three people show up. I try my darnedest to ignore all the empty chairs, then ask the three people to scootch in closer. In this way, we gather to have more of a chat. I arrive feeling a little sad this isn't going to be the big-selling event I had hoped, but leave knowing I just made friends with three good readers who will more than likely buy my next book too. It's about connection more than anything else. But it never hurts to tell your friends to show up if they want to still be your friends later.

Book Clubs

I'd heard many a famous author talk about their book tour being so hard—"Five cities in three days!" Or, "Twenty-five cities in three hours!" I suppose the latter is more how they felt. As much as my compassion went out to them, I envied that opportunity to get to share my book with the world. When *MoonPies* came out, the publicist assigned to me by my publisher prepared an itinerary for my tour stops. My tour was more of a seven-cities-in-twenty-days kind of tour, but that first stop was a doozy. The Pulpwood Queens Convention. The world's largest book club. This is no ordinary book club. They are hundreds of tiara-wearing, book-sharing book club members. Most of the attendees wear animal print and all are required to wear a tiara or a crown. When on Zoom, they wear pajamas with their tiaras.

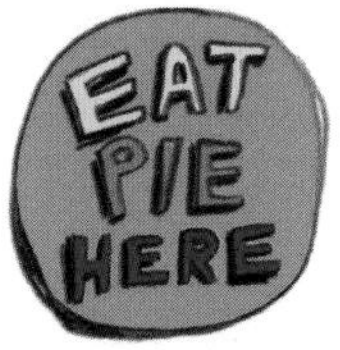
EAT
PIE
HERE

The in-person event was a hoot—everything about this convention was—except my publicist forgot to send my books. The day of the big book sale when the authors sat under a tent with their books stacked tall on their tables in front of them, I sat at an empty table passing out copies of my positive reviews and asking people to please buy my book when they got home. I watched everyone else's tower of books get shorter and smaller as they sold out. I won't share the full story of me panicking and begging to search the entire warehouse where the books were supposed to be shipped in case they were just misplaced. That part is embarrassing. I will share that I made some author friends who are still my good friends to this day. One is the author whose book deal announcement I had read about in *Publishers Marketplace* years earlier and reached out to his agent with my manuscript. We shared the same agent for years. We danced at the Pulpwood

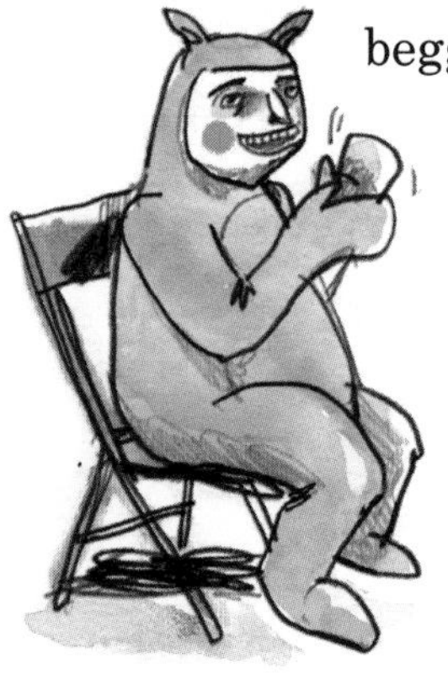

Queen Ball that weekend. I didn't sell any books, but I had more than enough fun for a queen.

The most endearing book club I was ever invited to was in the tiniest town about 120 miles from my home. I drove hours with just tumbleweeds and the horizon keeping me company to get to the little tea shoppe where I shared crumpets, iced tea, and my book with the members in a far-flung mountain outpost.

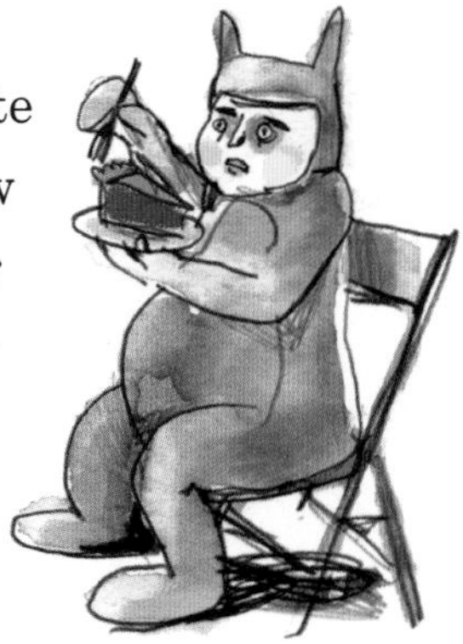

My favorite of all book events was an event to celebrate my memoir. The owner of Bookworks, a bookstore in New Mexico, had thought a book titled *When We Were Ghouls: A Memoir of Ghost Stories* would be an excellent reading event for Halloween. A friend of mine and memoirist, Jennifer Simpson, lived in Albuquerque. Jenn was a builder of community and a gatherer of writers. The day after Halloween, she hosted a Day of the Dead event at her home. The Mexican holiday celebrates the spirits of those who have gone before us and is a happy event with altars and remembrances. Many women gathered in her living room to eat posole and drink wine. By this point on my tour, I had been to so many book clubs and festivals and other events that I had run out of things to say that were new. I decided to turn the conversation around, and I asked the women in Jenn's living room if they had any ghost stories. I wish I would have recorded that night. The tales were stupendous, heartwarming, scary, funny, and each one unique. Every single person had a ghost story.

Book Festivals

Festivals and conventions can be found all over the world, but the ones close to home can be as magnanimous as the big ones in the fancy cities.

FREE THINGS

YOU GET WHEN YOU'RE A FAMOUS WRITER ON TOUR

(or even a NOT-SO-FAMOUS WRITER)

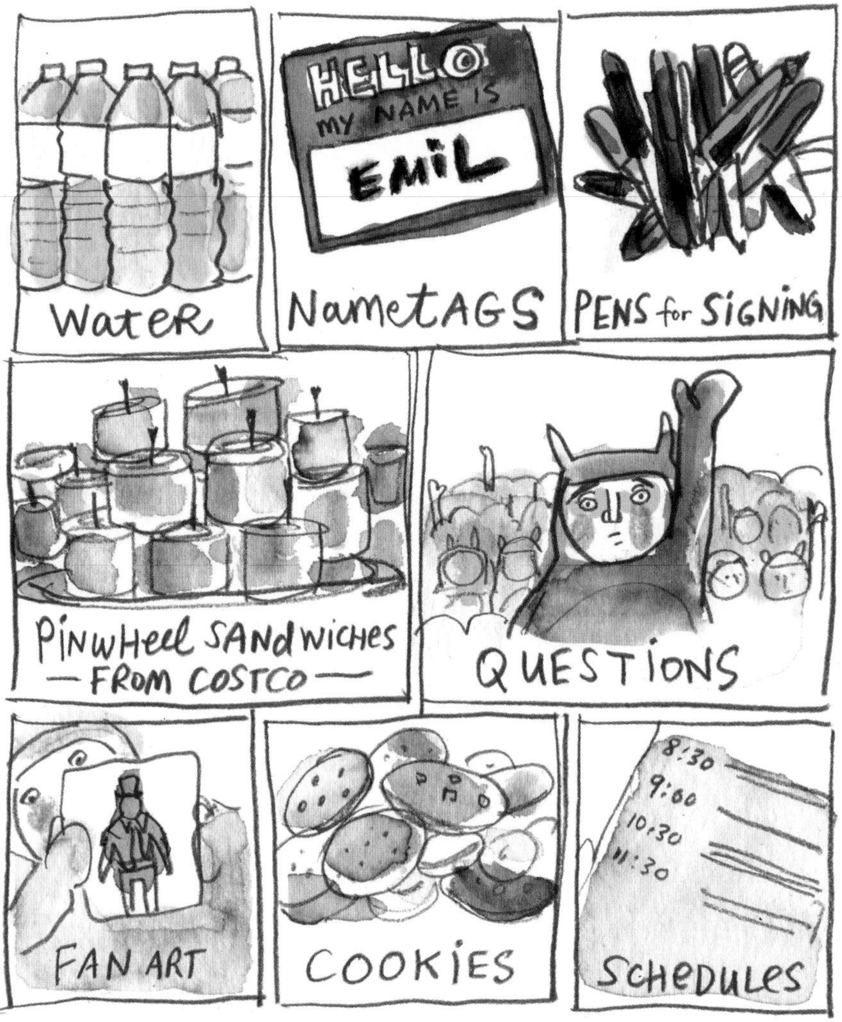

WATER
HELLO
MY NAME IS
EMIL
NAMETAGS
PENS for SIGNING
PINWHEEL SANDWICHES
— FROM COSTCO —
QUESTIONS
FAN ART
COOKIES
8:30
9:00
10:30
11:30
SCHEDULES

The smaller ones are great for getting to know your readers. I was lucky to be invited to the *Los Angeles Times* Festival of Books. My novel had been reviewed by the newspaper, and I was asked to be on a humor panel with three other authors. Only, I wasn't so funny because I was a nervous wreck. My fellow panelists could ad-lib and volley jokes back and forth. Me, I just opened my book and read aloud from the first chapter. Ack. I had nothing prepared. In front of three hundred people. Emil was in the audience, and afterward, when I slunk offstage and found him, he told me he overheard two women next to him, one said to the other, "The nicest one up there seems like that one on the far right." Whether he was just being kind, or telling me the truth, it's important to remember your friends are an important part of the process and the ego-assuaging. Especially post-publishing.

You get to be treated like royalty on these tours and events. The book festivals have greenrooms like movie stars have where all day you are served mini-tacos and éclairs. Bottled water is passed out like it's manna from the fountain of new books. You feel loved and appreciated. But even if the festival or reading is smaller and your greenroom is the storage closet at the bookstore, and you practice what you want to say to the vacuum cleaner, these events are still worthwhile. Everyone from the salesclerk to the woman who buys eight copies of your book to give to her family members makes you feel like all the hard work you put into your book was worth it. Even the vacuum seems to appreciate you.

And, yes, it does feel like twenty-five cities in three hours, mostly because it goes by so fast.

CARNITAS and HATCH CHILE PIE

The Hatch chile is a medium-spicy New Mexico chile grown in the Hatch Valley. They have festivals around the Hatch chile. Jenn would roast bushels of these and keep them in bags in her freezer to put together a pot of posole or chili for a group of friends and writers. Her door was always open for anyone and everyone to gather. Even if she didn't know you, she soon would. Jenn is a good example of how inviting writers to come together and be part of a nonjudgmental community (as opposed to writing groups who are helpful but are also focused on critiquing the writing) keeps us from feeling alone. It's important to have friends in the literary community who are there for support and camaraderie and to remind us we aren't alone. I kept Hatch salsa in my pantry for when Jenn came to visit so I could make her a Hatch chile chicken pot pie.

I made this recipe easy-peasy so you could throw it together at the last minute and invite your writer friends over to grouse about the hard toll of the Writing Life or to celebrate someone's (your!) book deal, or just to gather for no reason. Feel free to mix and match the chiles, cheeses, and even the meat.

CORNMEAL CRUST

2¼ cups all-purpose flour

½ cup cornmeal

8 tablespoons butter, cut into 1-inch pieces

8 tablespoons leaf lard

4 to 6 tablespoons sour cream

1 tablespoon flavored vinegar of your choice

FILLING

12 ounces carnitas (Mexican pulled pork)

2 cups roasted Hatch chiles, diced

1 (14 ounce) can whole kernel corn

1 (14 ounce) can black beans

1 tablespoon olive oil

1 chopped yellow onion

1 jar Hatch Chile salsa

1 can fire-roasted diced tomatoes

I find cornmeal crusts to have the kind of texture I want in a comfort food—a little crunch.

Place the flour and cornmeal into a large mixing bowl. Add the salt and stir until well mixed. Add the butter, leaf lard, and sour cream. By hand, mush the wet and dry ingredients until they become a shaggy mess of dough that when you squeeze a clump it holds together. Add the vinegar. I use a sweet habanero vinegar and it adds just the right amount of sweet and tart to go with the spicy. Of all the flavored vinegars out there, find one that sparks your interest. When the dough comes together enough to form a ball, make two disks, wrap them in plastic wrap, and stick them in the fridge while you write a new chapter and then begin the filling.

I love Trader Joe's Traditional Carnitas, Mexican-Style Oven-Roasted Pork. If you are the type who prefers to make things completely from scratch, or you have enormous amounts of time, or you just want to procrastinate, you can season and marinate your own carnitas. Shred the cooked meat into smaller bite-size pieces and place in a large bowl. Add the Hatch chiles, or if I don't have any of Jenn's chiles, I roast 6 sweet peppers, then slice open, remove the seeds, and slice into ¼-inch pieces. Add to the bowl with the meat. Strain and rinse the corn and beans in a colander. Dump these in with the meat and peppers. Heat the oil, then sauté the onion until soft, then add it to the bowl along with the Trader Joe's Double Roasted Salsa, or if you like more spice, Trader Joe's Hatch Valley Salsa. With a big wooden spoon, stir all the ingredients together until well mixed.

Preheat the oven to 425°F.

Roll out the bottom pastry. Place in a deep 9-inch pan. Pour and smooth the bowl of filling into the pastry. Roll out the top pastry and place on top, crimping around the edges. Slice a few steam vents around the center.

Bake for 30 minutes, then lower the temperature to 375°F and turn back of pie to face the front for even browning until the filling is bubbling out of the steam vents; remove it from the oven. Serve with guacamole and dollops of sour cream. This recipe is meant to please a crowd and you, so make it work for your taste buds. I like spicy, but maybe you like milder. Open your door, invite your friends and their friends over, and gather to celebrate all achievements, big and small, whether they arrive in a box or are still daydreams.

Here's a bonus recipe for a reminder as you step out into the world with your friends who aren't published yet.

HUMBLE PIE

1 lucrative book deal
1 ego, not too bruised
1 lifetime of friendships
8 tons of thanks and acknowledgments
3 ounces hubris
Juice of 1 lemon
2 pounds of humility

Bring the book deal to a full boil over high heat in a large sauté pan until excess water has evaporated. In a separate pot, reduce ego slowly to one quarter. Preserve friendships by spreading thanks and acknowledgments over book deal in sauté pan. Combine reduction of ego and reserved friendships into a large bowl and fold together gently. Allow to marinate until tender. Dice hubris fine with a sharp knife, then mix in a small bowl with the lemon juice. Let masticate until clear. Pour ingredients into a sweet crust and smother with humility. Bake slowly at low heat until humility is golden.

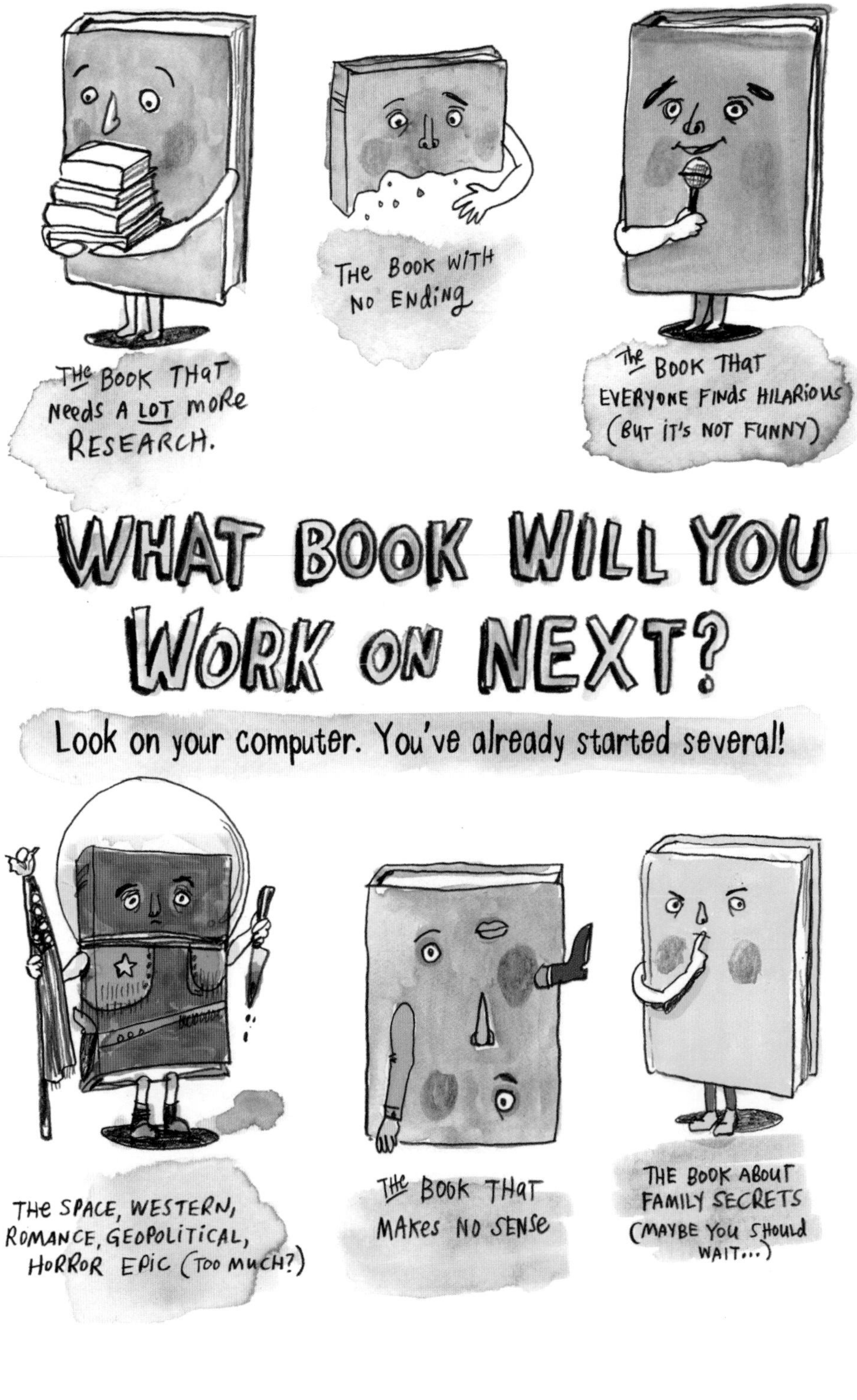
THE BOOK THAT NEEDS A LOT MORE RESEARCH.
THE BOOK WITH NO ENDING
THE BOOK THAT EVERYONE FINDS HILARIOUS (BUT IT'S NOT FUNNY)
WHAT BOOK WILL YOU WORK ON NEXT?
Look on your computer. You've already started several!
THE SPACE, WESTERN, ROMANCE, GEOPOLITICAL, HORROR EPIC (TOO MUCH?)
THE BOOK THAT MAKES NO SENSE
THE BOOK ABOUT FAMILY SECRETS (MAYBE YOU SHOULD WAIT...)

CHAPTER SEVENTEEN

Rumpus Room

The Next Book

The most popular questions by far at every reading, book club, or interview are, "What are you working on now? What's your next book?" Sometimes, it's an easy answer. Sometimes, it's complicated.

Watching all the authors out in the world who have made it—all the authors we see with large followings and tons of adoring fans can be debilitating when we wonder if we can ever accomplish what they have. They make it look so easy—just sit down and write. Wait, isn't that the advice I gave at the beginning of this book? I still stand by that advice, but I also know that sometimes we eat more pie slices than we fill pages. Sometimes we work on two or three books at one time and can't finish any of them. Sometimes, we feel we just have one book in us.

Most of my Writing Life, Harper Lee has been held as the author who wrote only one book, *To Kill a Mockingbird.* Everyone speculated on whether she wanted to write another but the fame and fortune of her initial success caused her to freeze. Others claimed her best friend, Truman Capote, really wrote *Mockingbird.* Years later, it came out that she also wrote *Go Set a Watchman* that didn't see the light of day until she baked her last pie (that's a baker's euphemism that I just made up for died). She obviously wasn't writing blogs and posting on Facebook while trying to type out another bestseller. To me, the Ms. Lee story is that we write the books we write. You may pop out many books, no problem, or the next one may be a struggle, or you may already have a trilogy in mind, or you may start and stop any number of books, or—and this is what happens to many writers—you may write more than one book that gets published while others sit in the proverbial bottom drawer, or in reality, a file on your laptop.

My second book started out as one thing, was asked to be another, then ultimately became a third thing. I have three books I hope to one day finish. I also know that those books may not see a place on the shelf. How do we know when to let go and when to keep trying? This book is about perseverance, so why would I ever suggest that you not finish a book? I've mentioned before, in regard to editing, that all books are never finished but are just abandoned. I hate the word *abandoned*, as it implies we left it all alone to just let the pages yellow and curl while we went about baking pies and publishing other books, never caring about the books left in a box in a dark, dank attic. Just as your newly published book came from an idea that took hold in your brain, the books that linger come from your imagination, and they stay in your imagination. I have a live-stream video where I can see inside my head, perhaps you do too, or if you don't, definitely set one up—it's easy. The live-stream video shows all my wannabe books inside a room where they play with the other books, romping and panting, occasionally stopping to bark out new scenes or character dialogue, or sometimes two books come together, or the characters chat across pages. Sometimes one book will sit in a corner and sulk that it's not getting any attention. Even this book you're holding in your hands went in there for a while. The place where these books hang out is not death row, not even a holding cell. I like to think of it as a rumpus room. The Rumpus Room inside our heads.

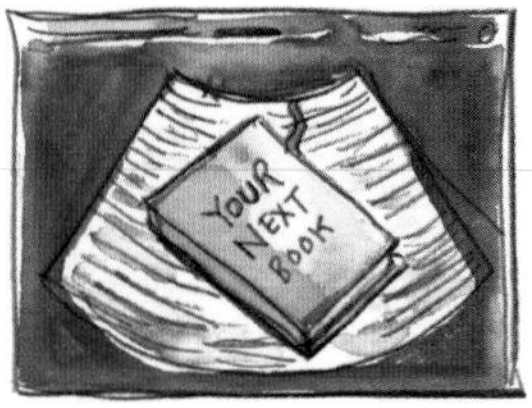
YOUR NEXT BOOK

Author's Life

I wrote this book because I know from personal experience, teacher observation, and friend support that when things get tough writing can make almost any other career, hobby, or even unemployment look preferable. Things can get tough often. Rejection can pull you down and make you not want to get up. The business side of things can be boring or seem more like an algebra problem than the way of life you dreamed of. Watching others soar to the top with their success while you know you're just as good of a writer can seem to affirm that you'll never have that chance. Even the creative part of writing can be debilitating when the right side of your brain stands you up on your writing date. I wanted to offer you an opportunity for play without letting go of how we must still persevere.

The art of writing should include play time! When your imaginings are doing the rumba across your hippocampus and the writing is do-si-do-ing from your fingertips onto the page, this is when we all aspire to have the Writing Life.

The Writing Life includes not only the joyous moments but also rejection, business, celebrating others, and lackluster imagination on occasion. You may not be able to wholly lock yourself inside the Rumpus Room, but it's a great place to set up your office. You can invite friends into your office—friends like Daydreams (often the life of the party), Critical Thinking (a great conversationalist), Bold New Ideas (often takes over the room), Allegories (sometimes a no-show), and Anecdotes (known to leave early). You can even have employee appreciation days in your Rumpus Room office—celebrate your five senses (sometimes six), sense of humor (even though it can be inappropriate), vulnerability (hiding out in your left ventricle), and that sometimes allusive, but very in demand, gut. Invite human friends inside your Rumpus Room

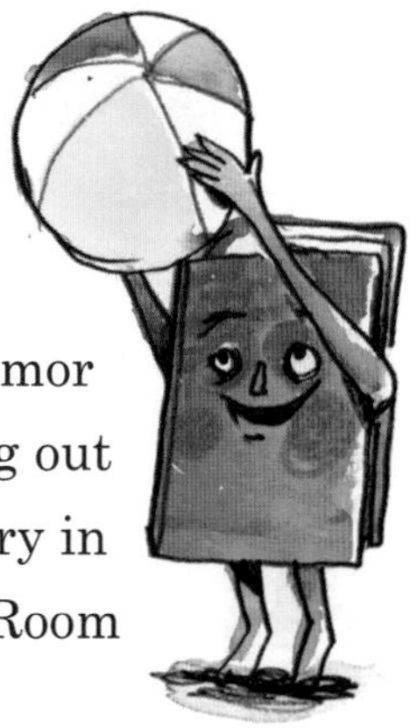

too—brainstorm ideas for new books, share critiques of your story, have a game of badminton with places you dance around in your writing, or even commiserate about the persistence of your novel at your heels. All of this celebrating and communing includes pie, of course.

Teaching

Teaching is part of the Writing Life for many authors. Teaching can provide a means for an income when publishing isn't enough, and it usually isn't. It's also a way to continue to learn the craft of writing, staying on top of what is most current, and building relationships with other writers, both wannabe and successful. Many of my students have gone on to be much more successful than I am, and I love watching that trajectory (with requisite doses of envy, of course). Relationships and connections are important in this solitary endeavor. Pies don't respond when you try to talk to them. At least mine don't—yet.

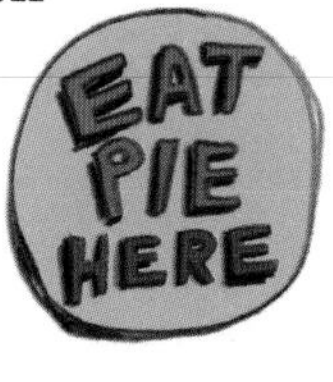
EAT
PIE
HERE

One of the reasons I teach is to share with other writers both the practical craft and how to stimulate the imagination. Teaching is a way of inviting others to play inside *my* Rumpus Room, and I also get to enter theirs to see how they've decorated, what games they play, and how together we can set up the Ping-Pong table and work on the best strategies for volleying ideas back and forth.

Savory Salons

You may also find your own niche that incorporates writing and your other passions. I created Savory Salons when I wanted to blend writing and pie. I knew that writing needed comfort food, so I brought together authors and writers and readers in my living room where I served pie to my guests.

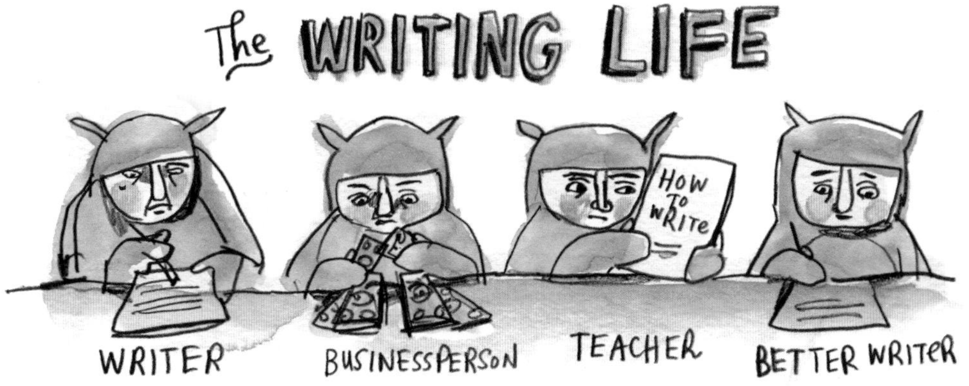
The WRITING LIFE
HOW TO WRITE
WRITER
BUSINESSPERSON
TEACHER
BETTER WRITER

Some of the guest of honor authors brought experiences to share with the readers and writers, which enlivened the group. One author, Dinah Lenney, brought objects for prompts. Everyone wrote short memoir pieces. The camaraderie and pie opened up the groups, and we explored and shared our personal experiences. I expounded on the salon idea and created Savory Workshops, collaborating with book critic David Ulin. By submissions, book-length writers submit their manuscripts to be accepted into an intimate group where we spend a weekend discussing and critiquing the accepted manuscripts. Two attendees who participated more than twice persevered and published their novels. I'm sure it was the pie that helped, but their tenacity on the road of writing probably had something to do with it too.

NaNoPieMo

You may have heard of NaNoWriMo, National Novel Writing Month. An exciting month every November where writers are challenged to write 50,000 words of a novel by the end of the month. That's about 1,700 words a day. Fifty thousand of those makes a novel. A messy novel, but one that counts as a novel nonetheless. It's like the biggest of all pie butts in chair. A few years ago, I decided I was going to join in on the challenge, but it was going to be pie. I achieved my goal—thirty pies in thirty days, even through Thanksgiving, I made a pie every single day. I did it again the next year. On Facebook, it became popular. I couldn't eat thirty pies, so I was giving them away. I had to set up an ice chest on my front porch. The next year, I turned it into a bake sale auction to raise money for charity, where each day social media friends bid on that day's pie. It was competitive, as some people really wanted a particular pie. People strategized and snuck their high bids in at the very last minute, raising the cost of a pie into the three-digit range. I was exhausted, and for a week after every time someone mentioned pie all I could think of was nap, but the energy and fun and support was overwhelming, making it clear I couldn't stop. It was hard, but I pushed through, and year after year have reached my goal. NaNoPieMo is now a tradition.

Pushing myself to do these challenges, and others pushing themselves on NaNoWriMo, creates a great sense of accomplishment. It's a small example of what it takes to write a complete book. Perseverance is essential, in my recipe for reaching a goal, but so is taking time to bake (or eat) a pie. Both are satisfying on their own, but eating the pie after reaching the goal is doubly satisfying. That's why my last pie every NaNoPieMo is mine alone to eat.

NaNoPieMo is when my Rumpus Room is lit up like a disco. If discos served pie.

Write First, Ask Questions Later

The Writing Life is about writing, of course, but like any job, it has its good and bad days, more serious and more tedious days, easier and harder days. Find your own niche, your own way of decorating your Rumpus Room, set up your desk, or your life, to follow your ideas of what you want your Writing Life to be. It's worth repeating that the best piece of advice I received from a mentor was when I asked her if I should get my MFA. "Write your book, then get published," she said. I've come to understand she meant my writing life would find its own path, but first, write.

Like pie, the Writing Life is made up of an infinite number of slices. Find what interests you most, what intrigues you, what drives you to want to know more. I've started many blogs, podcasts, and vlogs—*started* is the keyword there. They never went beyond maybe two entries, one recording, and a few goofy YouTubes. NaNoPieMo and Savory Salons stuck with me, probably because I like anything that has to do with pie. They both are ways of connecting with people, and since you can't eat pie through a computer screen or headphones, they worked best for me.

Write, be you, and, whatever you do, however you do it, make sure it gives you some kind of satisfaction and enjoyment. Make sure it's your favorite kind of pie.

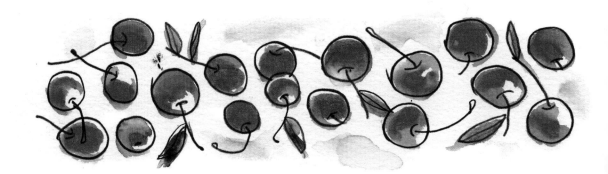

THE BEST CHeRRY PIe

When it's cherry season, I always pick up a few pounds of cherries every time I go to the store or farmers market until they are no longer in season. The season is too short, in my opinion, so I buy enough for several pies and then see what happens. What that means is, sometimes I make a four-cherry pie with sweet cherries, dried sour cherries, Rainier cherries, and Trader Joe's Dark Morello Cherries. I've never ever used the canned cherries in the red sticky syrup. I'm not judging if someone else likes that, but to me, cherries are superb on their own, stupendous in a pie, and don't need to come from a can. Why not savor them for the short season and dream of them the rest of the year? The BEST cherry pie I've ever made was with just fresh cherries—2 pounds sweet cherries and 1 pound Rainier cherries, which are sweeter than the "sweet" ones. Yes, I said pounds, not cups or ounces. I like a big cherry pie.

2 pounds sweet cherries

1 pound Rainier cherries

1 tablespoon lemon juice

1 teaspoon vanilla extract

½ cup plus 2 tablespoons
   granulated sugar, divided

3 tablespoons cornstarch

½ cup brown sugar

½ cup all-purpose flour

½ stick (¼ cup) butter

½ cup pecans

Prepare a single-crust pie dough. Let it rest while assembling the filling.

Through cherries, I enter my Rumpus Room. I pit all the cherries by hand. I find this meditative. Inside my imagination I go while my hands become stained a nice cherry red. I mull over what I'm working on in my writing, how I can fix a scene, whether my character needs a better job, or a different color hair, or a new boyfriend.

Add the lemon juice, vanilla, and ½ cup of the granulated sugar to the cherries and mix well. Let them sit for 15 minutes or so while they juice. In the meantime, mix the remaining sugar with the cornstarch in a small bowl.

To make the brown sugar topping, place the brown sugar in a food processor bowl with the flour, butter, and pecans. Pulse until the mixture has a grainy texture. Refrigerate until ready to use.

Add the cornstarch and sugar mixture to the cherries and mix until smooth.

Roll out the dough and insert it into an 8-inch pie pan. Add the cherry filling. Bake at 400°F (I should have said to preheat at the top) for 30 minutes. Sprinkle the brown sugar topping on and reduce the temperature to 375°F and bake for about 20 to 30 minutes until bubbling, oozing, and smelling oh so good. Let it rest for 20 minutes or until you just can't stand it any longer. Careful not to burn your tongue, then EAT.

Why is it the BEST? Because it's the best cherry pie I've ever made, and I've made so many different combinations. They all have a time and a place, like the four-cherry pie is sometimes necessary at the end of cherry season when cherries aren't as plentiful, so I have to add dried cherries. Rainiers, on the other hand, have a very short season, shorter than regular sweet cherries, so when Rainiers are available, I focus on them. If it's winter and I need to make a cherry pie—because let's face it, sometimes we NEED pie—I'll use the stockpile of cherries I pitted and froze earlier in the year. Cherries just make me happy, that's all.

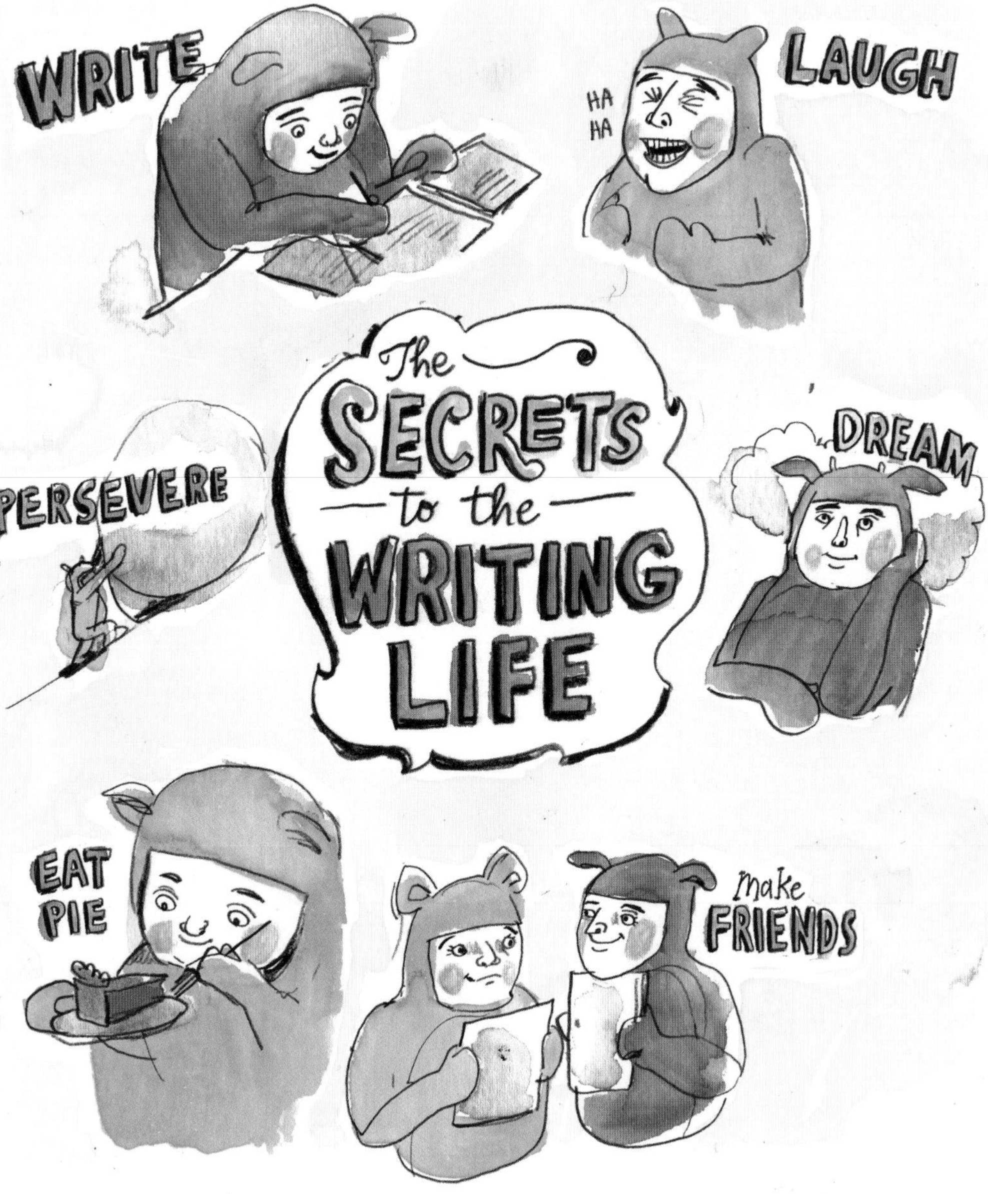
The SECRETS to the WRITING LIFE
WRITE
HA HA
LAUGH
PERSEVERE
DREAM
EAT PIE
Make FRIENDS

CHAPTER EIGHTEEN

E(PIE)logue

I hope this book inspired you to have fun along the way of writing your book and encouraged you to keep at it. At the beginning, I mentioned that perseverance and having fun must go hand in hand along your journey. I didn't say those words exactly, but I hope that you came to that conclusion on your own. Even if you just flipped through and looked at the illustrations, then you've taken a break filled with laughs—a meaningful break that may fill you up with new ideas. Maybe you only read the recipes, baked them, and gained a little weight. Sorry about that. You had fun, so I don't feel too guilty. Most of all, I hope you'll put down this book and pick up your pen. When you are down about your writing, or need a boost, or a laugh, or even just want to take a break, I hope you'll pick up this book like you might call a friend. This book won't mind giving you encouragement at any hour, while friends can be picky about the hours you call to whine.

Secrets to the Writing Life

The secrets to writing a book, no one knows those. But I did promise you the secrets to a Writing Life. Here you go.

Write.

Persevere.

Eat pie.

Make friends.

Laugh.

Dream.

Stir until the consistency feels right.

One last story, and one last recipe before I go. After *MoonPies*'s publication, I was asked to be the guest of honor at numerous book clubs. This thrilled me, and I always enjoyed the questions and impressions readers had of my work. But there was just one thing that I didn't enjoy. The book clubs always had a MoonPie theme. If you aren't familiar with MoonPies, they are two graham cookies covered in chocolate with a thick pile of marshmallow in between. Every book club would serve MoonPies. Unfortunately, I don't like MoonPies, but to be polite, I'd nibble on one end and put the rest in my purse. I promised myself next time I had food in my book it would be something I liked so I could eat it at every gathering. All the recipes in this book seem to make certain that I'll like anything served, but I'm going to stick in this recipe here at the end because if I were to redesign the MoonPie, I'd make it coconut custard instead of marshmallow. And, when I'm invited to book clubs, let me suggest this one just in case.

Coconut CREAM Pie in an OREO Cookie CRUST

Like the old advertising jingle used to say, "Sometimes you feel like a nut, sometimes you don't." Almond Joy candy bars were my favorite as a kid. I could get one for a nickel at the corner drugstore, when my mom wasn't paying attention that I'd snuck out of the house.

OREO CRUMB CRUST

20 Oreo cookies

2 tablespoons melted butter

2 teaspoons milk

FILLING

1 cup unsweetened shredded coconut

5 egg yolks

1 (13.5 ounce) can coconut milk

1 (13.5 ounce) can coconut cream

½ cup granulated sugar

¼ cup light brown sugar

⅓ cup cornstarch

½ teaspoon salt

1 tablespoon vanilla extract

½ cup almond slivers

2 cups heavy whipping cream

Preheat the oven to 325°F.

Place the Oreos in a food processor, and pulse until just crumbs are left. Add the melted butter and milk to the food processor. Pulse until the mixture starts to stick to the sides of the bowl. Pour the Oreo mixture into a 9-inch pie pan and smooth out and up the sides. Place in fridge to chill for 10 minutes. Bake for 7 minutes. Let cool while you prepare the filling.

Line a baking sheet with foil. Toast the shredded coconut for 5 minutes or until lightly browned. Set aside to cool.

In a large saucepan, combine the egg yolks, coconut milk, coconut cream, sugars, cornstarch, and salt. Heat to a boil over medium heat, whisking constantly. This requires the same patience you need to have for your book—it takes longer than it seems it should. You keep whisking and waiting for that boil to happen. It seems that it may never boil, that it will stay a thin liquid forever. You almost want to give up, but you keep at it to see if maybe in another minute or two the boil will start to happen. Finally, you see some bubbles, and the boil starts. Turn the burner down to medium-low and keep whisking for 2 more minutes. The mixture starts to thicken and you think it may be done, but there's still more whisking. Don't be tempted to scrape the sides of the pan, as this will make your custard lumpy. And don't be tempted to turn the heat up to make the boiling point arrive sooner, as this may cook the egg yolks too fast and curdle the custard. Just keep whisking and trusting that it will come together. Keep at it. After 2 minutes, remove the saucepan from the heat but keep whisking, as there's still more to go. There always is, isn't there? Whisk in the vanilla extract, $\frac{7}{8}$ cup of the coconut you toasted earlier, and the almond slivers. Now it's ready to be poured into the cooled Oreo crust right away. Cover with plastic wrap, letting it smooth over the top of the custard. Chill for 4 hours until set.

Beat the heavy whipping cream, or use coconut whipping cream if you want to keep it dairy-free. Beat until the cream begins to thicken and makes soft clouds. Spoon the cream over the coconut custard pie and sprinkle with the remaining toasted coconut and more slivered almonds.

Sometimes, writing a book can make you feel like a nut. I love nuts.

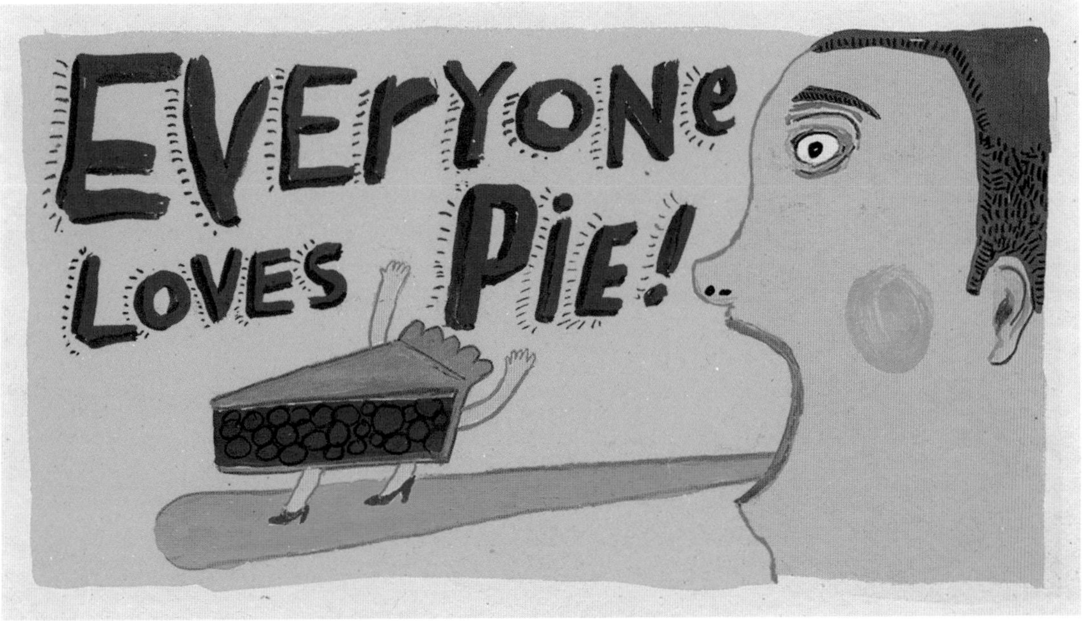
EVERYONE LOVES PIE!

Andrews McMeel Publishing
a division of Andrews McMeel Universal
1130 Walnut Street, Kansas City, Missouri 64106

www.andrewsmcmeel.com

Writing and recipes by Amy Wallen
www.amywallen.com

Comics, illustrations, and additional recipes by Emil Wilson
www.emilwilsonart.com

Editor: Lucas Wetzel
Art Director: Sierra S. Stanton
Production Editor: Meg Utz
Production Manager: Tamara Haus

22 23 24 25 26 TEN 10 9 8 7 6 5 4 3 2 1

ISBN: 978-1-5248-7565-7

Library of Congress Control Number: 2022936519

ATTENTION: SCHOOLS AND BUSINESSES

Andrews McMeel books are available at quantity discounts with bulk purchase for educational, business, or sales promotional use. For information, please e-mail the Andrews McMeel Publishing Special Sales Department: specialsales@amuniversal.com.